THE DENIAL OF STRESS

THE DENIAL OF STRESS

edited by
SHLOMO BREZNITZ

INTERNATIONAL UNIVERSITIES PRESS, INC.
New York

Library of Congress Cataloging in Publication Data

Main entry under title:

The Denial of stress.

    Bibliography: p.
    Includes index.
    1. Denial (Psychology) I. Breznitz, Shlomo.
BF175.D455 1982   155.9   82-13044
ISBN 0-8236-1185-X

Second Printing 1985

Manufactured in the United States of America

To my wife Tzvia

CONTENTS

Preface   ix
Acknowledgments   xi
Contributors   xiii

1. *The Costs and Benefits of Denial* — Richard S. Lazarus   1
   DISCUSSION: DENIAL IN VARIOUS FACETS OF HEALTH   31

2. *Preventing Pathogenic Denial by Means of*
   Stress Inoculation — Irving L. Janis   35
   DISCUSSION: WHEN TO INOCULATE AGAINST DENIAL   77

3. *The Concept and Mechanisms of Denial: A Selective*
   Overview — Leo Goldberger   83
   DISCUSSION: DEFINITIONAL PROBLEMS   97

4. *The Paradox of Denial* — Donald P. Spence   103
   DISCUSSION: IMPLICATIONS OF RESEARCH FINDINGS   125

5. *Psychological Response to Serious Life Events*
   — Mardi J. Horowitz   129
   DISCUSSION: "WORKING THROUGH" AS A PROCESS   161

6. *Information-Processing Aspects of Denial: Some*
   Tentative Formulations — Vernon Hamilton   167
   DISCUSSION: COGNITIVE VERSUS PSYCHODYNAMIC APPROACHES
        TO DEFENSE   197

7. *Denial in concentration camps: Some Personal Observations on the Positive and Negative Functions of Denial in Extreme Life Situations* — Leo Eitinger   199

8. *Denial and Religion* — R. S. Zwi Werblowsky   213
   DISCUSSION: WHICH "REALITY" IS DENIED?   223

9. *Anticipatory Stress and Denial* — Shlomo Breznitz   225

10. *The Seven Kinds of Denial* — Shlomo Breznitz   257
    DISCUSSION: THE DENIAL MODEL AS A FRAMEWORK FOR DEBATE   281

11. *Methodological Considerations in Research on Denial* — Shlomo Breznitz   287

12. *Denial Versus Hope: Concluding Remarks* — Shlomo Breznitz   297

Subject Index   303

Author Index   311

PREFACE

Stress and denial go hand in hand; our ability to cope with "the thousand natural shocks that flesh is heir to" is often based on the protective veil of illusion. In extreme forms, denial can be pathogenic, and yet sometimes it saves us from breaking under strain. How odd, then, that in view of the increasing interest in psychological stress, denial as such has received only minimal empirical and theoretical attention.

It was in order to contribute to this neglected area that a special international conference on "Denial of Stress" was organized in June 1979, by the newly inaugurated Ray D. Wolfe Centre for Study of Psychological Stress at the University of Haifa. For one entire week, scholars of psychological stress discussed the various aspects of denial and its role in stress management. This volume is based on that conference. It includes the papers presented as well as the major issues that surfaced during the relatively long discussion periods. Three of the chapters were written after the conference and consequently are not followed by discussion. The editing of the transcripts of the proceedings was done very stringently and points were included only if they represented substantive additions to the papers themselves.

There is no attempt to cover the entire spectrum of denial-relevant issues. Rather, it is the goal of this book to point out the areas in which our gaps of knowledge are particularly detrimental to a more complete understanding of behavior under stress, and to motivate the much-needed research effort in this domain. In addition to often being a dramatic and interesting phenomenon, denial occupies a strategic position in the as yet largely uncharted no-man's-land between stress and pathology. Our ignorance in this critical area has, therefore, particularly important ramifications.

Shlomo Breznitz, Ph.D.

ACKNOWLEDGMENTS

The Ray D. Wolfe Centre for Study of Psychological Stress and the conference on which this book is based could not have materialized without the generous help of the many Canadian friends and fellows who found this a most fitting way to honor one of their leading citizens. Mrs. and Mr. Ray Wolfe in fact participated in the opening session of the international conference on "Denial of Stress." Thanks are due to the administrative staff at the Centre, and particularly to Mrs. Ruth Maos and Mrs. Rachael Warburg. Mrs. Dina Katz was very helpful with the typing. My colleagues, and specifically H. Ben-Zur and Dr. G. Ben-Dov, gladly provided their much-needed assistance in the preparation of this volume. Part of the manuscript was written in the peaceful atmosphere of the Netherland Institute for Advanced Studies, where I spent a few weeks as a Visting Fellow.

CONTRIBUTORS

SHLOMO BREZNITZ, PH.D. — Lady Davis Professor of Psychology and Director, Ray D. Wolfe Centre for Study of Psychological Stress, University of Haifa.

LEO EITINGER, M.D. — Professor of Psychiatry, University of Oslo; Adjunct Professor, University of Haifa.

*JOEL ELKES, M.D. — Professor of Psychiatry, McMaster University; Adjunct Professor, University of Haifa.

*REUVEN GAL, PH.D. — Commander, Centre for Behavioral Sciences, Israeli Defense Forces.

*ZWI GIORA, PH.D. — Associate Professor of Clinical Psychology, Tel Aviv University.

LEO GOLDBERGER, PH.D. — Professor of Psychology and Director, Research Center for Mental Health, New York University.

VERNON HAMILTON, PH.D. — Reader in Psychology, University of Reading.

*ALEX HESS, PH.D. — Chief Psychologist, Israeli Air Force.

MARDI J. HOROWITZ, M.D. — Professor of Psychiatry, University of California, San Francisco.

IRVING L. JANIS, PH.D. — Professor of Psychology, Yale University.

*GIORA KENAN, PH.D. — Lecturer in Psychology, Tel Aviv University.

*ASHER KORIAT, PH.D. — Senior Lecturer in Psychology, University of Haifa.

*Discussants only.

xiii

RICHARD S. LAZARUS, PH.D. — Professor of Psychology, University of California, Berkeley.

*Noah Milgram, Ph.D. — Professor of Psychology, Tel Aviv University.

*Shmuel Nagler, Ph.D. — Kunin-Lunenfeld Professor of Special Education, University of Haifa.

*Michael Rosenbaum, Ph.D. — Senior Lecturer in Psychology, University of Haifa.

*Marilyn Safer, Ph.D. — Senior Lecturer in Psychology, University of Haifa.

Donald P. Spence, Ph.D. — Professor of Psychology, Rutgers University.

R. S. Zwi Werblowsky, Ph.D. — Professor of Comparative Religion, Hebrew University, Jerusalem.

*Discussants only.

1

THE COSTS AND BENEFITS OF DENIAL

RICHARD S. LAZARUS

Some years ago, to be sophisticated meant accepting *accurate reality testing* as the hallmark of mental health (Erikson, 1950; Maslow, 1954; Jahoda, 1958; Menninger, 1963). Everyone knew that self-deception was tantamount to mental disorder. If one wished to manage life successfully, it was not only necessary to know the truth, however painful, but to revel in it and even drown in it if need be. One recent form this doctrine has taken is that we must always be "in touch with our feelings" and absolutely honest about them with others. This outlook about reality is still dominant today (Haan, 1977; Vaillant, 1977). However, I no longer believe such a thesis is sound; one can argue, in fact, that illusion is necessary to positive mental health.

Clearly, illusion and self-deception are closely related con-

---

This paper was supported in part by a research grant from the National Institute on Aging (AG 00799).

Constructive criticisms of an earlier draft by Professor Gerald A. Mendelsohn and members of my research group are appreciatively acknowledged.

1

cepts. To have an illusion is to believe something that is not so; therefore, assuming that there is an adequate basis for assessing reality (an assumption often unwarranted), it is a self-deception. But if we were to equate having illusions with being crazy (as Freud did with the defense mechanism of denial), most or all of us would have to be condemned to asylums. We have collective illusions, for example, that our society is free, moral, just; that successful people work harder, are smarter, more favored by God than others, and so on. We believe in a God (which we capitalize to express the reification), just as the Greeks believed in many gods. And we believe that our God is the true one while someone else's is not, or that there is no god. We also believe, to some degree, in personal immortality; Becker (1973) has argued that all our striving and products stem from a single, powerful psychological force—the denial of death. True, these notions may be only partly illusory "working assumptions," but the line separating a working assumption from an illusion is indeed difficult to draw.

People not only have systems of belief that they share with others in their culture and social groups, but also maintain their own idiosyncratic set of beliefs about themselves and the world in which they live (Bem, 1970). Many of these beliefs are passed down from forebears and may never be challenged or examined; they are what Rokeach (1968) calls "primitive" beliefs. Other beliefs and belief systems are forged out of the experiences of living. Some are implicit and barely accessible to awareness; others are formal and fully conscious, and form central personal themes affecting expectations and commitments. Some run counter to accepted wisdom, while others fit in comfortably with those shared by peers.

In any case, one finds a genuinely unsettling discrepancy between the way most mental health professionals view reality testing and self-deception, and the outlook of many writers of fiction and poetry who maintain that life is intolerable without illusion. It is instructive to consider how these fiction writers have treated the issue.

ILLUSION AND REALITY IN FICTION

The idea that illusion is essential to life is the core theme of Eugene O'Neill's *The Iceman Cometh*. The protagonist of the play,

Hickey, who has unmasked himself and zealously wants to free the other blighted denizens of a saloon from their self-deceptions, destroys one man in the process and severely distresses all the others. An acceptable mode of living does not return until reality testing is abandoned in favor of illusion.

Henrik Ibsen's play *The Wild Duck* is built on the same theme that one must protect and nurture illusions, or in Ibsen's terms, "the saving lie." As with O'Neill's character Hickey, Ibsen creates the personage of Gregers, a neurotic moralist who presses his own destructive truths on a young peer, shattering the latter's illusions about his past and present, inadvertently encouraging the suicide of his 14-year-old daughter, and shattering his family's happiness and morale.

In *Man of La Mancha*, author Dale Wassermann tells us that instead of writing a cynical commentary on the remarkable human capacity for self-deception, his musical adaptation of Miguel de Cervantes' *Don Quixote* is a plea for illusion as an important and powerful sustaining force in life. We are urged to "dream the impossible dream," "fight the unbeatable foe." "Facts," says Wassermann's Don Quixote, "are the enemy of truth."

Consider also the vignette below from Allen Wheelis' (1966) *The Illusionless Man*, which clearly implies that without illusions our lives are empty. Speaking of the wedding to his bride-to-be, Lorabelle, for whom illusion is all, Henry, the illusionless man, says:

> God won't be there, honey; the women will be weeping for their own lost youth and innocence, the men wanting to have you in bed; and the priest standing slightly above us will be looking down your cleavage as his mouth goes dry; and the whole thing will be a primitive and preposterous attempt to invest copulation with dignity and permanence, to enforce responsibility for children by the authority of a myth no longer credible even to a child [p. 17].

At the end of the story, when Henry and Lorabelle are near the end of their lives, Wheelis clearly tells us that illusion is the only workable way of life:

...he could see himself striving toward a condition of beauty or truth or goodness or love that did not exist, but whereas earlier in his life he had always said, "It's an illusion," and turned away, now he said, "There isn't anything else," and stayed with it; and though it cannot be said that they lived happily, exactly, and certainly not ever after, they did live. They lived—for a while—with ups and downs, good days and bad, and when it came time to die Lorabelle said, "Now we'll never be parted," and Henry smiled and kissed her and said to himself, "There isn't anything else," and they died [p. 44].

Friedrich Dürrenmatt's powerful play *The Visit* is another illustration of how writers have often treated illusion and reality. The setting is a post-World War II town in Italy that has neither vitality nor economic viability. The townsfolk see hope in the anticipated return visit of an aging millionairess who had grown up there in poverty. They hope she will give them financial aid. As part of her offer of a huge sum, however, she stipulates a terrible condition, namely, the execution of her lover whose treachery had eventuated in the death of her child, imprisonment, and her ultimate banishment from the community. She now wants retribution, or "justice," as she puts it. At first the town leaders seem reluctant to accept the immoral bargain, but gradually it becomes apparent that everyone has been living on the anticipated windfall. The climax comes with the acceptance and formal celebration of the evil bargain and the execution of the lover. The town now thrives economically and socially. The mayor emphasizes that the money is not being accepted for its own sake, but for justice, and the townsfolk cheer. Dürrenmatt offers two social messages here: first, that prosperity and social vitality generally rest on evil; second, that evil is denied and disguised in the cloak of justice. In effect, he is saying that our most cherished social values depend on self-deception; they are illusions, little better than sugar-coated distortions of social reality, which is at root evil.

Perhaps the most celebrated modern literary figure to deal with illusion and reality and make it his trademark was Pirandello, whose plays offer multiple and complex variations on social- and self-deception. For example, *Henry IV* deals with a man who lives out the fantasy of being a long-dead monarch with hired retainers, advisors and the like, but who confuses all participants and on-lookers about whether he is really insane or merely play-acting. *It Is So! (If You Think So)* concerns the efforts of a townspeople to decipher the relationships of three people, a husband, a wife and her mother, each of whom has a very different conception of himself and the others. Not only do the husband and his mother-in-law view reality in diametrically opposed ways, but the wife, knowing that her spouse and mother cannot manage without their own self-deceptions, adapts herself to both simultaneously; thus, through a social deception, she engages in a humanitarian act toward those she loves. One of the townsfolk, who has insight into what is going on and probably speaks for the author, argues that each set of illusions is as real as any other. It is, therefore, impossible to know external reality without viewing it through the eyes of the individual person.

Summarizing Pirandello's outlook on illusion and reality in the play *Liolà*, Bentley (1952) states:

> The play is about appearance and reality and shows, in what readers have always regarded as Pirandello's characteristically tricky fashion, that reality is not more real than appearance. Further, there are real appearances and merely apparent appearances. And just as appearances may be more real than reality, so merely apparent appearance may be more real than real appearance.

> . . . for Uncle Simone, to appear to be a father is enough: appearance will establish his paternity more surely than actually having done the deed. However, strictly speaking, he does *not* appear to be a father; for the whole town knows the truth. He only appears to appear to be the father. That he appears to be the father is a kind of social pact or legal fiction [p. xiii].

Pirandello himself (Bentley, 1952) puts it as follows:

> The harder the struggle for life and the more one's weakness is felt, the greater becomes the need for mutual deception. The simulation of force, honesty, sympathy, prudence, in short, of every virtue, and of that greatest virtue veracity, is a form of adjustment, an effective instrument of struggle. The "humor-

ist" at once picks out such various simulations; amuses himself by unmasking them; is not indignant about them—he simply is that way!

And while the sociologist describes social life as it presents itself to external observation, the humorist, being a man of exceptional intuition, shows—nay, reveals—that appearances are one thing and the consciousness of the people concerned, in its inner essence, another. And yet people "lie psychologically" even as they "lie socially." And this lying to ourselves—living as we do, on the surface and not in the depths of our being—is a result of the social lying. The mind that gives back its own reflection is a solitary mind, but our internal solitude is never so great that suggestions from the communal life do not break in upon it with all the fictions and transferences which characterize them [p. xiv].

In a vigorous assault on the concept of reality, *How Real Is Real?*, communications psychologist Paul Watzlawick (1976) cites Fyodor Dostoevski and Franz Kafka as particularly good literary exemplars of the "dissolution of reality." He observes Hermann Hesse's suggestion that Prince Myshkin in Dostoevski's *The Idiot* "does not break the Tablets of the Law, he simply turns them round and shows the contrary to them is written on the other side." Moreover, Watzlawick considers the metaphysical argument between Alyosha and Ivan in *The Brothers Karamazov* as the supreme literary example of this dissolution of reality. Ivan speaks of the imaginary confrontation between the Grand Inquisitor and Jesus, whom he has arrested after the latter's descent once again to earth. In the Inquisitor's view of reality, Jesus has betrayed humankind by wanting people to be free to choose, by rejecting miracles, and by refusing to rule the world as one unanimous and harmonious "ant heap." These three ideological positions have made the lot of humans miserable. On the other hand, the organized Church, says the Grand Inquisitor, keeps people happy by providing miracles, mystery, and authority. Thus we see two diametrically opposite views of reality—Jesus versus the Grand Inquisitor, in which the same virtue, humanitarianism, leads to quite logically opposite conclusions.

Thus, the importance of illusions may well be, as Bentley (1952, p. viii) has observed, "the main theme of literature in general."

ILLUSION AND REALITY IN PSYCHOLOGICAL THOUGHT

Despite the longstanding dominant view of psychiatry and clinical psychology that accurate perception of reality is a hallmark of mental health, there have been numerous voices expressing the constructivist view that people create their own realities. The New Look movement of the 1950s also emphasized individual differences in the way events are perceived and cognized (Lazarus, 1978; Folkman, Schaefer, and Lazarus, 1979).

Some psychologists, such as Frankl (1955), have built entire psychological and therapeutic systems on the need for meaning in our lives, and have emphasized the devastating effects of the loss of such meaning. In a recent study of stress and coping in concentration camp survivors, my colleagues and I (Benner, Roskies, and Lazarus, 1980) also suggested that such meaning served as a coping resource during the Holocaust, and that its loss helps to account for the troubled pattern of adjustment among survivors. This also seems to be a time in the industrialized Western world characterized by widespread loss of meanings that once served as anchors in people's lives, although the concept of alienation, which includes meaninglessness as a core concept (Kanungo, 1979), was important in sociological thought before the turn of the century.

The important point, however, is that the kinds of beliefs on which people depend have an uncertain reality basis regardless of the fixity with which they may be held. One person's beliefs can be another's delusions. From a communications theory perspective, Watzlawick (1976) writes:

> The reader will have noticed that I have been unable to avoid the use of terms like "really," "actually," "actual fact," and thus have apparently contradicted the main thesis of the book: that there is no absolute reality but only subjective and often contradictory conceptions of reality.
>
> Very frequently, especially in psychiatry where the degree of an individual's "reality adaptation" plays a special role as the indicator of his normalcy, there is a confusion between two

very different aspects of what we call reality. The first has to do with the purely physical, objectively discernible properties of things and is intimately linked with correct sensory perception, with questions of so-called common sense or with objective, repeatable, scientific verification. The second aspect is the attribution of meaning and value to these things and is based on communication.

This domain of reality, however, says nothing about the meaning and value of its contents. A small child may perceive a red traffic light just as clearly as an adult, but may not know that it means "do not cross the street now." The first-order reality of gold — that is, its physical properties — is known and can be verified at any time. But the role that gold has played since the dawn of human history, especially the fact that its value is determined twice daily by five men in a small office in the City of London and that this ascription of value profoundly influences many other aspects of our everyday reality, has very little, if anything, to do with the physical properties of gold. But it is this second reality of gold which may turn us into millionaires or lead us into bankruptcy.

. . . It is a delusion to believe that there is a "real" second-order reality and that "sane" people are more aware of it than "madmen" [pp. 140–142].

Yet, in spite of the ambiguities in judging reality, strip us of beliefs in which we are heavily invested and we are deeply threatened, alienated, and perhaps even seriously disrupted in our life course and capacity for involvement and satisfaction. In effect, we pilot our lives by virtue of illusions that give meaning and substance to living. Life cannot easily be lived and enjoyed without a set of both shared deceptions and self-deceptions, that is, without beliefs that have no necessary relationship with reality.

Alfred Adler's concept of "fictional finalism" (see Ansbacher and Ansbacher, 1956), which suggests that human actions are pulled by future considerations rather than pushed from the past, and which draws on Hans Vaihinger's (1911) The Philosophy of "As If," is relevant here. Vaihinger argued that we live by fictional ideas that have no necessary connection with reality, for example, that "all men are created equal," "honesty is the best policy," and "the end justifies the means" (see also Hall and Lindsey, 1957, on Alfred Adler).

That living "as if" could be a workable strategy in the real world is not surprising when we realize that from early childhood on we are treated to two alternative and simultaneous modes of thought: fairy tales and magic on the one hand, and the "real world" on the other. Yet both modes seem capable of residing comfortably together, and even of being fused. In his theory of cognitive dissonance, not only did Festinger (1957) fail to help us understand and predict which of many dissonance-resolving strategies people use, but I think he was wrong in presuming that it is always urgent for people to resolve dissonances. Quite the contrary, though some of us are more sensitive to self-contradictions than others, we tolerate them very easily, and much of the time do not even notice when we or others engage in them. Moreover, as Freud emphasized, humans have a great capacity for rationalizing or dispelling apparent contradictions.

Rather than equating the use of illusion with pathology, a more appropriate and interesting conclusion would be that mental health *requires* some self-deception. Otto Rank (1936) has also adopted this position by suggesting that the problem of the neurotic person is that he or she senses the truth, but cannot deal with it. Rank wrote:

> With the truth, one cannot live. To be able to live one needs illusions, not only outer illusions such as art, religion, philosophy, science and love afford, but inner illusions which first condition the outer [i.e., a secure sense of one's active powers and of being able to count on the powers of others]. The more a man can take reality as truth, appearance as essence, the sounder, the better adjusted, the happier will he be...this constantly effective process of self-deceiving, pretending and blundering, is no psychopathological mechanism [pp. 251–252].

We must somehow face the seeming paradox that illusion or self-deception can be both adaptationally sound *and* capable of eliciting a heavy price. The paradox is: How is it possible for self-deception to be at once healthy and pathogenic? The paradox can be resolved by shifting to the more sophisticated question: What kinds and degrees of self-deceptions are damaging or constructive, and under what conditions, or as Becker (1973) has put it, "On what level of illusion does one live?" (p. 189). Alternatively, perhaps some illusions work better than others.

THE DENIAL PROCESS AS A FORM OF SELF-DECEPTION

Denial is the negation of something in word or act, or more properly, both, since thoughts and actions are apt to be conjoined in any defense process. Logically speaking, the negation can be either of an impulse, feeling or thought, or of an external demand or reality; but, as we shall see, both Sigmund and Anna Freud distinguished denial from repression as being focused on external rather than internal conditions. Examples of denial in the larger sense include: I am not angry; I do not love you; I am not distressed; I am not seriously ill, dying or facing extinction; I am not in danger; he doesn't mean any harm; she is not a competitor, etc. Some of these denials refer to environmental realities, others to intrapsychic forces.

In speaking of the denial process, one is immediately faced with multiple ambiguities. One of the most common sources of confusion is the equation of denial with *avoidance*. Behaviorally speaking, for example, one may exhibit denial by not paying attention to or not speaking of the threatening connotation of events. Thus, if we wish to deny that we are mortally ill, we will also avoid this idea in thought, deed or word. This is what Anna Freud seems to have meant by denial "in word and act." Therefore, it is not an illogical presumption that a cancer patient who does not mention the terminal nature of the illness, particularly when there is provocation, is denying the imminence of death. Although the presumption is not unreasonable, it is incomplete. A terminal patient may know full well that he or she is dying, but prefer not to think or talk about it. This is not denial, but avoidance; there is a world of difference between the two.

Another source of ambiguity is that one cannot deny what is not *known*. Therefore, if physicians have evaded communicating the diagnosis and prognosis, or have pussyfooted about it or been excessively subtle with a person who is not particularly perceptive, then the impression that this person is denying may be incorrect. Here, what is being revealed is ignorance rather than denial. There is a considerable difference between shading things a bit, and a full-fledged process of denying what clearly should be known and acknowledged. Only very careful, in-depth exploration is capable of providing the empirical basis for this distinction.

In saying this I have accepted the idea, at least provisionally, that there are "realities" to be denied, although we must be extremely careful about how we deal with this idea. Put differently, if we could not take this position, there would be no basis for speaking about denial or for doing research on it. We cannot become completely hamstrung by the metaphysical problems. Thus, while subject to the usual diagnostic reservations, a rapidly developing carcinoma or a clogged coronary artery offers reasonable (realistic) bases for an appraisal that one's life is threatened. Similarly, the death of a loved one involves a reality that needs to be taken into account in living and for which a grief process would be appropriate. Whether the absence of grief is inappropriate is somewhat more difficult to assess.

Still another important source of confusion has to do with the extent to which the process of denial is tentative or well-entrenched, or as clinicians used to say, *well-consolidated*. A well-consolidated denial is presumably unshakeable. Many, perhaps most, denials are tentative constructions, responsive to this or that bit of information, mood, or whatever. Many patients who seem not to "know" they are dying really do know at some level of awareness, perhaps only dimly; this idea is expressed in the concept of "middle knowledge" (Weisman, 1972). Somehow, their declining physical fortunes, leakage from what has been said to them, contradictions in word and fact, all conspire to give the patient a sense, however slight, of what is happening. As Oken (1961) has put it, "A patient who is sick enough to die knows it without being told," although he or she must often play along with the reassuring, denial-focused statements of physicians, friends and relatives (Hackett and Weisman, 1964). What is called denial in such cases may be, at best, only a *partial* denial process that depends on social circumstances to sustain it. A partial denial involves the capacity to bring the denied "reality" into awareness, or to act on the denied knowledge when it is necessary. It is not a full-fledged self-deception but only a tentative "suspension of belief."

In his treatment of denial in terminal cancer patients, Weisman (1972) also addresses the question, "What is being denied?" He describes first-order denial as a denial of *facts*, for example, that a loved one has died, that one has cancer, or that manifest symptoms imply an important life-threatening illness. Such denial is usually tentative because the facts in a life-threatening or progressive disease ultimately make the first-order denial process untenable. In second-order denial, the potentially damaging or threatening primary facts are accepted, but the worst *implications* are denied. The distinction here is very much like that made by Watzlawick (1976) of first- and second-order realities, noted earlier. After all, it is the ultimate meaning of the facts for one's well-being that constitutes the threat. Third-order denial refers to the refusal to accept the further implications of one's extinction or personal death.

We have had the unfortunate habit in the past of treating the processes of coping as static states of mind, as fixed cognitive achievements (or traits), expressing the idea that the person has arrived at a stable interpretation (or defense). A better way of thinking is that, except for relatively rare instances of consolidated defenses, people are constantly seeking a way to comprehend what is happening to them; this *ongoing process* of construing reality is a constantly changing one, depending on many variables within and outside of the person. Thus, when we consider denial, or any other kind of self-deception or illusion, we are dealing with flux, and we must always be aware of the slippery nature of the event we are trying to understand (Lazarus, 1978).

Consider the following excerpt of an interview from my own research on coping with stressful encounters, specifically the threat of being electrocuted:

> There I was alone vacuuming up this water near all the exposed wiring...I hoped I wouldn't get electrocuted. But then I thought: "Well, this thing is made to take water and I have on rubber soles," and so I felt I wouldn't get electrocuted and kept on doing it but made sure I didn't touch anything. As soon as Bernie came back I said, "You're sure this is safe: I'm

not going to get electrocuted doing this?" And he said, "I
hope not; I don't think so." I know he was kidding. At least I
hope he was. And he had been doing it before I arrived. He
has a lot of common sense about these things so I shook off
most of the fear and just ran the vacuum.

Then we drank our wine and laughed at each other and just let it
go...knowing we had to face it again tomorrow. We changed
the situation by working on it together. I got over my anxiety
about the wires by being very careful and knowing that Bernie
wouldn't have me do something dangerous. The glass of wine
really made me feel better. What else can you do? I don't like
to get all upset. That was the first time we'd had a glass of
wine at work. After all, life is just a game. It wasn't severe
anxiety and I moved to a safer spot and everything was okay.
I just let go of the fear. I did it by concentrating on what I was
doing. I am just glad I was wearing crepe soles.

Many things seem to be happening here, including recognition
of the danger, and efforts to bring the fear under control by brava-
do and avoidance. Still, the coping process seems also to contain
denial-like elements, including the effort to accept Bernie's reassurance ("He has a lot of common sense" and "Bernie wouldn't have
me do something dangerous"). To anyone (an observer) aware of
the danger of standing in water near exposed wiring, to be convinced so easily and reassured by the crepe soles seems to involve a
tremendous degree of denial. Yet how can we assess the actual
sense of danger the person speaking could have experienced on the
basis of what she saw and knew?

Another lesson of importance is that denial is not a single act,
but a highly *diverse set of processes* that respond to different external and internal conditions, and that are inferred with varying degrees of confidence on the part of the observer. There can be no
satisfactory answer to the question of the adaptational outcomes
of denial without there also being a sound basis for identifying, describing and measuring the defensive process itself. Hasty and superficial measurement is hardly the way to undertake research on
the problem (see Horowitz, Sampson, Siegelman, Wolfson, and
Weis, 1975, or Chapter 4 by Spence, for examples of an in-depth

process measurement approach).

A thorough exposition of the concept of denial in theoretical terms is impossible to undertake here. It would go back to Freud, follow his shifting conceptions of defense in general, and proceed to subsequent psychoanalytic writers. Such an account is currently available in a book by Sjöbäck (1973), who gives considerable space to the history of thought about denial. As was noted earlier, Freud actually saw denial as a "disavowal" (to use his term) of external reality. It was also assumed to occur only in psychosis. He and others, including Anna Freud (1936) and Otto Fenichel (1945), continued this conception in later writing. On the one hand, Anna Freud may have changed her view of the matter much later, and, at least by implication appeared to regard denial as capable of having positive clinical significance. In a book by Bergmann (1958), on which Anna Freud collaborated, a case is reported of a child with polio whose father's very strong denial was said to have potentiated remarkable feats of physical function in the sick child. About this, Bergmann wrote:

> It is interesting to realize that the physical and medical evaluation could not explain how this child managed to walk so well with or without the cane because tests of muscle strength revealed quite insufficient power for such an accomplishment. With Carl it was evidently a case of "mind over matter." What had also to be taken into account was the father's denial of the facts, his unfaltering belief that everything was going to be all right again. Actually, it must have been the influence of the father's unrealistic attitude (and not my sensible advice) which contributed to Carl's amazingly successful recovery, the degree of which could not be explained in physical terms [p. 111].

Still others (Jacobson, 1957) later extended the concept of denial to mean a defense against intrapsychic forces (i.e., instinctual fantasies, wishes and impulses). Such an enlargement of the concept, however, has produced confusion. For example, if denial is a defense against intrapsychic processes as well as external reality, how is it to be distinguished from repression? The problem has never been resolved satisfactorily, and is part of the continuing uncertainty and confusion about definition and measurement (Fine, Joseph, and Waldhorn, 1969; Lipowski, 1970). Whether it is more useful to distinguish among many types of denial, as I do here, as well as among related processes such as avoidance, or to speak of a generalized process, a family of denial, as it were, that includes a large range of specific patterns, remains at issue.

What then is the resolution of the seeming paradox, stated earlier, that the use of denial is both harmful and beneficial; that although we venerate reality testing as a hallmark of mental health, life is intolerable without illusion? The resolution takes two forms. First, we must recognize that denial consists of many diverse forms, some of which are disavowals of clear realities, and others merely implications of avoidance. The latter merges with affirmations or positive thinking in the face of ambiguous circumstances; in short, it is what we mean by illusion. By carefully making such distinctions, both definitionally and in assessment, we can ultimately justify the seemingly contradictory assertion that sometimes denial-related processes have positive outcomes and other times negative. Second, we can recognize that the costs and benefits of denial and denial-like coping processes depend on the context in which the processes occur. That is, the adaptational outcome must be considered in relation to the situational demands and constraints on action, and the resources available to the person, in short, the coping alternatives. In the section that follows, some of these contextual variables play important roles in producing positive or negative outcomes.

RESEARCH ON DENIAL-LIKE PROCESSES AND THEIR CONSEQUENCES

The definitional and conceptual confusion that surrounds denial, as it does most other defensive processes, makes the problem of evaluating its outcomes even more difficult. For example, although there are a substantial number of research studies of denial-like processes, it is difficult to compare them because of variations in the way the coping process is understood and measured.

In this connection, it is instructive to consider a rating scale designed by Hackett and Cassem (1974) to measure denial in coronary care patients; it is based on Anna Freud's concept that denial is a general psychological goal that can be achieved in many diverse ways. Hackett and Cassem's scale includes some items that express denial explicitly in words, and others in which the denial is implicit, as in the item, "The patient avoids talking about the disability." We have already seen that combining alternative tactics such as avoidance and denial in word under the same general rubric, risks confusion about which process is actually being used by the person. It may be a much better research strategy to carefully differentiate diverse denial-like processes so that their impact on adaptational outcome can also be distinguished.

Nevertheless, it is worth trying to wade into some of this research in an effort to extract whatever hypothetical principles we can, recognizing that they must be tentative at best. To undertake this I have chosen the device of examining two types of studies: those in which denial seems to have damaging adaptational outcomes, and those having constructive ones. In making this categorization I have had to overlook some definitional and measurement problems. This is why I have used the term "denial-like processes" in all headings in place of "denial" per se. The studies cited below vary greatly in their methods of assessing the coping process, although the word "denial" is used in all. Strictly speaking, one cannot treat them as studies of denial without evading the very definitional issues I raised earlier.

No attempt has been made to provide a thorough review of all research; the citations were chosen to be illustrative. However, a fuller list of studies has been offered previously (Wortman and Dunkel-Schetter, 1979).

STUDIES OF DENIAL-LIKE PROCESSES WITH DAMAGING OUTCOMES

An important line of thought about denial has come from the work of Lindemann (1944) and Bowlby (1961) on grieving. Lindemann found denial of pain and distress a common feature of the grief process among the bereaved. Other observers have suggested a similar pattern among those sustaining an incapacitating loss such as spinal cord injury (Dembo, Leviton, and Wright, 1956; Wright, 1960; McDaniel and Sexton, 1970). Implicit in Lindemann's concept of "grief work" was the notion that if the bereaved person was prevented by processes such as denial and avoidance from grieving fully, it would result in failure to negotiate the bereavement crisis; the latter requires emancipation from the emotional bondage to the deceased and the formation of new relationships.

A parallel theme was also stated later by Janis (1958, 1974) in the concept of the "work of worrying." Janis found that low fear prior to surgery was associated with high distress and behavioral difficulties during the later recovery period; this was consistent with the view that denial of threat prevented the patient from realistically anticipating and working through the post-surgical discomforts. Although there was no direct measure of denial, and the findings on which this concept was based have not been replicated, the concept has had good staying power because of its ring of truth and supportive findings from other types of investigations (Cohen and Lazarus, 1979).

In his more recent writings about decision-making (Janis and Mann, 1977), vigilance continues to be viewed as desirable because it potentiates a search for information and the weighing of alternative coping strategies in the face of threat. Research by Horowitz (1975) makes use of an idea similar to the "work of worrying," namely, the tendency for unresolved threats (in the form of thoughts and images) to enter into awareness as unwanted intrusions (see also Freud's concept of repetition compulsion). Breger's (1967) treatment of dreams as efforts by the person to cope cognitively with unresolved conflicts also clearly falls within the same conceptual tradition.

Another direct descendant of this line of thought is the series of studies generated and reviewed by Goldstein (1973), which uses a sentence completion test measure of vigilance (or sensitization) and avoidance (repression) as the opposite extremes of a coping continuum. Vigilants are those who accept and elaborate fully on the threatening meaning conveyed by incomplete sentence stems. (To the stem "I hate," they write: "my parents," "nosey people," "anyone who is smarter than me," etc.) Avoiders seem to evade or deny what the researcher presumes is the threatening content. (To the stem "I hate," they write: "to be caught in the rain without an umbrella," "no one.") Nonspecific defenders fall into neither extreme category, and are said to adapt their form of coping flexibly to the circumstances. To oversimplify this research (Andrew, 1970; DeLong, 1970), avoiders do not do well in anticipatory threat situations or when they are exposed to repeated threats (e.g., when they are shown the same stressful movie more than once). The assumption is that their characteristic mode of coping prevents coming to terms with the threat. Avoiders and vigilants also seem to be differentially benefited by diverse interventions in anticipatory stress situations—avoiders do better when left alone; vigilants respond best to detailed preparation. Although the data are more complicated and unclear than one would wish, they seem consistent with the concepts of grief work and the work of worrying, and point to avoidance or denial as processes that can interfere with successful mastery by preventing appropriate cognitive coping prior to a stressful confrontation.

A recent study of asthmatic patients (Staudenmayer, Kinsman, Dirks, Spector, and Wangaard, 1979) further supports the above ideas, but adds an important behavioral dimension. Asthmatics were divided into those who respond to symptoms with vigilance and those who disregard them. When the slightest sign of a developing attack is noticed, the former grow fearful and vigilant; the latter evade or deny the seriousness of the symptom and wait out the situation, expecting or hoping that the attack will not materialize and the symptoms will disappear. These authors found that the high-fear, vigilance patients were far less likely to be rehospitalized over a six-month period than the low-fear, denial-oriented patients. The former tended to take action quickly when breathing difficulties ensued, while the latter tended to disregard these difficulties, and hence allowed the attack to progress too far to treat short of hospitalization. Here too we see the value of vigilance and the high cost of avoidance and/or denial in a medical outcome; in this case the denial-like coping process leads to the failure to act in one's own best interest.

An oft-cited and even clearer demonstration of the theme that denial may interfere with actions necessary to survival may be found in the research of Katz, Weiner, Gallagher, and Hellman (1970) with women who discovered a breast lump. Denial, mixed with rationalization, was reported to have been the most common form of coping employed, being used by 11 out of 30 subjects. They found that there was often considerable delay in getting medical attention, which in the event the lump was malignant, added greatly to the danger of metastasis and reduced the chances for surgical care. Delays in seeking medical help for a heart attack have also been reported. Von Kugelgen (1975) and Hackett and Cassem (1975) cite cases of men who, while undergoing such an attack, did vigorous pushups or climbed flights of stairs to convince themselves that what they were experiencing was not a heart attack.

STUDIES OF DENIAL-LIKE PROCESSES
WITH CONSTRUCTIVE OUTCOMES

In recent years, clinical thought has shifted considerably from an emphasis on intrapsychic conflict to environmental conditions, such as catastrophic illness, as factors in adaptational crises in ordinary people (Lipowski, 1970). In all likelihood, this shift in part reflects the positive mental health movement and a retreat from a preoccupation solely with inner dynamics and pathology. A series of studies influenced by the research and theorizing of Roy Grinker, Sr. (Offer and Freedman, 1972) has been particularly influential in the growing acceptance of the idea that denial-like processes could have positive as well as negative adaptational consequences. Defensive processes are not treated as the exclusive property of "sick" minds, but as an integral feature of healthy coping as well.

Included in this research are studies of the victims of severe and incapacitating burns (Hamburg, Hamburg, and deGoza, 1953), of paralytic polio (Visotsky, Hamburg, Goss, and Lebovits, 1961), and other life crises, summarized analytically by Hamburg and Adams (1967). A major thesis has been that self-deception, for example, by denial of the seriousness of the problem, is often a valuable initial form of coping, occurring at a time when the person is confused and weakened and therefore unable to act constructively and realistically. In a severe and sudden crises, "time for 'preparation' is likely to be bought by temporary self-deception, in such a way as to make recognition of threatening elements gradual and manageable" (p. 283). Davis (1963) too has observed that denial of the gravity of the illness (polio) and its damaging implications permits the parents to have a longer time perspective about their child's recovery, and to be able to accept as milestones comparatively small steps toward recovery, such as being fitted with leg braces. And in writing about the atomic holocaust at Hiroshima, Lifton (1964) has suggested that early denial might facilitate ultimate adjustment by allowing the survivors to engage in a "psychic closing off" from "the threat [of psychosis] posed by the overwhelming evidence of actual physical death" (p. 208). The above, then, offers a stage-related concept of denial in which the "disavowal" of reality is temporary and helps the person to get through the devastating early period of loss and threat; it sets the stage for later acknowledgment (Kübler-Ross, 1969) of the situation and the mobilization of more realistic coping efforts.

A number of research studies have suggested that there is a high incidence of denial-like coping processes in severe, incapacitating illness, and that these coping activities can have positive adaptational consequences. Denial of the danger and its imminence has been reported as common in cancer (Cobb, Clark, McGuire, and Howe, 1954), with denial inferred from retrospective depth interviews and identified to some degree in 90% of a sample of 840 patients. In patients with spinal cord injuries, Dinardo (1971) used the Byrne questionnaire scale of repression-sensitization, a dimension akin theoretically to Goldstein's (1973) sentence completion measure; he found that repressors displayed greater self-esteem than sensitizers, although the latter type of injured persons were significantly less happy. Dinardo also obtained ratings of adjustment from physical therapists, occupational therapists and nurses, and found that repressors seemed to do better, although the difference was not statistically significant. In considering this type of evidence, we must be wary of the measure itself (see also Lefcourt, 1966). First, the Byrne scale is a trait rather than process measure. Second, it can be as readily regarded as a measure of anxiety as a coping process, though these concepts are quite interdependent. Third, there appears to be no correlation among the three diverse trait measures of presumably the same process (Lazarus, Averill, and Opton, 1974).

Stern, Pascale, and McLoone (1976), on the other hand, used interview techniques to assess the coping process following acute myocardial infarction. What are called "deniers" by the authors (representing 25% of the sample) were more generally optimistic, did very well in returning to work and sexual functioning, and suffered less from post-coronary depression and anxiety. This finding is consistent with Hackett, Cassem, and Wishnie's (1968) claim that denial of the danger of death may be associated with decreased mortality and better post-coronary adjustment in the coronary care unit.

Cohen and Lazarus (1973) have reported a study of vigilance and avoidance of relevant information by patients the night before surgery. Patients who avoided such information showed a more rapid recovery post-surgically, fewer minor complications, and less distress than vigilant patients, a finding quite opposite to that of Janis. The process measure did not correlate at all with a trait measure of repression-sensitization (similar to Byrne's), which in turn failed to correlate with outcome. The authors offer both an institutional and psychological interpretation. With respect to the former, it is possible that physicians were guided in their decision to send patients home by virtue of their manifest attitude; polly-anna avoider-deniers would seem better candidates for early dismissal than worried, complaining vigilants. As to the psychological interpretation, a hospital environment encourages passivity and conformity, which would make vigilance a useless coping strategy since little or nothing one does will affect one's actual fate.

More equivocal concerning the outcome of denial is the research of Wolff, Friedman, Hofer, and Mason (1964) with the parents of children dying of leukemia. This well-known study found that parents who were "well-defended" (largely through denial-like forms of cognitive coping) showed lower levels of corticosteroid secretion during the child's illness than those who were poorly defended. Thus, to the extent that lowered stress levels can be considered a positive consequence, denial-like coping had positive adaptational value. On the other hand, a follow-up study with the same parents (Hofer, Wolff, Friedman, and Mason, 1972) obtained data suggestive of a later reversal: Those who had high secretion levels prior to the child's death showed lower levels many months after; alternatively, those who had low prior levels had higher ones later.

If this finding turns out to be solid and does not merely represent regression to the mean, it also points up the idea that one must be time-oriented in evaluating adaptational outcomes of coping. One might say, for example, that the well-defended parents benefited *during* the illness, but were more vulnerable *after* the child's death because they failed to do "grief work"; in contrast, those who continued consciously to struggle with the impending tragedy were better off later because of the anticipatory coping. To complicate matters further, a later study by Townes, Wold, and Holmes (1974) suggests that fathers did the work of grieving prior to the child's death while mothers did not, so that subsequent mourning was sustained and more intense for the latter. Although such data as these are suggestive (the difference did not reach statistical significance in the study by Townes et al.), none of the studies cited in this research arena is capable of clearly settling the issue of denial and the passage of time. Nevertheless, they are consistent with the concepts of anticipatory coping and with the antithetical role denial might play in it. We are still left with the possibility that denial may be helpful only in a limited time frame, and might exact a price later on.

Recent observations by Levine and Zigler (1975) on denial in stroke victims may also be considered here. Measuring denial idiosyncratically by examining their real- versus ideal-self disparity, stroke victims were found to have the greatest use of denial (i.e., showed a larger discrepancy between presumed loss of function and how it was appraised) compared with two other handicapped groups, namely, victims of lung cancer and heart disease. Denial, assessed in this way, appeared to produce a comparative state of emotional equanimity in the stroke patients despite the fact that they actually suffered the greatest damage to functioning among the three disorders. One could argue, moreover, that a more realistic self-assessment by the stroke victims would have had little value, adaptationally speaking, since little or nothing more could have been done about their deficits even with a more realistic appraisal. Perhaps it could be said in such an instance that ignorance is more functional than the bitter truth.

Before leaving studies in which denial has proved constructive, it is worth noting a recent neurohumoral discovery that, with a small leap of the imagination, seems to have a bearing. Biochemists (Guillemin, Vargo, Rossier, Minick, Ling, Rivier, Vale, and Bloom, 1977) have discovered that, simultaneous with the secretion under stress of ACTH by the pituitary gland, another hormone called endorphin-B is also secreted. ACTH stimulates secretion of corticosteroids by the adrenals; endorphin-B seems to affect morphine-sensitive brain tissue, presumably acting like an analgesic and psychedelic. A severely wounded animal, or a badly frightened or enraged one, might well be expected to produce not only corticosteroids (as in Selye's GAS stage of resistance), but also this morphine-like substance. This may help explain why Beecher (1957) and others have observed a remarkable absence of pain in wounded soldiers, or why in battle men sometimes throw themselves into combat seemingly oblivious of the consequences. It may not be altogether fanciful to suggest that chemicals such as endorphin-B could be the neurohumoral analogue of denial and other comforting cognitions (Mechanic, 1962) or, as I have elsewhere referred to them, palliative forms of coping. The analogy could be reassuring to those who take seriously the thesis that palliative forms of coping, denial among them, might play a valuable part in the overall human armamentarium of coping.

Principles Concerning Costs and Benefits of Denial-like Coping Processes

In accordance with these analyses and the research cited above, a useful summary of the adaptational consequences of denial-like processes is offered, which contains four principles:

(1) The first is a version of an old truth, namely, that circumstances alter cases. Put more pedantically, denial can have positive value under certain conditions and negative value under others. Specifically, if direct action to change the damaging or threatening person-environment transaction is adaptationally essential or useful, the family of processes called denial (when they undermine such action by avoiding or disavowing the threat or danger) will be destructive. On the other hand, when direct action is irrelevant to the adaptational outcome, then denial-like processes have no necessarily damaging consequences, and could even be of value by reducing distress and allowing the person to get on with other matters.

This principle also allows us to extrapolate to other damaging circumstances, for example, illnesses such as kidney failure and diabetes. Control of these illnesses depends on vigilant attention to diet and exercise, and to behavioral and bodily signals of the need for dialysis or insulin. To the extent that successful denial of fact or damaging implications pushes the person to overlook such signals and therefore to evade suitable actions, it is counterproductive and could even be fatal. However, depression and disengagement are also enemies of efforts to stay alive and functioning well, and to mobilize the necessary vigilance over a long time requires relatively good morale and the feeling of hope. It could be argued, therefore, that some positive thinking in the face of a severe hardship might also prove of value and even be necessary.

The distinction implied in principle one is between what my colleagues and I have been calling *problem-focused coping* and *emotion-focused coping*, and which I had earlier spoken of as direct action and palliation (Lazarus and Launier, 1978). They represent two of the most important functions of coping, namely, that of changing a damaging or threatening relationship between person and environment (problem-focused) and regulating the emotional distress produced by that relationship (emotion-focused). In current research in my laboratory, Folkman and Lazarus (1980) found that in every complex stressful encounter people use a mixture of both kinds of coping. Moreover, when an encounter is appraised as permitting little or nothing to be done, there is a pull toward emotion-focused coping; and when it is appraised as permitting constructive actions, the shift is to problem-focused modes. Folkman also found that work pulls for more problem-focused modes, and illness pulls for emotion-focused ones. Denial clearly falls within the emotion-focused function, and as noted below in principle four, when denial is partial, tentative or minimal in scope, it does not necessarily undermine the *simultaneous* use of problem-focused forms of coping when these might have relevance to the person's plight.

(2) The second principle is that when a given type of stress must be encountered again and again, then denial (which could keep up morale and keep down distress) will prevent ultimate mastery. In effect, there are *time-related* implications in the use of denial.

(3) The third principle is also *time-related*. Denial can have positive value at an early stage of coping when the person's resources are insufficient to cope in a more problem-focused way. Severely injured patients gain from denial when their life hangs in balance, when they are too weak or shocked to act constructively and so need to be supported by others.Thus, the patient with spinal cord injury is helped for a while by believing that bodily functions that have been lost will return, or that the incapacitation is not as severe as it seems. Only later will the person be strong enough to come to terms with the reality of the condition and ultimately struggle to cope in a practical, problem-focused sense.

There is no contradiction between principles two and three. Both agree that denial is valuable, but only in an early stage. Principle two concerns the price of denial for later similar encounters, while principle three treats denial as a temporary preservative before more problem-focused forms of coping can be brought to bear.

(4) Principle four is that some *kinds* of denial are more or less fruitless and dangerous, while others may have considerable value. For example, of two objects of denial, emotional distress and the harm or threat inherent in some encounter, the former has less utility because it provides little reason for the person actually to feel better — while denying, the person still feels upset. On the other hand, if we can believe that we are not seriously ill, or not in some danger, there is no reason to be upset; the threat has been shortcircuited (Lazarus and Alfert, 1964; Lazarus, Opton, Nomikos, and Rankin, 1965). Furthermore, logically it would seem to be far more dangerous to deny what is clear and unambiguous than to deny what cannot be known for certain. The most obvious example is the difference between denial of *fact* and denial of *implication*. The fact that one is sick is harder to deny successfully than the implication that one is going to die soon, and still harder to deny than the notion that one will in some sense live on after death. There is an insightful joke that wherever one goes after death can't be such a bad place since no one has ever returned to complain about it. If one denies what is ambiguous, the fiction is more easily sustained and is apt to be less pernicious adaptationally.

The last principle above also concerns instances in which denial is partial, tentative, or minimal in scope (as in Lipowski's, [1970], term "minimization"). Then it should be far less pernicious, and often quite useful. I started by noting some of the self-deceptions or illusions people live by and how important they are for mental health. It is useful to remember that these self-deceptions are not usually challenged by evidence, nor do we even try to test them by the methods of science. This kind of denial is closer to the sense of "as if," to illusion in the more literary usage, or to working fictions or assumptions.

Moreover, throughout human history such working fictions have been regarded as useful not only in maintaining morale, but in aiding effective adaptation. An example from stress and coping theory is the distinction between two ways in which the same demanding or troubling event can be appraised. One person is *threatened* by it, the other *challenged* (e.g., Lazarus, 1978; Lazarus and Launier, 1978; Lazarus, Cohen, Folkman, Kanner, and Schaefer, 1979). Some people appear to have the happy faculty of viewing harsh experiences in a positive, challenging light while others seem constantly to view them dourly as threats. There is even reason to think that the former persons feel better and perform more effectively in the face of adversity than the latter. It is an important and practical research issue.

The discussion of threat and challenge above might remind us of a popular inspirational book of several decades past, Norman Vincent Peale's *The Power of Positive Thinking*, which exhorted the reader to think positively even about life's travails and setbacks as the most serviceable way of life. To propose that it is better to appraise a stressful encounter as a challenge than as a threat is not very different from arguing that we would all lead happier, more productive lives if we could learn to think positively. Such an outlook is nicely expressed in the Hebrew expression common to Israelis, *yiheyeh beseder* (it will be all right). The problem with Peale's inspirational message is not that he was altogether wrong about this, but, as in the case of all advice and inspirational messages, those who need them most are least able to use them effectively.

REFERENCES

Andrew, J. M. (1970), Recovery from surgery with and without preparatory instruction for three coping styles. *J. Pers. Soc. Psychol.*, 151: 223–226.

Ansbacher, H. L. & Ansbacher, R. R., Eds. (1956), *The Individual Psychology of Alfred Adler*. New York: Basic Books.

Becker, E. (1973), *The Denial of Death*. New York: Free Press.

Beecher, H. K. (1957), The measurement of pain. *Pharmacol. Rev.*, 9: 59–209.

Bem, D. (1970), *Beliefs, Attitudes and Human Affairs*. Belmont, Cal.: Brooks/Cole.

Benner, P., Roskies, E. & Lazarus, R. S. (1980), Stress and Coping under extreme conditions. In: *Survivors, Victims and Perpetrators: Essays on the Nazi Holocaust*, ed. J. E. Dimsdale. Washington, D.C.: Hemisphere, pp. 219–258.

Bentley, E., Ed. (1952), *Naked Masks: Five Plays by Luigi Pirandello*. New York: Dutton.

Bergmann, T. (in collaboration with A. Freud) (1958), *Children in the Hospital.* New York: International Universities Press.

Bowlby, J. (1961), Process of mourning. *Internat. J. Psycho-Anal.*, 42: 317–340.

Breger, L. (1967), Functions of dreams. *J. Abnorm. Psychol. Monogr.*, 72.

Cobb, B., Clark, R. L., McGuire, C. & Howe, C. D. (1954), Patient-responsible delay of treatment in cancer. *Cancer*, 7:920–926.

Cohen, F. & Lazarus, R. S. (1973), Active coping processes, coping dispositions, and recovery from surgery. *Psychosom. Med.*, 35:357–389.

_____ _____ (1979), Coping with the stress of illness. In: *Health Psychology*, ed. G. C. Stone, F. Cohen, & N. E. Adler. San Francisco: Jossey-Bass, pp. 217–254.

Davis, F. (1963), *Passage through Crisis: Polio Victims and Their Families.* Indianapolis: Bobbs-Merrill.

Delong, D. R. (1970), Individual differences in patterns of anxiety arousal, stress-relevant information and recovery from surgery. Unpublished doctoral dissertation, University of California, Los Angeles.

Dembo, T., Leviton, G. L. & Wright, B. A. (1956), Adjustment to misfortune—a problem of social psychological rehabilitation. *Artificial Limbs*, 3:4–62.

Dinardo, Q. E. (1971), Psychological adjustment to spinal cord injury. Unpublished doctoral dissertation, University of Houston, Texas.

Erikson, E. H. (1950), *Childhood and Society.* New York: Norton.

Fenichel, O. (1945), *The Psychoanalytic Theory of Neurosis.* London: Routledge & Kegan Paul.

Festinger, L. (1957), *A Theory of Cognitive Dissonance.* New York: Harper & Row.

Fine, B. D., Joseph, E. D. & Waldhorn, H. F., Eds. (1969), *The Mechanism of Denial.* Monograph III, Monograph Series of the Kris Study Group of the New York Psychoanalytic Institute. New York: International Universities Press.

Folkman, S. & Lazarus, R. S. (1980), An analysis of coping in a middle-aged community sample. *J. Health Soc. Behav.*, 21:219–239.

_____, Schaefer, C. & Lazarus, R. S. (1979), Cognitive processes as mediators in stress and coping. In: *Human Stress and Cognition: An Information-processing Approach,* ed. V. Hamilton & D. M. Warburton, pp. 265–298.

Frankl, V. E. (1955), *The Doctor and the Soul.* New York: Knopf.

Freud, A. (1936), *The Ego and the Mechanisms of Defense.* New York: International Universities Press, 1946.

Goldstein, M. J. (1973), Individual differences in response to stress. *Amer. J. Commun. Psychol.*, 1:113–137.

Guillemin, R., Vargo, T., Rossier, J., Minick, S., Ling, N., Rivier, C., Vale, W. & Bloom F. (1977), B-endorphin and adrenocorticotropin are secreted concomitantly by the pituitary gland. *Science*, 197:1367–1369.

Haan, N. (1977), *Coping and Defending*. New York: Academic Press.

Hackett, T. P. & Cassem, N. H. (1974), Development of a quantitative rating scale to assess denial. *J. Psychosom. Res.*, 18:93–100.

———— ———— (1975), Psychological management of the myocardial infarction patient. *J. Human Stress*, 1:25–38.

———— ———— & Wishnie, H. A. (1968), The coronary-care unit: An appraisal of its psychologic hazards. *New England J. Med.*, 279:1365–1370.

———— & Weisman, A. D. (1964), Reactions to the imminence of death. In: *The Threat of Impending Disaster,* ed. G. H. Grosser, H. Wechsler & M. Greenblatt. Cambridge, Mass.: MIT Press, pp. 300–311.

Hall, C. S. & Lindsey, G. (1957), *Theories of Personality*. New York: Wiley.

Hamburg, D. A. & Adams, J. E. (1967), A perspective on coping behavior: Seeking and utilizing information in major transitions. *Arch. Gen. Psychiat.*, 17:277–284.

————, Hamburg, B. & deGoza, S. (1953), Adaptive problems and mechanisms in severely burned patients. *Psychiat.*, 16:1–20.

Hofer, M. A., Wolff, E. T., Friedman, S. B., & Mason, J. W. A. (1972), A psychoendocrine study of bereavement, Parts I and II. *Psychosom. Med.*, 34: 481–504.

Horowitz, L. M., Sampson, H., Siegelman, E. Y., Wolfson, A. & Weiss, J. 1975), On the identification of warded-off mental contents: An empirical and methodological contribution. *J. Abnorm. Psychol.*, 84:545–558.

Horowitz, M. (1975), Intrusive and repetitive thoughts after experimental stress. *Arch. Gen. Psychiat.*, 32:1457–1463.

Jacobson, E. (1957), Denial and repression. *J. Amer. Psychoanal. Assn.*, 5:61–92.

Jahoda, M. (1958), *Current Conceptions of Positive Mental Health*. New York: Basic Books.

Janis, I. L. (1958), *Psychological Stress*. New York: Wiley.

———— (1974), Vigilance and decision-making in personal crises. In: *Coping and Adaptation*, ed. G. V. Coelho, D. A. Hamburg, & J. E. Adams. New York: Basic Books, pp. 139–175.

———— & Mann, L. (1977), *Decision-making*. New York: Free Press.

Kanungo, R. N. (1979), The concepts of alienation and involvement revisited. *Psychol. Bull.*, 86:119–138.

Katz, J. L., Weiner, H., Gallagher, T. G. & Hellman, L. (1970), Stress, distress, and ego defenses. *Arch. Gen. Psychiat.*, 23:131–142.

Kübler-Ross, E. (1969), *On Death and Dying*. New York: Macmillan.

Lazarus, R. S. & Alfert, E. (1964), The short-circuiting of threat. *J. Abnorm. Soc. Psychol.*, 69:195–205.

————, Averill, J. R. & Opton, E. M., Jr. (1974), The psychology of coping: Issues of research and assessment. In: *Coping and Adaptation*, ed. G. V. Coelho, D. A. Hamburg, & J. E. Adams. New York: Basic Books, pp. 249–315.

_____ (1978), The stress and coping paradigm. Presented at Conference on the Critical Evaluation of Behavioral Paradigms for Psychiatric Science, Gleneden Beach, Oregon, November 3–6.

_____ , Cohen, J. B., Folkman, S. K., Kanner, A., & Schaefer, C. (1979), Psychological stress and adaptation: Some unresolved issues. In: *Guide to Stress Research*, ed. H. Selye. New York: Van Nostrand Reinhold.

_____ & Launier, R. (1978), Stress-related transactions between person and environment. In: *Perspectives in Interactional Psychology,* ed. L. A. Pervin & M. Lewis. New York: Plenum, pp. 287–327.

_____ , Opton, E. M., Jr., Nomikos, M. S. & Rankin N. O. (1965), The principle of short-circuiting of threat: Further evidence. *J. Pers.*, 33:622–635.

Lefcourt, H. M. (1966), Repression-sensitization: A measure of the evaluation of emotional expression. *J. Consult. Clin. Psychol.*, 30:444–449.

Levine, J. & Zigler, E. (1975), Denial and self-image in stroke, lung cancer, and heart disease patients. *J. Consult. Clin. Psychol.*, 43:751–757.

Lifton, R. J. (1964), On death and death symbolism: The Hiroshima disaster. *Psychiat.*, 27:191–210.

Lindemann, E. (1944), Symptomatology and management of acute grief. *Amer. J. Psychiat.*, 101:141–148.

Lipowski, Z. J. (1970), Physical illness, the individual and the coping process. *Internat. J. Psychiat. Med.*, 1:91–102.

Maslow, A. H. (1954), *Motivation and Personality*. New York: Harper & Row.

McDaniel, J. W. & Sexton, A. W. (1970), Psychoendocrine studies of patients with spinal cord lesion. *J. Abnorm. Psychol.*, 76:117–122.

Mechanic, D. (1962), *Students under Stress*. Madison: University of Wisconsin Press, 1962.

Menninger, K. (1963), *The Vital Balance*. New York: Viking.

Offer, D. & Freedman, D. X. (1972), *Modern Psychiatry and Clinical Research: Essays in Honor of Roy R. Grinker, Sr.* New York: Basic Books.

Oken, D. (1961), What to tell cancer patients: Study of medical attitudes. *J. Amer. Med. Assn.*, 175:1120–1128.

Pirandello, L. (1939), *Saggi*. Milano, Italy: Mondadori.

Rank, O. (1936), *Will Therapy and Truth and Reality*. New York: Knopf.

Rokeach, M. (1968), *Beliefs, Attitudes and Values*. San Francisco: Jossey-Bass.

Sjöbäck, H. (1973), *The Psychoanalytic Theory of Defensive Processes*.

New York: Wiley.
Staudenmayer, H., Kinsman, R. A., Dirks, J. F., Spector, S. L. & Wangaard, C. (1979), Medical outcome in asthmatic patients: Effects of
airways hyperactivity and symptom-focused anxiety. *Psychosom.
Med.*, 41:109–118.
Stern, M. J., Pascale, L. & McLoone, J. B. (1976), Psychosocial adapta-
tion following an acute myocardial infarction. *J. Chronic Dis.*, 29:
513–526.
Townes, B. D., Wold, D. A., & Holmes, T. H. (1974), Parental adjustment to childhood leukemia. *J. Psychosom. Res.*, 18:9–14.
Vaihinger, H. (1911), *The Philosophy of "As If."* New York: Harcourt,
1925.
Vaillant, G. (1977), *Adaptation to Life.* Boston: Little, Brown.
Visotsky, H. M., Hamburg, D. A. Goss, M. E. & Lebovits, B. Z. (1961),
Coping behavior under extreme stress. *Arch. Gen. Psychiat.*,
5:423–448.
Von Kugelgen, E. (1975), Psychological determinants of the delay in de-
cision to seek aid in cases of myocardial infarction. Unpublished
doctoral dissertation, University of California, Berkeley.
Watzlawick, P. (1976), *How Real Is Real?* New York: Random House.
Weisman, A. D. (1972), *On Dying and Denying.* New York: Behavioral
Publications.
Wheelis, A. (1966), *The Illusionless Man: Fantasies and Meditations.*
New York: Norton.
Wolff, C. T., Friedman, S. B., Hofer, M. A. & Mason, J. W. (1964), Re-
lationship between psychological defenses and mean urinary
17-hydroxycorticosteroid excretion rates, Parts I and II. *Psycho-
som. Med.*, 26:576–609.
Wortman, C. B. & Dunkel-Schetter, C. (1979), The importance of social
support: Parallels between victims and the aged. Presented at Work-
shop on the Elderly of the Future, Committee on Aging, National
Research Council, Annapolis, Maryland, May 3–5.
Wright, B. A. (1960), *Physical Disability: A Psychological Approach.*
New York: Harper.

DISCUSSION

DENIAL IN VARIOUS
FACETS OF HEALTH

The discussion following Dr. Lazarus' presentation focused on the role of denial in health, which led to the question of the various facets of health. On the basis of Dr. Elkes' remarks, a distinction was made between morale, social functioning, and somatic well-being as separate aspects of a broader view of health.

Dr. Lazarus: We do not know much about the relations between these facets of health in nature. We do not know, for example, to what extent someone functioning well socially will also have good morale and good somatic health. They may often be dissociated. Certain forms of denial, or denial under certain conditions, will produce good morale, yet produce damage in some somatic sense. Individuals with the Type-A behavior pattern might be a case in point. These people live their lives as striving, hardworking, time-oriented and competitive, many of them liking what they do very much, and unable to think of any other way to live. Nevertheless, they are paying a price in somatic health.

The possible dissociation of the various facets of health in the

31

context of denial was illustrated by some concrete examples.

Dr. Spence recalled a patient whose main symptom was telling the truth: She inevitably lost friends by telling them just what she thought, and just what they didn't want to hear. One reason why it took her years to realize that this was maladaptive was her intolerance of ambiguity. Her compulsive truth-telling was quite like that of Hickey in *The Ice Man Cometh.*

Dr. Horowitz took exception to principle four (that denial of emotion is useless). He claimed that denying the expression of anger may well protect patients following serious life events: Trainees in psychotherapy often come with the notion that by getting the people to express their emotions, they will get better. In fact, we have seen negative effects from the pursuit of techniques based on this principle. Anger is a good example. After serious life events, people frequently try to avoid recognition of their anger, or avoid expressing it even if they consciously know about it; this is for very good reasons. Once they enter states which we call "righteous rages" which have self-propelled, out-of-control properties, they may demolish their social support systems and cause grief and humiliation.

Dr. Breznitz considered the issue of denial following bereavement, cautioning against the generality of principle three (that denial may be particularly effective during the initial, impact phase of a stressful experience). The point also related to the need to distinguish between the above three facets of adjustment: Often, during the initial impact phase the individual receives a substantial amount of social support. Thus, following bereavement, for instance, the extended family and friends converge on the person trying to support him. During the later phase of the bereavement process, however, he is often left very much on his own. Denial during the initial phase and delay of the "grief work," while possibly conducive to morale, may thus deprive the person of important social support when he needs it most. Observations on delayed depression of Israeli widows who took a stoic posture during the critical impact phase bear witness to this difficulty.

The possible interrelationships among the various facets of health were commented upon, including the positive function of denial.

Dr. Janis, referring to the production of endorphins by the human brain, mentioned the famous case of Norman Cousins, who overcame fatal illness by actually engaging in pleasure-producing (anti-stress?) behavior: That particular case has stimulated a great deal of interest, along with the scientific developments on placebo effects. We have reached the stage where the term "placebo effects" is no longer being used; it is now called "nonspecific forms of therapy," because there are a well-documented series of cases where the so-called "placebo effect" actually does bring about a cure. Some of the consequences of denial-like behavior could actually have biochemical effects.

Dr. Elkes: Belief has been found to be an extraordinarily effective way of getting people well. Man is not a stupid animal; he would not have preserved belief systems if they did not have adaptive value. Denial is part of a deeply ingrained biological adaptive process which would not have been invented by an organism if it did not have adaptive functions.

2

PREVENTING PATHOGENIC DENIAL BY MEANS OF STRESS INOCULATION

IRVING L. JANIS

VARIETIES OF DENIAL

The term "denial" is somewhat ambiguous because it is used to refer to a wide variety of psychotic, neurotic, and normal psychological processes (A. Freud, 1936; Lindemann, 1944; Federn, 1952; Janis, 1958; Adler, Cohen, and Stone, 1979; Cohen and Lazarus, 1979; Mages and Mendelsohn, 1979). The common feature of behavior that is labeled "denial" is a tendency to minimize or fail to appraise correctly an undesirable personal characteristic or event. In circumstances of extreme stress, this tendency is observed in normal persons and may have adaptive value. It is necessary to distinguish between those instances when a person ignores ambiguous signs of threat and those when he disregards clear-cut evidence of loss or danger. Only the latter are likely to be

Preparation of this paper was supported in part by Grant No. 1R01 MH32995-01 from the National Institute of Mental Health.

35

regarded as "pathological denial." The behavioral consequences are quite different for those highly ambiguous situations of potential adversity where the probabilities of loss or danger cannot be accurately ascertained at the moment, but must await subsequent events. Intellectual denial of any such potential danger will be referred to as "minimization" of the threat. Typical examples of minimization are to be found in any hospital ward where patients are waiting to be taken to an operating room (Hamburg, 1953; Janis, 1958; Cohen and Lazarus, 1979).

Denial in the form of minimizing the magnitude or imminence of the threat may prove to be an adaptive type of response, even when the dangers are nonambiguous, if there is little realistic basis for hope of survival—as in the case of patients suffering from inoperable cancer, and combat troops being attacked by a vastly superior force.

At the opposite extreme from adaptive denial are clear-cut instances of pathological denial, which include all instances where a person rejects a painful fact about his present environment even though it can be clearly perceived and is generally regarded by others in his community as unquestionable. Typical instances of pathological denial have been described in the literature on the delusions and morbid elations of the chronically ill and the bereaved (Wittkower, 1952; Weinstein and Kahn, 1955; Parkes, 1972). Thus, for example, a patient who is suffering from tuberculosis might deny being ill and refuse to stay in a hospital; a widow might deny that her husband is dead after attending his funeral.

The distinction between the two categories, "pathological" and "nonpathological," is important insofar as it enables correct predictions to be made about the personality characteristics of anyone who is displaying one or another form of denial. When a person's denial reaction is diagnosed as "pathological," the term carries the implication that he will prove to have an abnormally low degree of stress tolerance in general, and that he can be expected to display other grossly pathological symptoms of severe neurosis or psychosis.

Pathological denial reactions lead to maladaptive behavior, such as incautious exposure to danger, as in the Old Sergeant syndrome observed among seasoned infantrymen who are "old" in combat experience and have witnessed the death of many buddies

(Sobel, 1949; Janis, 1971). They become apathetic, ignore elementary safety precautions, and even fail to take cover during artillery attacks. Such reactions are characterized as pathological denial because they involve personality disorganization. The denial tendency is accompanied by a variety of other psychological symptoms, and the maladaptive behavior continues even when the environmental circumstances improve.

Somewhere in between the two extremes of *adaptive denial* and *pathological denial* is a third major type, which I call *pathogenic denial*. This third type occurs in somewhat ambiguous circumstances of potential adversity. Like adaptive denial, it involves *minimization* of the threat. Unlike pathological denial, however, it does not involve a break with reality testing, even though real dangers are being ignored. The probabilities of loss or danger are fairly high, but are difficult for anyone to ascertain until further developments occur. A person who displays this nonpathological form of denial is likely to be highly responsive to changes in the environment that provide new clues as to what is likely to happen, and is also responsive to social communications that are intended to correct his or her temporary misinterpretation of "reality." Thus, after being exposed to advice or persuasion from a respected authority figure, a person who has been minimizing oncoming danger will change his or her appraisals and no longer fail to take precautionary action. But if the person is not exposed to corrective information, he or she will continue to minimize the threat and be psychologically unprepared for the danger if it materializes. In this respect, such nonpathological denial is *pathogenic*.

Many normal persons characteristically fail to take advantage of opportunities to learn about future dangers that might someday materialize. When unavoidably exposed to warnings or other cues pertaining to danger, they tend to ignore the ominous significance of those unfavorable signs which lend themselves to alternative interpretations; or they selectively recall and give most weight to favorable signs that permit them to maintain a relatively unperturbed attitude about what the future holds in store for them.

Pathogenic denial can be conceptualized as a component of the pattern of defensive avoidance, which involves suppression of disturbing thoughts, selective inattention to cues that arouse anxiety or guilt, and biased information-processing of messages that deal with the emotionally disturbing issue. Janis and Mann's (1977) analysis of coping patterns specifies two essential conditions for defensive avoidance: (1) the decision-maker is in a state of relatively high decisional conflict resulting from awareness of threatening consequences that make it seem impossible for him to adopt any easy resolution; and (2) the decision-maker has lost hope of finding a solution better than the defective ones he is considering. Antecedent conditions that contribute to loss of hope include being exposed to the following stimuli or circumstances: (1) markedly diminishing returns from prolonged information search, indicating that the information supply has been exhausted; (2) impressive warnings about unacceptable losses from adopting any of the proposed alternatives; and (3) a consensus of pessimism among advisors about finding any promising new way to resolve the conflict.

When the conditions making for defensive avoidance are present (namely, awareness of serious losses from any alternative that might be selected, together with loss of hope of finding a satisfactory solution), the individual becomes closed-minded and biased in his or her information preferences. There are three defensive avoidance subpatterns, and each involves a characteristic type of information preference:

(a) *Procrastination*, the pattern that emerges when there are no deadline pressures, is associated with information *evasion*. There is a slight degree of passive interest in reassuring information along with a strong tendency to avoid all challenging information. The decision-maker is mainly interested in deferring the decision; information that provokes him to think about the decision is neither sought nor welcomed. The person would prefer to *ignore* the vast majority of relevant messages (a phenomenon rarely, if ever, observed in the laboratory, where subjects are generally required to look at or listen to the communications offered by the experimenter, however much they might prefer to ignore them).

(b) When the additional conditions that make for *shifting of responsibility* obtain (namely, strong deadline pressures together with the opportunity to foist the decision onto someone else), the dominant tendency will be to limit information gathering to the activity of *seeking out others*, such as a superior or an expert, who will either take over entirely or instruct the person on what to do, and thereby take responsibility.

(c) When the additional conditions that foster the *bolstering* form of defensive avoidance are present (namely, strong deadline pressures along with little or no opportunity to shift responsibility), the classic pattern of *selective exposure* becomes dominant, marked by active search and preference for information that supports the least objectionable alternative, and avoidance of discrepant information.

Despite these biased information preferences, people who display the pathogenic form of minimization of potential danger along with other manifestations of defensive avoidance can generally be influenced by corrective information. Stress inoculation is one of the major means of presenting corrective information to prevent or counteract pathogenic denial.

PRIOR RESEARCH ON STRESS INOCULATION

Stress inoculation involves giving preparatory communications designed to increase a person's level of tolerance for unpleasant events by preventing denial and promoting adherence to adaptive courses of action. Field studies provide suggestive evidence supporting the expectation that preparatory communications containing forewarnings combined with reassurances and coping suggestions will function as stress inoculation to increase adherence to difficult decisions (see reviews of the research literature in Janis, 1971; Girodo, 1977; Janis and Mann, 1977; Meichenbaum, 1977). Preparatory information is said to function as a form of stress inoculation if it enables a person to increase his or her tolerance for subsequent stress as manifested by behavior that is relatively efficient and stable, rather than disorganized, impulsively vacillating, and dominated by acute anxiety symptoms or defensive symptoms such as denial of real threats. Stress inoculation is usually administered shortly after a person makes a commitment to carry out a stressful decision, such as undergoing surgery, but before he or she implements it. The process is called stress inoculation because it may be analogous to what happens when antibodies are induced by injections of attenuated strains of virulent viruses.

Janis' (1958) study of surgical patients first called attention to the potential value of inoculation for stressful decisions made by patients agreeing to undergo elective surgery and postoperative regimens. His correlational results indicated that those surgical patients who received information about the unpleasant consequences beforehand were less likely than those given little information to overreact to setbacks during the postoperative period. Subsequently, supporting evidence for the effectiveness of stress inoculation has come from a variety of controlled field experiments with people who decided to undergo surgery (Egbert, Battit, Welch, and Bartlett, 1964; Johnson, 1966; Schmidt, 1966; Delong, 1971; Schmitt and Wooldridge, 1973; Vernon and Bigelow, 1974). Although some of these studies did not use adequate controls and there are some partial inconsistencies among the findings, all of them provide evidence indicating that when someone on the hospital staff gives preoperative information about the stresses of surgery and ways of coping with those stresses, adult patients show more favorable reactions after the operation. They display less anger, less postoperative regret, more adherence to the postoperative medical regimen, and sometimes better recovery from surgery. Two other studies of surgical patients (Field, 1974; Langer, Janis, and Wolfer, 1975) reported no significant effect of very brief messages describing operative procedures or expected sequelae.

Positive results on the value of stress inoculation have been found in studies of childbirth (Levy and McGee, 1975; Breen, 1975) and noxious medical examinations requiring patients to swallow tubes (Johnson and Leventhal, 1974). Field experiments with children on pediatric surgery wards yielded similar results (Moran, 1963; Melamed and Siegel, 1975; Wolfer and Visintainer, 1975). Preparatory communications given prior to relocation of elderly patients to a new nursing home or to a hospital have reportedly been effective in reducing protests and debilitation (Schulz, 1976).

In a completely different area—work decisions—there is also evidence that stress inoculation can lessen postdecisional stress and minimize the tendency to reverse the decision when setbacks are encountered (Gomersall and Myers, 1966; Wanous, 1973). New employees given realistic preparatory information at the time they are offered a job, or immediately after they accept it, have been found to be more likely to stay with the organization. All of these findings support the conclusion that many people will display higher stress tolerance in response to undesirable consequences of their decisions if they have been given warnings in advance about what to expect, together with sufficient reassurances, so that fear does not mount to an intolerably high level.

We know that there are bound to be exceptions, of course, such as neurotic personalities who are hypersensitive to any threat cues (Janis, 1971). Stress inoculation may also be inappropriate for some types of unmitigated personal disaster — incurable cancer and severe burns, for example, requiring painful treatments that leave their victims only "withered remnants of their former selves" (Hamburg, Hamburg, and DeGroza, 1953). Among these victims, blanket denial may be the only effective means of avoiding overwhelming anxiety and depression. But such considerations do not preclude the possibility that techniques of stress inoculation might prove effective in preventing pathogenic denial and mitigating the impact of a wide variety of anticipated stressful events, especially when a chosen course of action requires undergoing temporary losses in order to achieve long-term goals. Although the evidence so far comes from only a few types of decisions, it seems plausible that stress inoculation might be applied successfully to all consequential decisions.

In his account of stress inoculation for pain and phobic situations, Meichenbaum (1977) distinguishes between two different aspects of coping with anticipated stress: (1) handling each stressor effectively so that the person is not overwhelmed; and (2) coping with the feeling of being overwhelmed by one or more stressors. A comparable distinction can be made when stress inoculation is applied for purposes of preventing pathogenic denial of the potentially adverse consequences of a difficult decision, such as undergoing painful medical treatment or surgery.

A number of interrelated cognitive and motivational processes that may mediate the effects of stress inoculation are suggested by case studies describing how hospitalized men and women react to severe postdecisional setbacks after having decided to permit surgeons to operate (Janis, 1958). Some of the case studies deal with surgical patients who for one reason or another were not psychologically prepared. These patients were so overwhelmed by the usual pains, discomforts, and deprivations of the postoperative convalescence period that they manifestly regretted their decision, and on some occasions actually refused to permit the hospital staff to administer routine postoperative treatments. Before the disturbing setbacks occurred, these patients typically received relatively little preparatory information. They retained unrealistic conceptions of how nicely everything was going to work out, which enabled them to set their worries aside. They sincerely believed that they would not have bad pains or undergo any other disagreeable experiences. But then, when they unexpectedly experienced incision pains and suffered from all sorts of other unpleasant deprivations that are characteristic of postoperative convalescence, their blanket type of reassurance was undermined. They thought something had gone horribly wrong, and could neither reassure themselves nor accept truthful reassurances from doctors or nurses.

Like someone traumatized by an overwhelming accident or disaster, psychologically unprepared patients experience acute feelings of helplessness, and overreact with symptoms of acute fright or aggrievement. It is precisely in this respect that nonpathological denial of impending threat during the preoperative period is pathogenic.

The process of mentally rehearsing anticipated losses while in a somewhat agitated state and developing reassuring conceptions that can at least partially alleviate fear, is referred to as the "work of worrying." It is assumed to be stimulated by preparatory information concerning any type of impending threat to one's physical, material, social, or moral well-being (Janis, 1958). Essentially the same cognitive and emotional changes that were discerned in the case studies of surgical patients have been noted in comparable case studies of people who have encountered setbacks following other types of decisions, including choosing a career, taking legal action to obtain a divorce, and making policy decisions on behalf of an organization (Janis and Mann, 1977).

Stress inoculation is pertinent to the problem of *backsliding*, which plagues those practitioners who try to help their clients to improve their eating habits, stop smoking, cut down on alcohol consumption, or change their behavior in other ways that will promote health (Janis and Rodin, 1979). The evidence on the high incidence of backsliding has been appalling to those behavioral scientists who have reviewed the research literature on adherence.

Like many other psychologists, I believe that research on psychological preparation for subsequent stress is needed in order to understand how and why backsliding can be prevented. Without an understanding of the basic psychological processes involved, little progress is to be expected in the practical sphere of solving the problems of backsliding. Numerous prior studies have shown that the positive results achieved by counselors in anti-smoking clinics and weight-reduction clinics are frequently not sustained after termination of supportive contact (Ball, 1965; Mausner, 1966; Keutzer, Lichtenstein, and Mees, 1968; Schwartz and Dubitzky, 1968; Bernstein, 1969; McFall and Hammen, 1971; Atthowe, 1973; Hunt and Matarazzo, 1973; Shewchuk, 1976; Sackett and Haynes, 1977; Flaxman, 1978). In their review of the pertinent literature on cigarette smoking, heroin, and alcohol relapse rates, Hunt and Matarazzo (1973) found that many people start to abstain in response to whatever program of clinical treatment they receive, but a very high percentage of the temporary abstainers rapidly relapse between the first and second month after starting the program.

Stress inoculation might be able to facilitate long-term adherence to all sorts of difficult decisions, including those pertaining to many spheres of life in addition to health problems (Janis and Mann, 1977). One major function of stress inoculation might be to stimulate vigilance by counteracting current pathogenic denial and other defensive avoidance tendencies. As long as the expected losses remain somewhat vague and ambiguous, a person is likely to indulge in wishful thinking by denying the potentially adverse consequences of adopting a new course of action. But when exposed to impressive information about those consequences, the person would no longer minimize the impending losses and would begin the constructive work of worrying.

A second major function of stress inoculation for difficult decisions might be to prevent overreactions to subsequent setbacks and crises that might lead to pathogenic denial or other maladaptive reactions, such as hypervigilance, at some time in the future. In order for the first function (counteracting current denial tendencies) to be successful, it is necessary to take account of a set of communication problems involving appropriate dosage of fear-arousing information. The second function (preventing denial and other maladaptive reactions from arising in the future) requires taking account of an additional set of problems concerning long-term effects, including such factors as commitment, self-confidence, and sustained hope for coping adequately with new setbacks as they arise. I shall discuss each set of problems in turn.

Obviously, we cannot expect all preparatory communications to be effective. Very brief preparatory messages about impending threats may be too weak to stimulate the development of effective reassurances, and therefore have no effect at all (Langer, Janis, and Wolfer, 1975; Meichenbaum, 1977). At the opposite extreme, when a preparatory communication is too strong, it can unintentionally stimulate expectations in the receiver of being helpless to avert intolerable losses. Like an overdose of antigens, an overenthusiastic inoculation attempt might produce the very condition it is intended to prevent.

DOSAGE OF FEAR-AROUSING INFORMATION

In order to produce successful stress inoculation, it is necessary to interfere with the person's spontaneous denial tendencies and related efforts to ward off awareness of signs of impending danger. Unwelcome information has to be given in order to convey a realistic picture of the disturbing events each person is likely to experience. How can this be done without running the risk of provoking either panic or adverse avoidance reactions, such as an increase in defensive denial?

Some tentative answers can be inferred from extensive investigations on the effects of warnings and fear appeals by social psychologists. Although a large number of relevant experiments have been reported, we cannot yet formulate any definitive rule about the intensity of emotional arousal that is most likely to be effective (Janis, 1967; McGuire, 1968; Janis, 1971; Leventhal, 1973; Rogers and Mewborn, 1976). Some, but not all, attitude change experiments show less acceptance of precautionary health recommendations when strong fear appeals are used in warning messages than when milder ones are used. In the initial experiment on the problem, Janis and Feshbach (1953) gave equivalent groups of high school students three different versions of a dental hygiene communication, all of them containing the same set of recommendations about when and how to brush their teeth. The results showed that there were diminishing returns as the level of fear increased. A number of subsequent studies have supported the conclusion that when fear is strongly aroused by a communication but is not fully relieved by reassurances, the recipients will be motivated to ignore, minimize, or deny the importance of the threat (Janis and Terwilliger, 1962; Rogers and Thistlethwaite, 1970).

There have been similar experiments, however, that show a gain in effectiveness when strong threat appeals are used, and these experiments point to the facilitating effects of fear arousal (Insko, Arkoff, and Insko, 1965; Leventhal, Singer, and Jones, 1965). Changes in feelings of vulnerability to a threat and adoption of a recommended course of action apparently depend upon the relative strength of facilitating and interfering reactions, both of which are likely to be evoked whenever a warning by an authority arouses fear. Consequently, we cannot expect to discover any simple generalization applicable to all warnings given by authoritative sources that will tell us whether strong fear-arousing presentations that vividly depict the expected dangers, or milder versions that merely allude to the threats, will be more effective in general. Rather, we must expect the optimal level of fear arousal to vary for different types of threat, for different types of recommended action, and for different personalities.

There is general agreement among social psychological investigators that the effectiveness of any fear-arousing communication depends partly upon three content variables that interact in complex ways (Hovland, Janis and Kelley, 1953; McGuire, 1969; Rogers and Mewborn, 1976):

1. Magnitude of the threat (if it were to materialize).
2. Probability of the threat materializing (if no protective action is taken).
3. Probable effectiveness of the recommended protective action or other reassurances about averting or reducing the threat.

These three components are similar to the constructs of expectancy-value formulations that a number of social psychologists have proposed to account for attitude change in general (Rosenberg, 1956; Fishbein, 1967; Rogers, 1975), and which have been applied directly to health education and patient compliance (Hochbaum, 1958; Rosenstock, 1966; Becker and Maiman, 1975). According to this model, people suffering from an illness will not adhere to their physicians' orders unless they believe that the consequences of doing what is recommended, despite all the costs in terms of money, time, effort, and discomfort, are preferable to the consequences of the illness. But, as I shall indicate later, this model can be expected to hold only when certain conditions are present that make for a vigilant pattern of coping with threat.

For anyone who comes to a clinic or hospital, the third component listed above (efficacy) would include not only the anticipated effectiveness of whatever treatments are prescribed, but also the person's general level of confidence in the staff and the degree to which the person obtains reassuring social support (Howard and Strauss, 1975; Caplan and Killilea, 1976). The crucial role of statements about the efficacy of the recommended means for averting or reducing the threat is repeatedly borne out by social psychological studies of the effects of public health messages that contain fear-arousing warnings (Leventhal, Singer, and Jones, 1965; Chu, 1966; Rogers and Thistlethwaite, 1970; Leventhal, 1973; Rogers and Deckner, 1975). Utilizing three different public health communications dealing with well-known hazards that produce preventable human suffering—lung cancer, automobile accident injuries, and venereal disease, Rogers and Mewborn (1976), for example, found that assertions about the efficacy of recommended protective actions had a significant effect on college students' intentions to adopt them.

The findings just cited appear to be consistent with the hypothesis that when a stress inoculation procedure presents realistic information about unpleasant consequences to be expected from a difficult course of action—going on a diet, giving up smoking, or undergoing medical treatment—it is more likely to have positive effects on adherence if it also contains a second component, i.e., impressive information about the expected efficacy of the recommended course of action. (Theoretical grounds for this two-component conception of stress inoculation will be discussed when I summarize the model of coping patterns.)

PREVENTING MALADAPTIVE REACTIONS TO SUBSEQUENT SETBACKS AND CRISES

Why do many people decide to do what physicians or public health authorities recommend, then break off before completing the prescribed regimen, or backslide after having temporarily changed their behavior? Why are other people able to adhere successfully? No definite answer can be given on the basis of existing research, but some of the pertinent factors have been identified. Obviously, a major factor in backsliding is the actual suffering or deprivation imposed, which is especially hard to take if it continues over a long period of time. But psychological factors affect a person's tolerance for pain, frustration, and unpleasant experiences. Some of the factors that influence adherence are suggested by social psychological research on *commitment* and *cognitive coping devices* that enter into psychological preparation for subsequent stress (Janis and Rodin, 1979). Research on commitment, for example, indicates that if a person is induced to announce his or her intention to an esteemed other, such as a counselor in a weight-reduction clinic or in an anti-smoking clinic, the person is anchored to the decision not just by anticipated social disapproval, but also by anticipated self-disapproval (Kiesler, 1971; McFall and Hammen, 1971; Brehm, 1976; Janis and Mann, 1977). The stabilizing effect of commitment, according to Kiesler's (1971) research, is enhanced by exposure to a mild challenging attack, such as counterpropaganda that is easy to refute. A stress inoculation procedure might serve the function of providing a mild challenging attack by calling attention to the obstacles and drawbacks to be expected, and providing impressive suggestions about how those obstacles and drawbacks can be overcome.

A number of social psychological experiments provide evidence of the positive long-term effects of *predicting adverse events in advance*. These experiments show that advance warnings and accurate predictions can have an emotional dampening effect when subsequent setbacks or crises occur, including relatively impersonal events of an undesirable character, such as the bad news that the Soviet Union has increased its capabilities for producing atomic weapons (Janis, Lumsdaine, and Gladstone, 1951). McGuire (1964) has extended the analogy of inoculation or immunization against attitude change to inducing resistance to the effects of mass communications that attack widely held cultural truisms, such as those that argue against brushing one's teeth regularly or against being X-rayed for screening purposes. Several laboratory experiments indicate that a person is less likely to display strong emotional reactions or extreme changes in attitude when confronted with an unpleasant event if he previously has been exposed to a preparatory communication that predicted the disagreeable experience

(Lazarus and Alfert, 1964; Epstein and Clarke, 1970; Staub and Kellett, 1972). These findings support the generalization that giving realistic preparatory information about any potential threat that is likely to materialize will dampen the impact of a subsequent confrontation with the predicted adverse event. But whether prediction of the unfavorable events alone is sufficient to enable the warned person to cope more effectively remains an open question.

There is no general agreement as yet among research investigators about the esential conditions for effective stress inoculation, or about the crucial psychological processes that mediate the positive effects that have been observed. The theoretical rationales that have been suggested include the assumptions that accurate preparatory information about an impending crisis gives a person the opportunity to anticipate the loss, to start working through his anxiety or grief, to make plans, and to develop reassurances that might enable him to cope more adequately. The processes involved in effective psychological preparation are thought to include correcting faulty beliefs, reconceptualizing the threat, engaging in realistic self-persuasion about the value of protective action, and developing concepts and self-instructions that enable the person to avoid being overwhelmed by setbacks (Janis, 1971; Meichenbaum and Turk, 1976; Girodo, 1977; Meichenbaum, 1977).

Perhaps one of the most important effects of the preparatory communications used for purposes of stress inoculation is the person's gain in *perceived control* over distressing environmental events. There is now a sizable literature indicating that perceived personal control sometimes plays an important role in coping with stress (Pervin, 1963; Bowers, 1968; Staub, Tursky, and Schwartz, 1971; Houston, 1972; Averill, 1973; Kanfer and Seider, 1973; Pranulis, Dabbs, and Johnson, 1975; Seligman, 1975; Janis and Rodin, 1979). Several investigators cite evidence which they interpret as indicating that increased sense of control in the face of uncertain threats is associated with increased predictability, which is stress-reducing (Weiss, 1970; Ball and Vogler, 1971). Some interventions that are regarded as control-enhancing give people a great deal of preparatory information, including precise descriptions of expected emotional reactions, as in the stress inoculation procedure used by Johnson and Leventhal (1974) with medical patients who had agreed to undergo gastroendoscopy. The important point is that stress inoculation may be successful in promoting long-term adherence partly because it enhances feelings of control as well as predictability.

Johnson (1975) argues that preparatory information not only increases expectancies about likely sensations; it also decreases expectancies about unlikely ones. Some interventions may make patients feel less helpless by making them more active participants, increasing their actual behavioral commitment and personal involvement in the treatment. Pranulis et al. (1975), for example, redirect patients' focus of attention away from their own emotional reactions as passive recipients of treatments, to information that makes them feel more in control as active collaborators with the staff. The value of directing attention to coping capabilities has been suggested by a study of effectiveness of a cognitive reappraisal technique with surgical patients (Langer, Janis, and Wolfer, 1975). Without encouraging denial of realistic threats, the technique encourages each patient to feel confident about being able to deal effectively with whatever pains, discomforts, and setbacks are subsequently encountered. I shall say more about this confidence-enhancing technique shortly.

Meichenbaum (1977) has developed a stress inoculation training program based on the concepts of cognitive-behavior modification. It involves three main steps: (1) discussing the nature of stress reactions with the clients in order to provide them with a conceptual framework and also to motivate them to acquire new coping skills; (2) teaching and inducing rehearsal of coping skills, such as collecting information about what is likely to happen, and arranging for ways to deal effectively with anxiety-engendering events; and (3) encouraging the client to practice and apply the newly acquired coping skills to stressful conditions, either by means of role-playing in imagined stress situations or actual exposures to real-life stresses. This type of stress inoculation training has been found to be at least partially successful for a number of anxiety-arousing situations (Meichenbaum and Cameron, 1973), and for experimentally induced pain (Turk, 1978; Turk and Genest, 1979).

Some negative results, however, are reported among college women with fear of flying (Girodo and Roehl, 1976). After reviewing the positive and negative outcomes of studies employing stress inoculation training, Girodo (1977) suggests that the successful components are those that induce the person to reconceptualize the threat into nonthreatening terms, and that all other components merely serve as attention-diversion mechanisms. Any such generalization, however, gives undue weight to a limited set of findings; therefore, it is premature until we have well-replicated results from a variety of investigations that carefully test the effectiveness of each component of stress inoculation. It remains for the next phase of research to determine which components are the necessary and sufficient ingredients for promoting effective coping in stressful situations.

Related types of psychological intervention also need to be investigated, including those that may help clients to reconceptualize the stresses engendered by a stressful course of action. For example, the coping device developed by Langer, Janis, and Wolfer (1975) involves encouraging an optimistic reappraisal of anxiety-provoking events. It appears to build up realistic hope of dealing effectively with whatever suffering or setbacks might be encountered. Such an approach was tested in a field experiment with surgical patients by utilizing it in a brief interview conducted by a psychologist. Each patient was given several examples of the positive or compensatory consequences of his or her decision to undergo surgery (for example, improvement in health, extra care and attention in the hospital, temporary vacation from outside pressure). Then the patient was invited to think up additional examples that pertained to his or her individual case. Finally the patient was given the recommendation to rehearse these compensatory consequences whenever he or she started to feel upset about the unpleasant aspects of the surgical experience. Patients were urged to be as realistic as possible about the compensatory features, so as to emphasize that what was being recommended was not equivalent to trying to deceive oneself. The instructions were designed to promote warranted optimism and awareness of the anticipated gains that outweighed the losses expected from the chosen course of action.

The findings from this controlled experiment supported the prediction that cognitive reappraisal would reduce stress both before and after an operation. Patients given the reappraisal intervention scored lower on nurses' blind ratings of preoperative stress, and on unobtrusive postoperative measures of the frequency with which pain-relieving drugs and sedatives were requested. Coping procedures like this one may help patients avoid becoming discouraged and losing confidence in the hospital staff, which can result in their making personal decisions during the postoperative period that are antithetical to the medical regimen prescribed by their physicians and to their own best interests.

That similar coping procedures may be effective for other types of decision, such as dieting, is suggested by the findings from a doctoral dissertation by Riskind (1982), which was carried out in a weight-reduction clinic under my research program. Riskind found that clients with a relatively high initial level of self-esteem responded favorably when they were given instructions to adopt a day-by-day coping perspective as compared with the usual long-term perspective. They showed a greater sense of personal control and more adherence to the diet, as measured by weight loss over a period of two months. Coping devices like the ones used by Riskind (1982) and Langer, Janis, and Wolfer (1975) could be incorporated into stress inoculation procedures and might prove to enhance their effectiveness.

Although warnings and coping suggestions may be helpful for dealing with subsequent stresses, potential dangers that are predicted in advance frequently do not materialize. When a danger does not materialize the prior warnings about it prove to be false alarms. In military threat situations, for example, a realistic threat of an enemy invasion may not occur because of last-minute peace negotiations. Troops may be given a red-alert warning because of malfunctions in sensitive radar instruments for detecting unidentified aircraft or because of errors made by human operations. Breznitz' (1967, 1976) laboratory experiments using the threat of electric shock indicate that false alarms tend to reduce fear reactions to a subsequent similar threat, whether the false alarm involves postponement or cancellation of the danger. The fear-reducing effect of a warning about a potential danger that proves to be a false alarm obviously could have a "cry wolf" effect that reduces the impact of any subsequent attempts at stress inoculation for the same kind of potential danger.

A THEORETICAL MODEL OF COPING PATTERNS

Additional factors that might prevent pathogenic denial and

promote long-term adherence to difficult decisions are suggested by a theoretical analysis of the way people cope with decisional conflict, which has been developed by Janis and Mann (1977). This theoretical model provides a basis for formulating hypotheses concerning the mediating processes that might help to explain when, how, and why stress inoculation is effective.

Janis and Mann describe five basic patterns of coping with realistic threats, each of which is assumed to be associated with a specific set of antecedent conditions and a characteristic level of stress. These patterns were derived from an analysis of the research literature on how people react to emergency warnings and public health messages that urge protective action. The five coping patterns are:

1. *Unconflicted adherence.* The decision-maker complacently decides to continue whatever he or she has been doing, ignoring information about the risks of losses.

2. *Unconflicted change.* The decision-maker uncritically adopts whichever new course of action is most salient or most strongly recommended.

3. *Defensive avoidance.* The decision-maker evades the conflict by procrastinating, shifting responsibility to someone else, or constructing wishful rationalizations that bolster the least objectionable alternative, minimizing the expected unfavorable consequences and remaining selectively inattentive to corrective information.

4. *Hypervigilance.* The decision-maker searches frantically for a way out of the dilemma and impulsively seizes upon a hastily contrived solution that seems to promise immediate relief, overlooking the full range of consequences of his or her choice because of emotional excitement, repetitive thinking, and cognitive constriction (manifested by reduction in immediate memory span and simplistic ideas). In its most extreme form, hypervigilance is referred to as "panic."

5. *Vigilance.* The decision-maker searches painstakingly for relevant information, assimilates it in an unbiased manner, and appraises alternatives carefully before making a choice.

While the first two patterns are occasionally adaptive in saving time, effort, and emotional wear-and-tear, especially for routine or minor decisions, they often lead to defective decision-making if the person must make a vital choice. Similarly, defensive avoidance and hypervigilance may occasionally be adaptive, but they generally reduce one's chances of averting serious losses. Consequently, all four are regarded as defective patterns of decision-making. The fifth pattern, vigilance, although occasionally maladaptive if danger is imminent and a split-second response is required, generally leads to careful search and appraisal, effective contingency planning, and the most adequate psychological preparation for coping with unfavorable consequences that might otherwise induce postdecisional regret.

According to Janis and Mann's (1977) analysis of research on psychological stress, the coping pattern selected is determined by the presence or absence of three conditions: (1) awareness of serious risks for whichever alternative is chosen (that is, arousal of conflict); (2) hope of finding a better alternative; and (3) belief that there is adequate time to search and deliberate before a decision is required. Janis and Mann assume that the vigilance pattern occurs only when all three of these conditions are met. They assume further that if the first condition (conflict) is not met, unconflicted adherence or unconflicted change is to be expected; if the second condition (hope) is not met, defensive avoidance will be the dominant coping pattern; if the third condition (adequate time) is the only one that is not met, hypervigilance will be the dominant coping pattern.

This model differs in one fundamental respect from value-expectancy models of decision-making under conditions of uncertainty derived from the work of Kurt Lewin (1935), such as Rosenstock's (1966) health belief model. According to the Janis and Mann model, people will weigh the benefits of a recommended course of action against the perceived costs or barriers to taking that action, as is assumed by value-expectancy models, *only when their coping pattern is vigilance.* To put it another way: When any of the four defective coping patterns is dominant, the decision-maker will *fail* to engage in adequate information search and appraisal of consequences, overlooking or ignoring crucial information about relevant costs and benefits.

Although the conflict-theory model has not yet been fully tested, a review by Janis and Mann (1977) of the social-psychological studies bearing on openness to nonsupporting information, postdecisional regret, and a number of other aspects of decisional behavior, indicates that the findings generally are consistent with predictions about the behavioral consequences of vigilant versus nonvigilant coping patterns. Janis and Mann claim that the theory has heuristic value in that it calls attention to some neglected research problems that should be systematically explored, if our understanding of psychological stress and personal decision-making is to advance beyond its current fragmented state.

One of the values of the conflict model is that it suggests a number of ways advisers can help people make more vigilant decisions. Several new intervention procedures have been developed that attempt to bring about the conditions necessary for the vigilant coping pattern. The "balance-sheet" procedure, for example, is a predecisional exercise that requires a decision-maker to confront and answer questions about potential risks and gains he or she had not previously contemplated. Preliminary evidence of the effectiveness of several of these new types of intervention is consistent with a major assumption of conflict theory: A decision-maker in a state of decisional conflict is much more likely to display adaptive behavior when making a difficult decision if his or her dominant coping pattern is vigilance rather than defensive avoidance. When the vigilance pattern is dominant and persists, the decision-maker engages in careful search and appraisal before implementing a new course of action, and thereafter remains relatively unshaken by setbacks that challenge the decision.

The three essential conditions making for vigilance (conflict, hope of finding an adequate solution, and lack of extreme time urgency) are assumed to be determinants of successful stress inoculation. When one or more of these conditions is not met, we would expect the information contained in a stress inoculation procedure to be ignored, minimized, or misinterpreted by the person as a result of complacency (defective coping patterns #1 and #2), defensive avoidance (defective coping pattern #3) or hypervigilance (defective coping pattern #4). Insofar as the information in a stress inoculation procedure is assimilated by a partially vigilant decision-maker, it will increase the dominance of the vigilance pattern over the defective coping patterns, thus creating a positive feedback loop.

A major implication of this theoretical analysis is that stress inoculation will be maximally effective in preventing backsliding when it contributes to a sustained coping pattern of vigilance by: (1) making the person *aware of the risks of losses* entailed by the chosen course of action; (2) providing information that enables the person to build up a sustained attitude of *hope* about finding a satisfactory solution for the new problems that will be encountered as a consequence of carrying out the new course of action; and (3) fostering up sustained expectations of having *sufficient time* to work out solutions before being overwhelmed by a crisis.

Observations from our prior studies in weight-reduction and anti-smoking clinics indicate that clients often decide to go on a diet or to cut down on smoking without engaging in vigilant search and appraisal of the alternative courses of action open to them (Janis, 1982). The dominant pattern in many cases appears to be defensive avoidance: deciding without deliberation to adopt the recommended course of action which appears to be the least objectionable alternative at the moment, and bolstering it with rationalizations that minimize the difficulties expected in carrying it out. In some cases, unconflicted change appears to be the dominant coping pattern. Hypervigilance, however, has rarely been encountered among the hundreds of subjects in our prior field experiments who decided to carry out a preventive course of action beneficial for their health. (Ill patients, however, who are under time pressure to decide whether or not to accept the treatments prescribed by their physicians, may frequently show hypervigilance.)

In order to prevent unconflicted change and defensive avoidance among people who seek help in carrying out a difficult decision, an advisor's communications need to meet at least the first two of the three essential conditions for promoting a vigilant coping pattern (making the clients aware of the problems to be expected and fostering hope of solving those problems). These two conditions are also essential for *maintaining* a vigilant problem-solving approach to whatever frustrations, temptations, or setbacks subsequently occur when the decision is being implemented. A major purpose of stress inoculation is to prevent reversals of decision in the face of challenge. When people decide to go on a diet, for example, the probability of backsliding is reduced if they do not lose hope about solving whatever problems arise and respond to each major challenge by carefully appraising all the consequences of the alternatives open to them. They would then be most likely to take account of all the various pro-dieting considerations that originally led them to decide to go on a diet. If those same persons, as a result of insufficient psychological preparation, were to lose hope of overcoming the obstacles encountered, their coping pattern would be defensive avoidance.

Our prior studies of smokers and overweight people lead us to believe that backsliding most often occurs when one or more major setbacks make the clients lose hope about finding an adequate solution (Janis, 1982). Although we have no direct evidence, we surmise from the clients' retrospective interviews that those who become demoralized during a postdecisional crisis are likely to regard reverting to the old course of action as the least objectionable alternative, and to develop rationalizations to bolster their backsliding; this is in line with the theoretical analysis of defensive avoidance.

In summary, the theoretical analysis, with its strong emphasis on the hope factor, differs from the view that the only important component of stress inoculation is predicting the adverse consequences in advance. Rather, at least two essential components are presumably needed in a stress inoculation procedure in order to increase the chances of promoting successful adherence: (1) information about problems or obstacles to be expected that may create postdecisional regret, and incline the person to reverse the decision; and (2) information about coping resources, including specific devices that will prevent or reduce the impact of potentially adverse events, and provide reassurance about coping with whatever obstacles or setbacks are encountered. The latter type of information would help to maintain the person's hope when he or she encounters subsequent stress; it might also prevent the well-prepared person from feeling that there is insufficient time to find an adequate solution.

THREE ESSENTIAL STEPS

The theoretical analysis of the cognitive and emotional changes that enter into successful stress inoculation points to three steps that a counselor can initiate to induce psychological preparation for postdecisional setbacks:

Step 1: *Call the client's attention to information about im-*

pending losses and risks that he or she is selectively forgetting or unrealistically discounting in efforts to bolster the new decision. The counselor can gently but firmly challenge the client's unwarranted reassurances by frankly presenting his own views or by quoting from authoritative warning communications. It might also be helpful to ask the client to engage in psychodramatic enactments of the main setbacks that can be anticipated. In one way or another, the counselor can make the client keenly aware of specific points of vulnerability for which he or she needs to be prepared and stimulate the work of worrying (see Janis, 1958; Breznitz, 1971).

Step 2: *Encourage the person to work out ways of reassuring himself* about the ultimate success of the course of action he is pursuing each time a major setback is encountered. The counselor can remind the client of his personal assets and of the resources available from his family, his social network, and his community, all of which can prevent feelings of helplessness in a future crisis. The counselor can also go over the positive entries in the balance sheet to enable the client to work out realistic answers that he can give himself at moments of grave doubt as to whether the new course of action is worth the costs. By discussing the client's imaginings of the future, asking pertinent questions, and emphasizing well-known reassuring facts, a skilled counselor can help the client develop a balanced outlook. This will enable him to continue to be reasonably confident about the success of his chosen course of action in the long run, and at the same time maintain realistic expectations about the numerous ways in which it could be temporarily troublesome and unsatisfying.

Step 3: *Supplement the client's spontaneous efforts to arrive at effective reassuring beliefs* by supplying new information about how potential setbacks can be handled or their effects mitigated (e.g., with surgical patients, reassuring medical facts about pain-killing drugs; with clients facing marital or career crises, reassuring information about the availability of the counselor for emergency sessions if they should subsequently feel the need for more consultations).

In general, the learning process whereby unrealistic reassurances are gradually replaced by a more effective set of reassuring beliefs tends to be facilitated when the person is given concrete information concerning the nature of the potential losses or set-backs, the ways in which the setbacks can be surmounted, and the mitigating or protective aspects of his environment. By presenting the decision-maker with an accurate blueprint of the stresses that are in store for him and the coping resources at his disposal, a preparatory message can help him to build a basic attitude of self-confidence and develop specific beliefs that will have a reassuring effect during and after each crisis (Janis and Mann, 1977).

INDIVIDUAL DIFFERENCES AND PREDISPOSITIONAL FACTORS

For certain types of persons, stress inoculation might have no effect or possibly adverse effects. The Janis and Mann theoretical model of coping patterns has some implications for personality differences in responsiveness to stress inoculation. Some people can be expected to be highly resistant to communications that attempt to induce the three conditions that are essential for vigilant search and appraisal: conflict, hope, and belief that there is adequate time. A person who is generally unresponsive to authentic information that promotes one or another of these conditions would be expected to show a consistently defective coping pattern. This generally would lead either to no change at all or to a poorly worked-out decision without adequate contingency planning. This, in turn, would soon be followed by a reversal of the decision in response to acute postdecisional regret.

There is suggestive evidence from prior research on personali-ty differences that appears to be in line with these assumptions. For example, a number of studies employing Byrne's (1964) Repression-Sensitization Scale and Goldstein's (1959) closely related Coper-versus-Avoider Test suggest that persons diagnosed as chronic re-pressors or avoiders tend to minimize, deny, or ignore any warning that presents disturbing information about impending threats. Such persons appear to be predisposed to display the characteristic features of defensive avoidance. Unlike those who are predisposed to be vigilant, they do not respond adaptively to preparatory infor-mation that provides realistic forecasts and reassurances about stressful experiences to be expected.

Some confirmatory findings are found in two field experi-ments conducted on surgery wards (Andrew, 1970; DeLong, 1971). In both studies, patients awaiting surgery were given Goldstein's test in order to assess their preferred mode of coping with stress, and were then given preparatory information. The reactions of the following three groups were compared: (1) copers, who tended to display vigilance or sensitizing defenses; (2) avoiders, who displayed avoidant or denial defenses; and (3) nonspecific defenders, who showed no clear preference. In Andrew's (1970) study, preparatory information describing what the experience of the operation and the postoperative convalescence would be like had an unfavorable effect on the rate of physical recovery of avoiders, but a positive effect on nonspecific defenders. Copers recovered well irrespective of whether they were given the preoperative information. In DeLong's (1971) study, avoiders had the poorest recovery regardless of preparatory information; copers showed the greatest benefit from such information.

Although not completely consistent with each other, the findings from the two studies appear to agree in indicating that persons who display defensive avoidance tendencies do not respond well to preoperative counseling that presents preparatory information. This conclusion seems to be in line with evidence on stress tolerance obtained in some (though not all) of the laboratory stress experiments in which differences between repressors (or avoiders) versus sensitizers have been studied. For example, Davidson and Bobey (1970) found that repressors showed a decrease in tolerance for experimentally induced pain following an initial exposure to the painful stimulus, whereas sensitizers showed a trend in the opposite direction. In a laboratory experiment by Olson and Zanna (1979), which required subjects to make a minor decision, repressors avoided exposing themselves to dissonance-producing perceptions, whereas sensitizers did not.

Evidence from a correlational study of surgical patients (Cohen and Lazarus, 1973) appears to contradict the implications of the predispositional studies just discussed. Patients who were rated as "vigilant" before their operation showed more negative postoperative reactions than those rated as "avoidant." This finding also goes against the expectation of conflict theory that vigilant individuals will cope better with unfavorable consequences of their decisions than those displaying either a defensive-avoidant or hypervigilant coping pattern. However, a careful examination of Cohen and Lazarus' procedures reveals that these investigators did

not differentiate between hypervigilance and vigilance. They classified as vigilant any patient who sought out information about his
operation (which a hypervigilant person does even more than a
vigilant one), or who was sensitized in terms of remembering the
information and displaying readiness to discuss his thoughts about
the operation. (Again, the hypervigilant people tend to be much
more preoccupied with information about threatening consequences than those who are vigilant.) The one example Cohen and
Lazarus give of a so-called vigilant reaction would be classified as
"hypervigilant" according to Janis and Mann's (1977) criteria: "I
have all the facts, my will is all prepared [in the event of death]...
you're put out, you could be put out too deep, your heart could
quit, you can have shock...I go not in lightly." Consequently, the
correlation observed by these investigators might be attributable to
the relationship between preoperative *hypervigilance* and low tolerance for postoperative stress, which has been observed by other
investigators (Janis, 1958; Leventhal, 1963).

Sime (1976) attempted to replicate Cohen and Lazarus'
(1973) finding using the same categories, but was unable to do so.
Such discrepancies are likely to arise because of unrecognized differences in procedures, or because the relationship between the
two variables is determined by an uninvestigated third variable,
such as severity of the patient's illness.

When opportunities for stress inoculation are made available,
personality factors may play a role in determining who will (and
who will not) choose to take advantage of them. A study by Lapidus (1969) of pregnant women indicates that when preparatory information about the stresses of childbirth is offered free of charge,
passive-submissive women who are most in need of stress inoculation are unlikely to obtain it if it is left up to them to take the initi-
ative. On various indicators of field dependence-independence,
cognitive control, and flexibility, the pregnant women who chose
to participate in a program that offered psychological preparation
for childbirth differed significantly from those who chose not to.
The participants were more field-independent and showed stronger
tendencies toward active mastery of stress than the non-partici-
pants, many of whom showed strong dependency and denial tendencies.

In order to reach those persons who prefer not to learn anything about the unpleasant aspects of stressful experiences in store for them, it may be necessary to set up a preparation program as a standard part of admission procedures in clinics and hospitals. The clients should probably be screened in advance for their knowledge about the consequences of their prospective treatment as well as for their capacity to assimilate unpleasant information. The same considerations apply to any other large organization, such as an industrial plant, where a stress inoculation program might be introduced to prevent overreactions to job stress and high turnover rates among new employees.

The evidence from the various studies I have just cited is suggestive, but bears only indirectly on the main implications of the conflict-theory analysis of coping patterns with respect to personality predispositions. The following three propositions specify how, according to the theory, personality predispositions are conducive to faulty decision-making in response to warnings.

1. If a person has a consistently high threshold for assimilating information about risks that would induce most other people to change their behavior (e.g., low intellectual ability, which prevents comprehension of warnings about impending threats; lack of vivid imagery, which dampens the emotional impact and subse-ᐉuent salience of warnings), he or she will show (a) *unconflicted adherence* to the old course of action in response to challenging events or communications; or (b) *unconflicted change* to a new course of action, without adequate preparation for avoiding acute postdecisional regret. (The latter will occur when two conditions are present: [i] the challenge is so powerful that it is above the person's high threshold for assimilating the information about the risks of continuing the same old course of action and [ii] the information about the risks entailed by the new course of action is not sufficiently impressive to be above the person's high threshold.)

2. If a person has a consistently high threshold for assimilating information that for most people promotes optimism about available opportunities and resources for finding an acceptable solution to the challenging event or communication (e.g., pessimistic expectations resulting from a chronic mood of depressive self-disparagement), he or she will generally display a *defensive avoidance* pattern in the form of chronic procrastination, shifting responsibility to someone else, or bolstering the least objectionable alternative

with rationalizations; this involves denying or minimizing the risks, and interferes with developing plans that lead to stable changes in behavior.

3. If a person has a consistently high threshold for assimilating information that leads most people to expect to have sufficient time for search and appraisal before being required to make a choice among alternative courses of action (e.g., a chronic sense of time urgency, as in "type A personalities" who are at high risk for coronary heart disease [Glass, 1977]), *hypervigilance* will frequently be displayed in response to challenging events or communications, which leads to impulsive and ill-considered decisions that are unstable.

The examples of predispositional variables given in the above three propositions refer to personality traits that are so broad in scope that they would affect all types of decisions—health, career, marriage, social affiliations, or even policy-making in an executive role. But most psychologists have learned to be skeptical about making predictions on the basis of such broad attributes. Much prior research shows that personality traits, as measured by the most widely used tests and rating scales, do not show high consistency across different situations or account for very much of the variance in observable behavior change (Mischel, 1968). Some recent studies, however, indicate that general personality traits are more promising than they formerly seemed (Sechrest, 1976). In any case, the three propositions need not be so imperialistic in scope; they can be reformulated as less sweeping predispositions that pertain to more limited domains of decision-making. In such a version, the propositions could be confined to the one type or subtype of decision, e.g., health risks.

There is no reason, in my opinion, to be pessimistic about the prospects of finding consistent individual differences in each of the above thresholds. I expect that in some persons such thresholds may be consistently high and in others consistently low for a variety of reasons, including current social circumstances and exposure to demoralizing or sensitizing events affecting responsiveness to particular decision-related information.

The theoretical analysis based on the Janis and Mann model provides a basis for reinterpreting some seemingly paradoxical findings. Consider, for example, studies of patients who have recently had a heart attack, and are temporarily depressed, worried about the possibility of having another attack, and preoccupied with the poor prospects for recovering fully. There is some evidence suggesting that these patients are less likely to adopt the recommended course of rehabilitative action than equally ill patients who are not as depressed and anxious (Hackett, Cassem, and Wishnie, 1968; Gentry, Foster, and Haney, 1972; McGill, 1975). This observation has been interpreted as suggesting that those heart patients who deny their illness do better in rehabilitation programs than those who do not. This formulation creates a paradox because other observations cited indicate that denial of illness generally has adverse effects on patients' decision-making, and can be pathogenic. However, I suspect that "denial" *versus* "non-denial" may not be appropriate terms to describe patients' reactions; rather, the crucial difference may be between developing and maintaining some degree of *hope* about solving the health problem despite current suffering *versus* remaining *hopeless*. That is, the defensive avoidance pattern (as described in Proposition #2) might provide an explanation: Those coronary heart disease patients who become pessimistic about finding a satisfactory solution to their current health problem—whether their pessimism is attributable to lifelong personality predispositions, recent untoward events, authoritative pessimistic communications from a physician, or current suffering and lack of social support—would tend to be relatively unresponsive to encouraging information. As a result, they procrastinate, shift responsibility onto their physicians, or bolster a business-as-usual stance, which consists of doing nothing about the hazards.

Consider, for example, the toxicological disaster that occurred in Atlanta in 1951 (Powell, 1953). Hundreds of lower-income people unknowingly poisoned themselves by drinking methyl alcohol (methanol), and developed symptoms of illness, including feelings of nausea, weakness, and impaired vision. Some rushed to a hospital in a hypervigilant state; others ignored the symptoms even to the point where, after becoming half-blind, they denied that there was anything wrong with their eyesight.

In terms of the conflict model, we assume that every physical symptom a person notices in himself constitutes a warning signal. The person asks himself if the symptom (or combination of symptoms) means that he is in a dangerous condition and in need of help. In the present example, if his initial answer concerning the very first, mild symptom of nausea is *no*, he goes on with business as usual. But if his symptoms become worse, the stricken person would give a positive response to the first question and would immediately start to think about what protective action he should take, for example, phoning a doctor, going to the emergency room of a hospital, or telling a relative about the worrisome symptoms. As he contemplates such actions, the images conjured up in his mind might involve very grave threats, such as being subjected to frightening, painful medical procedures, being humiliated and mistreated as a black person in a Southern white hospital, and other extremely high costs.

In this momentary state of conflict, the person would also ask himself whether he could hope to find a better way to escape the dilemma than just waiting for the symptoms to go away. A negative response would lead to a defensive avoidance pattern, including distracting oneself and developing rationalizations to explain away the unusual illness. One Atlanta woman developed acute symptoms of poisoning shortly after having been told about the toxic whiskey, but, while trying to help two other stricken victims in her household, she dismissed her own illness as merely a typical stomach upset and decided to take a home remedy for it. She continued to deny the danger until she became, as she put it, "blind as a bat," which suddenly made her feel "scared to death." Speaking about the period of denial, she said, "I think if I would've ever thought that it could've happened to me, I would've had a heart attack."

After a short time, a stricken person's defensive avoidance pattern might abruptly change to hypervigilance, if he or she encounters a new, dramatic danger signal (e.g., if a relative tells the victim that others in the neighborhood are going blind from having drunk the methyl alcohol, and that victims die unless they get immediate help from a doctor). When a decision to do nothing at all about a threat is based on a pattern of defensive avoidance, the decision-maker is likely to respond in an ineffective way to new signs of threat.

Some of the evidence on level of self-esteem that was reviewed earlier in this chapter is also pertinent to Proposition #2 (concerning pessimism and defensive avoidance). Among overweight persons who come to our weight-reduction clinic, the majority of cases who obtain low self-esteem scores may not be asserting a lack of confidence about succeeding on the diet; rather, they may be expressing feelings of guilt or shame about their past failures to control overeating, which is a different component of low self-esteem. Nevertheless, in a minority of clients who obtain low self-esteem scores, we have observed a similar syndrome of pessimism combined with manifestations of defensive avoidance, which usually takes the form of procrastination or shifting responsibility to others. The relatively hopeless cases, who expressed very low confidence about reducing their weight and sustaining the loss, became more dependent on the counselor, and after a few weeks were less likely to adhere to the recommended diet than those who were more hopeful (Quinlan and Janis, 1982; Janis and Quinlan, 1982). This observed phenomenon might again be explained by Proposition #2, which is compatible with the recent re-emphasis by Bandura (1977) and other behavior theorists on *self-efficacy* as a key determinant of successful behavior change.

In future research, investigations of individual differences in self-confidence and in feelings of hope should provide the type of data needed for more rigorous testing of the second proposition. By using appropriate questions in pretreatment interviews and questionnaires, it should be possible to determine whether such individual differences are related to manifestations of the defensive avoidance pattern, and whether those manifestations in turn are predictive of failure to adhere to a counselor's recommendations.

Appropriate questions could also be devised for use in pretreatment interviews and questionnaires in order to assess individual differences in the predispositional variables specified by the first and third propositions. Obviously, it would be worthwhile to begin by using measures that are already in the literature. If such measures fail to discriminate, the next step should be the development of new measures designed to tap more directly the predispositional factors specified in the three propositions. Some of the theoretically based measures might prove to be more predictive of behavior change than the predispositional measures currently used in research on counseling, therapy, and attitude change.

WHERE SHOULD RESEARCH GO FROM HERE?

Sufficient research has already been conducted on the effec-

tiveness of stress inoculation to warrant moving on to a new stage
— attempting to identify the factors that are responsible. There is
an extensive clinical and assessment literature regarding the effects
of psychological preparation on adherence to health-related decisions. However, this research literature is not very satisfactory for
two reasons: first, the psychological treatments are generally a
complicated mixture of procedures that potentially implicate a
large number of confounded, independent variables that investigators seldom follow up; and second, methodological weaknesses
make for uncertainty about the reported effects investigated. Critical reviews of the literature on psychological preparation and adherence to public health recommendations or to medical regimens
typically find most studies of questionable value on methodological grounds, such as lack of adequate specification of the psychological procedures used, dubious comparability of the experimental and control groups, and lack of objective criteria for assessing
adherence (Enelow and Henderson, 1974; Kasl, 1975; Weiss, 1975).

Obviously, future research should be designed to avoid both
types of limitation. Analytic experiments are needed that attempt
to determine the effective variables by testing hypotheses based on
theoretical concepts about basic processes. With regard to the
problems of internal validity and replicability of the findings, investigators can use standard methodological safeguards that have
evolved in experimental social psychology and personality research
during the past three decades. The major goal should be to pin
down as specifically as possible the key variables (and their interactions) that are responsible for the positive effects of stress inoculation in preventing pathogenic denial and promoting long-term adherence to adaptive courses of action.

Systematic field experiments are needed to test the explanatory hypotheses that have emerged from prior research, applying
analysis of variance designs, and assigning subjects on a purely
random or stratified random basis to different treatment conditions. It is possible to control for the influence of extraneous
sources of error that could impair the internal validity of the findings by adopting essentially the same techniques used in social psychological laboratory experiments. For example, in field experiments investigators can use more than one experimenter operating
"blind" to hypotheses and, for as much of the procedure as possi-

ble, "blind" to experimental conditions. Instructions and recommendations can be presented in an invariant way by using tape recordings or videotapes. Other standardized procedures can be used that also help to eliminate the influence of artifacts, such as differential demand characteristics and unintended experimenter effects that could become confounded with the independent variable under investigation. Through the use of control groups, investigators can hold constant self-monitoring and other "non-treatment" factors that have been found capable of producing positive effects in anti-smoking clinics (McFall and Hammen, 1971; Mahoney, 1977).

Some unique advantages are to be expected when the rigorous procedures developed during the past quarter-century in the fields of experimental social psychology and personality research are brought to bear in field investigations of real-life decisions (rather than laboratory studies of hypothetical decisions that typically evoke none of the ego-involvement or stress that characterizes actual decision-making). By using behavioral measures, such as weight loss among persons who decide to go on a low-calorie diet, we would have little need to worry about unauthentic responses based on demand characteristics or apprehension about being evaluated.

One obvious ethical constraint on field experiments conducted in community clinics is that no new procedure can be tried out for which there is reason to suspect potentially adverse effects on even a small percentage of the clients. Another less obvious one is that everyone who participates in a study as a client in a community clinic must be given some genuine help, even though he or she might be assigned to a control group. This usually requires a baseline control condition in which we use procedures that, in light of existing knowledge, are expected to help the clients achieve their goals. But these constraints do not prevent us from investigating the effects of various innovative psychological treatments that, on the basis of theoretical analysis, are expected to be more effective then the tried-and-true treatment given to the baseline control group.

In field experiments of the type I am advocating, the subjects do not have to be deceived. The investigators can honestly state that they are studying the effectiveness of different forms of psychological treatment that are expected to be helpful. Subjects in the control groups can be given treatments that have already been found to be effective, which provide a baseline against which any new treatment is assessed. Since no deception is involved and every client receives a genuine clinical treatment, there is no need for debriefing afterwards.

In my own field experiments in community clinics, I have noticed that most clients are highly ego-involved and very conscientious about doing whatever is requested of them, including time-consuming "homework" assignments. For the same reason, many are willing to return for follow-up assessments, which enable investigators to study long-term effects of the interventions.

EXAMPLES OF HYPOTHESES TO BE INVESTIGATED

The Janis and Mann (1977) conflict model generates a number of testable hypotheses about potentially significant variables in successful stress inoculation. I shall single out those that pertain most directly to promoting long-term adherence to difficult decisions by preventing pathogenic denial and other maladaptive reactions from occurring in the future. According to the theoretical analysis, adherence to a new decision will increase under each of the following five conditions:

(1) The decision-maker has become aware of the main potential challenges (including temptations as well as setbacks) that could make him regret the decision, and makes plans to avoid being exposed to them.

(2) The decision-maker has anticipated in advance the majority of challenges he will encounter, and has developed cognitive defenses that enable him to regard them as being surmountable.

(3) Each time the decision-maker encounters an effective challenge that does generate regret, he is highly aware of the losses (of utilitarian values, social esteem, and self-esteem) that will ensue if he were to break his commitment to the decision; this prevents impulsive reversals, and increases the likelihood that he will take account of the net advantages of sticking with his prior choice.

(4) The decision-maker has previously become aware of and rehearsed the long-term and short-term gains (that outweigh the anticipated losses) expected from the original course of action; thus, when he encounters an effective challenge that evokes intense

postdecisional regret, he has little hope of finding an alternative that will be better.

(5) The decision-maker has previously become aware of and rehearsed various ways of coping with anticipated losses so that when he encounters an effective challenge that evokes intense postdecisional regret, he maintains a high level of confidence that he will be successful in achieving his original goals.

The following are some of the testable hypotheses that follow directly from these five assumptions:

Stress inoculation will be maximally effective in preventing subsequent pathogenic denial and other stress reactions that interfere with adherence to an adaptive course of action if:

(1) the stress inoculation procedures contain additional information about realistic means for coping with subsequent adverse consequences of the course of action, rather than being restricted to information that predicts subsequent adverse consequences;

(2) the standard stress inoculation procedures deal with the full set of problems that are likely to arise in the future as a result of implementing the new decision (including problems not yet encountered), rather than being restricted to problems that the decision-maker already knows about;

(3) the standard stress inoculation procedures are supplemented by auxiliary interventions that help to build up a sustained attitude of self-confidence about overcoming obstacles that interfere with the new decision. Examples of such auxiliary interventions are: (1) guided self-talk that focuses on an optimistic outlook (Meichenbaum, 1976; Girodo, 1977); and (b) cognitive reappraisal to make salient the anticipated gains that outweigh the anticipated losses (Langer, Janis, and Wolfer, 1975);

(4) the standard stress inoculation procedures are supplemented by interventions that encourage the decision-maker to feel personally responsible for adhering to the new decision;

(5) the standard stress inoculation procedures are supplemented by inducing commitment statements from the decision-maker, for example, by drawing up a contract.

These hypotheses illustrate the type of research focus I believe is needed to determine the conditions under which stress inoculation will be most effective.

References

Adler, N. E., Cohen, F., & Stone, G. C. (1979), Themes and professional prospects in health psychology. In: *Health Psychology,* ed. G. C. Stone, F. Cohen, & N. E. Adler. San Francisco: Jossey-Bass.

Andrew, J. M. (1970), Recovery from surgery, with and without preparatory instruction, for three coping styles. *J. Pers. Soc. Psychol.,* 15: 223–226.

Atthowe, J. (1973), Behavior innovation and persistence. *Amer. Psychol.,* 28:34–41.

Averill, J. R. (1973), Personal control over aversive stimuli and its relationship to stress. *Psychol. Bull.,* 80:286–303.

Ball, K. (1965), First year's experience in anti-smoking clinic. *Brit. Med. J.,* 1:1651–1653.

Ball, T. S. & Vogler, R. E. (1971), Uncertain pain and the pain of uncertainty. *Percept. Motor Skills,* 33:1195–1203.

Bandura, A. (1977), Self-efficacy: Toward a unified theory of behavioral change. *Psychol. Rev.,* 89:191–215.

Becker, M. H. & Maiman, L. A. (1975), Sociobehavioral determinants of compliance with health and medical care recommendations. *Medical Care,* 13:10–24.

Bernstein, D. A. (1969), Modification of smoking behavior: An evaluative review. *Psychol. Bull.,* 71:418–440.

Bowers, K. G. (1968), Pain, anxiety, and perceived control. *J. Consult. Clin. Psychol.,* 32:596–602.

Breen, D. (1975), *The Birth of a First Child: Towards an Understanding of Femininity.* London: Tavistock.

Brehm, S. (1976), *The Application of Social Psychology to Clinical Practice.* New York: Wiley.

Breznitz, S. (1967), Incubation of threat: Duration of anticipation and false alarm as determinants of fear reaction to an unavoidable frightening event. *J. Exp. Res. Pers.,* 2:173–180.

—— (1971), A study of worrying. *Brit. J. Soc. Clin. Psychol.,* 10:271–279.

—— (1976), False alarms: Their effects on fear and adjustment. In: *Stress and Anxiety,* Vol. III, ed. I. G. Sarason & C. D. Spielberger. New York: Wiley & Sons.

Byrne, D. (1964), Repression sensitization as a dimension of personality. In: *Progress in Experimental Personality Research.* Vol. 1, ed. B. A. Maher. New York: Academic Press.

Caplan, G. & Killilea, M., Eds. (1976), *Support Systems and Mutual Help.* New York: Grune & Stratton.

Chu, C. C. (1966), Fear arousal, efficacy, and imminency. *J. Pers. Soc. Psychol.,* 4:517–524.

Cohen, F. & Lazarus, R. S. (1973), Active coping processes, coping disposition, and recovery from surgery. *Psychosom. Med.,* 35:375–389.

——— ——— (1979), Coping with the stresses of illness. In: *Health Psychology*, ed. G. C. Stone, F. Cohen, & N. E. Adler. San Francisco: Jossey-Bass.

Davidson, P. O. & Bobey, M. J. (1970), Repressor-sensitizer differences on repeated exposure to pain. *Percept. Motor Skills*, 31:711–714.

DeLong, R. D. (1971), Individual differences in patterns of anxiety arousal, stress-relevant information, and recovery from surgery. *Diss. Abstr. Internat.*, 32:554.

Egbert, L., Battit, G., Welch, C., & Bartlett, M. (1964), Reduction of postoperative pain by encouragement and instruction. *New England J. Med.*, 270:825–827.

Enelow, A. J. & Henderson, J. B., Eds. (1974), *Applying Behavioral Science to Cardiovascular Risk*. Proceedings of a Conference, Seattle, Washington, June 17–19. American Heart Association, 1975.

Epstein, S. & Clark, S. (1970), Heart rate and skin conductance during experimentally induced anxiety: Effects of anticipated intensity of noxious stimulation and experience. *J. Exp. Psychol.*, 84:105–112.

Federn, P. (1952), *Ego Psychology and the Psychoses*. New York: Basic Books.

Field, P. (1974), Effects of tape-recorded hypnotic preparation for surgery. *Internat. J. Clin. Exp. Hypnosis*, 22:54–61.

Fishbein, M. (1967), Attitude and the prediction of behavior. In: *Readings in Attitude Theory and Measurement,* ed. M. Fishbein. New York: Wiley.

Flaxman, J. (1978), Quitting smoking now or later: Gradual, abrupt, immediate and delayed quitting. *Behav. Therapy*, 9:260–270.

Freud, A. (1936), *The Ego and Mechanisms of Defense*. New York: International Universities Press, 1946.

Friedman, S. (1972), Role-playing with rehabilitation clients. *Gr. Psychother. Psychodram.*, 25:53–55.

Gentry, D., Foster, S. & Haney, T. (1972), Denial as a determinant of anxiety and perceived health in the coronary care unit. *Psychosom. Med.*, 34:39–43.

Girodo, M. (1977), Self-talk: Mechanisms in anxiety and stress management. In: *Stress and Anxiety*, Vol. 4, ed. C. D. Spielberger & I. G. Sarason. New York: Wiley & Sons.

——— & Roehl, J. (1976), Preparatory information and self-talk in coping with the stress of flying. Unpublished manuscript, University of Ottawa.

Glass, D. (1977), *Behavioral Antecedents of Coronary Heart Disease*. New York: Erlbaum.

Goldstein, M. J. (1959), The relationship between coping and avoiding behavior and response to fear-arousing propaganda. *J. Abnorm. Soc. Psychol.*, 58:247–252.

Gomersall, E. R. & Meyers, M. S. (1966), Breakthrough in on-the-job training. *Harvard Bus. Rev.*, 44:62–72.

Hackett, T. P., Cassem, N. H. & Wishnie, H. A. (1968), The coronary care unit: An appraisal of its psychological hazards. *New England J. Med.*, 279:1365–1370.

Hamburg, D. (1953), Psychological adaptive processes in life-threatening injuries. *Symposium on Stress.* Washington, D.C.: National Research Council & Walter Reed Army Medical Center.

———, Hamburg, B. & DeGroza, S. (1953), Adaptive problems and mechanisms in severely burned patients. *Psychiatry*, 16:1–20.

Hochbaum, G. (1958), *Public Participation in Medical Screening Programs: A Socio-psychological Study* (PHS Publication No. 572). Bethesda, Md.: U.S. Public Health Service.

Houston, B. K. (1972), Control over stress, locus of control, and response to stress. *J. Pers. Soc. Psychol.*, 21:249–255.

Hovland, C. I., Janis, I. L. & Kelley, H. H. (1953), *Communication and Persuasion.* New Haven: Yale University Press.

Howard, J. & Strauss, A., Eds. (1975), *Humanizing Health Care.* New York: Wiley.

Hunt, W. A. & Matarazzo, A. (1973), Three years later: Recent developments in the experimental modification of smoking behavior. *J. Abnorm. Psychol.*, 81:107–114.

Insko, C. A., Arkoff, A. & Insko, V. M. (1965), Effects of high and low fear arousing communications upon opinions toward smoking. *J. Exp. Soc. Psychol.*, 1:256–266.

Janis, I. L. (1958), *Psychological Stress: Psychoanalytic and Behavioral Studies of Surgical Patients.* New York: Wiley.

——— (1967), Effects of fear arousal on attitude change: Recent developments in theory and experimental research. In: *Advances in Experimental Social Psychology,* Vol. 3, ed. L. Berkowitz. New York: Academic Press.

——— (1971), *Stress and Frustration.* New York: Harcourt Brace Jovanovich.

———, Ed. (1982), *Counseling on Personal Decisions: Theory and Research on Short-term Helping Relationships.* New Haven: Yale University Press.

——— & Feshbach, S. (1953), Effects of fear-arousing communication. *J. Abnorm. Soc. Psychol.*, 48:78–92.

———, Lumsdaine, A. H. & Gladstone, A. I. (1951), Effects of preparatory communication on reactions to a subsequent news event. *Public Opin. Quart.*, 15:488–518.

——— & Mann, L. (1977), *Decision Making: A Psychological Analysis of Conflict, Choice, and Commitment.* New York: Free Press.

——— & Quinlan, D. M. (1982), What disclosing means to the client: Comparative case studies. In: *Counseling on Personal Decisions: Theory and Research on Short-term Helping Relationships,* ed. I. L. Janis. New Haven: Yale University Press.

——— & Rodin, J. (1979), Attribution, control, and decision making:

Social psychology and health care. In: *Health Psychology,* ed. G. C. Stone, F. Cohen, & N. E. Adler. San Francisco: Jossey-Bass.

_____ & Terwilliger, R. (1962), An experimental study of psychological resistance to fear-arousing communications. *J. Abnorm. Soc. Psychol.,* 65:403–410.

Johnson, J. E. (1966), The influence of purposeful nurse-patient interaction on the patient's postoperative course. *A. N. A. Monograph Series No. 2: Exploring Medical-Surgical Nursing Practice.* New York: American Nurses' Association.

_____ (1975), Stress reduction through sensation information. In: *Stress and Anxiety,* Vol. 2, ed. I. Sarason & C. Spielberger. New York: Wiley.

_____ & Leventhal, H. (1974), The effects of accurate expectations and behavioral instructions on reactions during noxious medical examinations. *J. Pers. Soc. Psychol.,* 29:710–718.

Kanfer, F. & Seider, M. L. (1973), Self-control: Factors enhancing tolerance of noxious stimulation. *J. Pers. Soc. Psychol.,* 25:381–389.

Kasl, S. V. (1975), Issues in patient adherence to health care regimens. *J. Human Stress,* 1:5–17.

Keutzer, C. S., Lichtenstein, E. & Mees, H. L. (1968), Modification of smoking behavior: A review. *Psychol. Bull.,* 70:530–533.

Kiesler, C. A., Ed. (1971), *The Psychology of Commitment.* New York: Academic Press.

Langer, E., Janis, I. & Wolfer, J. (1975), Reduction of psychological stress in surgical patients. *J. Exp. Soc. Psychol.,* 1:155–166.

Lapidus, L. B. (1969), Cognitive control and reaction to stress: Conditions for mastery in the anticipatory phase. Proceedings, 77th Annual Convention, American Psychological Association.

Lazarus, R. S. & Alfert, E. (1964), The short-circuiting of threat by experimentally altering cognitive appraisal. *J. Abnorm. Soc. Psychol.,* 69:195–205.

Leventhal, H. (1963), Patient responses to surgical stress in regular and intensive care units. Progress Report on Divisional Hospital Medical Facilities, U.S. Public Health Service. (Mimeographed.)

_____ (1973), Changing attitudes and habits to reduce chronic risk factors. *Amer. J. Cardiol.,* 31:571–580.

_____ , Singer, R. E. & Jones, S. (1965), Effects of fear and specificity of recommendations. *J. Pers. Soc. Psychol.,* 2:20–29.

Levy, J. M. & McGee, R. K. (1975), Childbirth as crisis: A test of Janis' theory of communication and stress resolution. *J. Pers. Soc. Psychol.,* 31:171–179.

Lewin, K. (1935), *A Dynamic Theory of Personality.* New York: McGraw-Hill.

Lindemann, E. (1944), Symptomatology and management of acute grief. *Amer. J. Psychiat.,* 101:141–146.

Mages, N. L. & Mendelsohn, G. (1979), Effects of cancer on patients' lives: A personological approach. In: *Health Psychology,* ed. G. C. Stone, F. Cohen, & N. E. Adler. San Francisco: Jossey-Bass.

Mahoney, M. J. (1977), Self-reward and self-monitoring techniques for weight-control. In: *Behavioral Treatments of Obesity*, ed. J. P. Foreyt. Elmsford, N.Y.: Pergamon Press.

Mausner, B. (1966), Report on a smoking clinic. *Amer. Psychol.*, 21: 251–255.

McFall, R. M. & Hammen, L. (1971), Motivation, structure, and self-monitoring: Role of nonspecific factors in smoking reduction. *J. Consult. Clin. Psychol.*, 37:80–86.

McGill, A. M. (1975), Review of literature on cardiovascular rehabilitation. In: *Proceedings of the National Heart and Lung Institute Working Conference on Health Behavior*, ed. S. M. Weiss. Washington, D.C.: DHEW (Publication No. NIH 76-868).

McGuire, W. J. (1964), Inducing resistance to persuasion: Some contemporary approaches. In: *Advances in Experimental Social Psychology*, Vol. 1, ed. L. Berkowitz. New York: Academic Press.

_____ (1968), Selective exposure: A summing up. In: *Theories of Cognitive Consistency: A Sourcebook,* ed. R. P. Abelson et al. Chicago: Rand McNally.

_____ (1969), The nature of attitudes and attitude change. In: *The Handbook of Social Psychology,* Vol. 3, ed. G. Lindzey & E. Aronson. Reading, Mass.: Addison-Wesley.

Meichenbaum, D. (1976), A cognitive-behavior modification approach to assessment. In: *Behavioral Assessment: A Practical Handbook*, ed. M. Hersen & A. S. Bellack. New York: Pergamon Press.

_____ (1977), *Cognitive-Behavior Modification: An Integrated Approach.* New York: Plenum.

_____ & Cameron, R. (1973), An examination of cognitive and contingency variables in anxiety relief procedures. Unpublished manuscript, University of Waterloo, Ontario.

_____ & Turk, D. C. (1976), The cognitive-behavioral management of anxiety, anger, and pain. In: *The Behavioral Management of Anxiety, Depression and Pain*, ed. P. O. Davidson. New York: Brunner/ Mazel.

Melamed, B. G. & Siegel, L. J. (1975), Reduction of anxiety in children facing hospitalization and surgery by use of filmed modeling. *J. Consult. Clin. Psychol.*, 43:511–521.

Mischel, W. (1968), *Personality and Assessment.* New York: Wiley.

Moran, P. A. (1963), An experimental study of pediatric admission. Unpublished Master's thesis, Yale University School of Nursing, New Haven.

Olson, J. M. & Zanna, M. P. (1979), A new look at selective exposure. *J. Exp. Soc. Psychol.*, 15:1–15.

Parkes, C. M. (1972), *Bereavement: Studies of Grief in Adult Life.* New York: International Universities Press.

Pervin, L. A. (1963), The need to predict and control under conditions of threat. *J. Pers.*, 34:570–587.

Powell, J. W. (1953), A poison liquor episode in Atlanta, Georgia. In *Conference on Field Studies on Reactions to Disasters.* Chicago: National Opinion Research Center.

Pranulis, M., Dabbs, J. & Johnson, E. J. (1975), General anesthesia and the patient's attempts at control. *Soc. Behav. Pers.*, 3:49–54.

Quinlan, D. M. & Janis, I. L. (1982), Unfavorable effects of high levels of self-disclosure. In: *Counseling on Personal Decisions: Theory and Research on Short-term Helping Relationships,* ed. I. L. Janis. New Haven: Yale University Press.

Riskind, J. (1982), The clients' sense of personal control: Effects of time perspective and self-esteem. In: *Counseling on Personal Decisions: Theory and Research on Short-term Helping Relationships,* ed. I. Janis. New Haven: Yale University Press.

Rogers, R. W. (1975), A protection motivation theory of fear appeals and attitude change. *J. Psychol.*, 91:93–114.

_____ & Deckner, W. C. (1975), Effects of fear appeals and physiological arousal upon emotion, attitudes, and cigarette smoking. *J. Pers. Soc. Psychol.*, 32:220–230.

_____ & Mewborn, C. R. (1976), Fear appeals and attitude change: Effects of a threat's noxiousness, probability of occurrence, and the efficacy of coping responses. *J. Pers. Soc. Psychol.*, 34:54–61.

_____ & Thistlethwaite, D. L. (1970), Effects of fear arousal and reassurance upon attitude change. *J. Pers. Soc. Psychol.*, 15:227–233.

Rosenberg, M. (1956), Cognitive structure and attitudinal affect. *J. Abnorm. Soc. Psychol.*, 35:362–372.

Rosenstock, I. M. (1966), Why people use health services. *Milbank Memorial Fund Quart.*, 44:94.

Sackett, D. L. & Haynes, R. B. (1977), *Compliance with Therapeutic Regimens.* Baltimore: Johns Hopkins University Press.

Schmidt, R. L. (1966), An exploratory study of nursing and patient readiness for surgery. Unpublished Master's thesis, Yale University School of Nursing, New Haven.

Schmitt, F. E. & Wooldridge, P. J. (1973), Psychological preparation of surgical patients. *Nursing Res.*, 22:108–116.

Schulz, R. (1976), Effects of control and predictability on the physical and psychological well-being of the institutionalized aged. *J. Pers. Soc. Psychol.*, 33:563–573.

Schwartz, J. L. & Dubitzky, M. (1968), One year follow-up results of a smoking cessation program. *Canad. J. Public Health*, 59:161–165.

Sechrest, L. (1976), Personality. In: *Annual Review of Psychology,* Vol. 27, ed. M. R. Rosenzweig & L. W. Porter. Palo Alto, Calif.: Annual Reviews.

Seligman, M. E. P. (1975), *Helplessness: On Depression, Development, and Death.* San Francisco: Freeman.

Shewchuk, L. A. (1976), Special report on smoking cessation programs of the American Health Foundation. *Prev. Med.*, 5:454–474.

Sime, A. M. (1976), Relationship of preoperative fear, type of coping, and information received about surgery to recovery from surgery. *J. Pers. Soc. Psychol.*, 34:716–724.

Sobel, R. (1949), Anxiety-depressive reactions after prolonged combat experience: The "old sergeant syndrome." *Bull. U.S. Army Med. Dept.*, 9:137–146.

Staub, E. & Kellett, D. (1972), Increasing pain tolerance by information about aversive stimuli. *J. Pers. Soc. Psychol.*, 21:198–203.

———— , Tursky, B. & Schwartz, G. E. (1971), Self-control and predictability: Their effects on reactions to aversive stimulation. *J. Pers. Soc. Psychol.*, 18:157–162.

Turk, D. C. (1978), Cognitive-behavioral techniques in the management of pain. In: *Cognitive Behavior Therapy: Research and Application,* ed. J. P. Foreyt & D. J. Rathgen. New York: Plenum.

———— & Genest, M. (1979), Regulation of pain: The application of cognitive and behavioral techniques for prevention and remediation. In: *Cognitive-Behavioral Interventions: Theory, Research and Practices,* ed. P. Kendall & S. Hollon. New York: Academic Press.

Vernon, D. T. A. & Bigelow, D. A. (1974), The effect of information about a potentially stressful situation on responses to stress impact. *J. Pers. Soc. Psychol.*, 29:50–59.

Wanous, J. P. (1973), Effects of a realistic job preview on job acceptance, job attitudes, and job survival. *J. Applied Psychol.*, 58:327–332.

Weinstein, E. & Kahn, R. (1955), *Denial of Illness.* Springfield, Ill.: Thomas.

Weiss, J. M. (1970), Somatic effects of predictable and unpredictable shock. *Psychosom. Med.*, 32:397–409.

Weiss, S. M., Ed. (1975), *Proceedings of the National Heart and Lung Institute Working Conference on Health Behavior.* Washington, D.C.: DHEW (Publication No. NIH 76-868).

Wittkower, E. (1952), Psychological aspects of physical illness. *Canad. Med. Assn. J.*, 66:220–224.

Wolfer, J. A. & Visintainer, M. A. (1975), Pediatric surgical patients' and parents' stress responses and adjustment as a function of psychologic preparation and stress-point nursing care. *Nursing Res.*, 24: 244–255.

DISCUSSION

WHEN TO INOCULATE
AGAINST DENIAL

*The purpose of stress inoculation as conceived in Dr. Janis'
presentation is to prevent pathogenic denial and enhance vigilance.
Part of the discussion focused on the desirability of promoting vigilance in various circumstances.*

Dr. Lazarus: What I heard was that denial and avoidance are
bad because they prevent the individual from obtaining what he
needs to know in order to cope effectively. My own position is that
sometimes such information is not useful; quite the contrary, denial and avoidance are useful. Life is full of instances — not just the
extreme instances of terminal illness — in which one does not have
the resources to take any effective action against anxiety, depression or pain. Under such circumstances information is not constructive, since the individual cannot use it and indeed operates
within the context of denial.

Dr. Janis: There is a class of facts that cannot be denied effectively, namely those concerning *unpleasant experiences that in all
probability are going to be encountered*. When this happens with-

out prior preparation, a person's confidence in his ability to continue in his course of action can be shattered. There is by no means a narrow class of facts that we encounter from time to time, where our blanket reassurances are going to be rudely shattered by experiencing some real loss and for which we need to be prepared, and that's where stress inoculation comes in. On the other hand, we are actually confronted by a variety of low probability threats about which it is hopeless to worry. The latter is in the category of situations in which I regard denial tendencies as serving a very adaptive function. Thus, the probability of occurrence of loss is the critical factor.

Dr. Goldberger was also struck by the different positions about the use of denial, especially in relation to the issue of how much ambiguity versus clarity are advisable: Dr. Janis was advocating as much clarity as possible, anticipating what might happen when the person is actually confronted with the stress, whereas Dr. Lazarus was proposing a transitional state where the person could be allowed illusions and some leeway within which he might feel more comfortable, at least for a limited time. The clarity/ambiguity issue is of special relevance when dealing with the kinds of addictive behavior that Dr. Janis studied. Smoking and eating are both strongly overlearned habits. We seem to need some taxonomy of stressors, not just in terms of probability, but also in terms of availability of learned habits.

Dr. Janis: In low probability threats we all must rely on ambiguity in order to keep our minds off of the improbable dangers.

EMOTION-FOCUSED VERSUS PROBLEM-SOLVING MODES OF COPING

Dr. Lazarus: Under what conditions is it appropriate to use problem-solving modes of coping, and under what conditions is it appropriate to use emotion-focused modes of coping? The Western value system prescribes action. If there is a problem, we should do something about it. I think people have failed to recognize the range of sources of stress for which there is no action solution. That is why it is important to turn the whole problem around and recognize that *emotion-focused coping such as denial is not pathological, but is often responsive to the many occasions in which there is no direct action possibility.*

This argument should be taken one step further. The definition of stress is not a matter of what is external to the individual, but is a balance between demands made by the environment and resources of the individual to do something about the problem. No one looking from the outside can say: "You are powerful enough; you are capable enough of doing it." This is an appraisal that a person makes himself. With an individual who is highly vulnerable, even a mild stressor is likely to lead to the judgment that: "I lack the resources to cope." *Such appraisal pushes this person toward an emotion-focused mode of coping with the problem because he feels, correctly or incorrectly, relatively helpless.* The same would apply to addictions when people may hold the conviction that there is no way they can stop their behavior. While this may be an unrealistic appraisal of addictions, as long as it occurs, we should expect emotion-focused forms of coping with denial to be extremely prominent.

Dr. Janis: You have now specified a further condition under which a denial-like type of response is going to have adaptive value, namely, *even when there is a high probability of confrontation with loss, if there is nothing one can do about it, the denial-like tendencies might have a positive adaptive value.*[1] For instance, once a person has committed himself to a flight and boarded the aircraft, there is no point for him in watching whether the engine is going to stay in place or not. The nature of that circumstance turns vigilance into a maladaptive mode of coping.

Dr. Safer: Can stress inoculation also enhance a person's ability to accept the unchangeable? That is the question.

THE ROLE OF COMMITMENT TO ACTION

Dr. Breznitz: The issue of commitment to a certain difficult action might be crucial in determining the efficacy of stress inoculation. The instances mentioned by Dr. Janis, such as going on a diet, stopping smoking, or even awaiting surgery, all relate to anticipated threats and problems as a consequence of a situation which the person entered more or less voluntarily. Stress inoculation prior to firm commitment might actually lead a person to reverse his decision. *Once committed, however, it may be worthwhile to show him that what is in store for him is not going to be*

[1] The principles concerning the conditions for effectiveness of denial will be further discussed in the last chapter of this volume.

easy. This is reminiscent of the cognitive dissonance argument. In the absence of such commitment, or in cases where a person did not voluntarily enter a threatening situation, stress inoculation may actually be counterproductive.

The Role of Auto-Inoculation

Dr. Breznitz: Following commitment, people sometimes engage in what one may call *self-imposed stress inoculation*. Thus, for instance, a student before an examination will rehearse a variety of low probability threats, which may reduce the anticipated disappointment, and consequently somewhat reduce the stressful nature of the examination itself. Such *vicarious confrontations with anticipated difficulties* can act as a minor provocation leading to self-administered reassurances. Their possible adaptive function may perhaps account for their prevalence.

The Role of Information

Dr. Rosenbaum: Dr. Janis stated that stress inoculation is usually administered shortly after the person makes a commitment to carry out a stressful decision, but before he or she implements it. My conception of stress inoculation is somewhat broader, including preparing people to cope with *unforseen stress*. In such a case there is no specific information available, and the aim is to inoculate against anxiety or depression.

Dr. Janis: You are perfectly right that the problem is to prevent subsequent reactions like anxiety, depression, pain and feelings of helplessness, which is what makes denial pathogenic. In connection with dieters or smokers, depression is by no means a minor problem. Backsliding has to do almost entirely with anxiety and depression. The person says: "What am I going to do with myself? I have encountered this crisis situation at work or at home and I've got to smoke."

The attempt to inoculate against depression can be illustrated by the theme that *nobody is perfect*. There is no such thing as anybody ever being able to live up to a diet 100% of the time. There are bound to be social situations where the hostess is serving very delicious homemade cakes, and one feels called upon to respond positively to the offer, then realizes that one has broken the diet. At that point feelings of depression become precisely the problem.

We predict in advance that such a situation will be encountered, and tell our clients what the typical emotional response to it is. We ask them to *role-play* it, and clearly go beyond the simple forms of informational input. We have them rehearse it in the form of emotional role-playing to see what their feelings are like in that situation, and they enact their feelings of depression and self-castigation. Then we say: "Now look, when you talk to yourself like that and say all those nasty things about yourself, that is not going to help you. You have to change that script. You have to say something else if you encounter this experience." Going through this kind of emotional learning process they come up with something new that we hope will serve them better when they in fact deviate from their diet. The process is by no means limited to getting early information.

BACKSLIDING AS A FORM OF DENIAL

Dr. Milgram asked whether a person backsliding to his usual behavior must be denying the original threats which motivated him to try the program.

Dr. Janis: There is a sense in which this is true. Some of the backsliders show the most extreme kind of denial attempts such as: "I have decided that does not apply to me," and so on. Most people, however, develop new rationalizations to support their decision to go back to heavy smoking or overeating. Sometimes it takes the form of saying: "It's an addiction; it's impossible to cure it. There is no hope for me, and I just have to live with it and take my chances."

There is a lot of interesting evidence to be derived from studying how people respond to their own backsliding, from which we can learn a great deal about defenses.

STRESS INOCULATION WITH CHILDREN

Dr. Nagler: Is there any substantial research in this field on children?

Dr. Janis: The research that I know about dealing with children is primarily in the sphere of preparation for surgery. Tonsilectomies have been very heavily studied, indicating positive results. Some of them, rather than using purely verbal means, are done through doll-play. Quite a number of clinicians have been trying out various modes of stress inoculation with children facing separation from parents, including even such things as going off to camp for the summer, which makes many children very homesick and unhappy. A lot of work is going on these days, but no systematic research that I am aware of, such as preparation for divorce and having the children face up to some aspects of what they are going to encounter. Very little systematic field research is being done in those spheres in contrast to the medical sphere.

3

THE CONCEPT AND MECHANISMS
OF DENIAL:
A SELECTIVE OVERVIEW

LEO GOLDBERGER

Just the other day I came across a newspaper column entitled
"Coping with an Age of Stress." It was written by a Boston colum-
nist named Melvin Maddocks (1979), and I quote:

> It seems to have been decreed that we live in the Age of Stress
> — whatever that is. Once you declare the Age of..., the new
> term has to become so all-inclusive that nobody can define it
> any longer. All that's known is: everybody's got it, and we had
> better act accordingly. The Age of Stress can be roughly
> located as one screw-turn up from the Age of Anxiety which
> we were all declared to be living in before.

The column goes on to say:

> The inhabitants of any Age soon would be immobilized by
> this malaise they have invented if they didn't quickly invent an

antidote. The antidote for the Age of Anxiety, it will be recalled, was 'a good sense of humor.' The antidote for the Age
of Stress, in case you haven't heard, is anger.

Have we moved up another screw-turn to the Age of Denial? I
was beginning to wonder when my search through the so-called
mental health literature produced an abundance of references to
the term "denial" in many diverse contexts. There are the lofty
treatments of the denial of death by authors such as Kübler-Ross
(1969), Becker (1973), Lifton (1968), and Weisman (1972). There
are the more technically toned reports of denial of illness found especially in the medical and psychosomatic journals, beginning with
the classic work of Weinstein and Kahn (1955). Then there is the
rather anemic version of denial reflected in psychological journals,
in which denial in an experimental subject is usually operationally
gauged by a simple verbal report instrument or the more complex
MMPI types, and it tends to get linked up with such terms as "repression-sensitization," "social desirability," or the L or K scales.
    Certainly not to be overlooked are the core references in the
psychoanalytic literature, notably in the writings of Sigmund Freud
(1924, 1927, 1938, 1940) and Anna Freud (1936); also Bertram
Lewin (1950), Robert Waelder (1951), and Edith Jacobson (1957),
among others. The Kris Study Group monograph entitled *The
Mechanism of Denial* (Moore and Rubinfine, 1969) is particularly
helpful for an orientation here, as is Sjöbäck's (1973) theoretical
analysis of defense mechanisms.
    Denial is obviously a much overworked term with an underly-
ing construct that needs clarification and specification. The questions posed by the term are similar to those confronting us in the
conceptual realm of stress. And here the fundamental work of
Janis (1958) and Lazarus, Averill, and Opton, Jr. (1974), to whom
I'm sure we're all indebted, is of immense help. How are we to define "denial"? What are its referents? Is it a dispositional trait or an
episodic response? What are its situational and ecological parameters? What are the conditions underlying the successful or
adaptive use of denial? These are just some of the obvious questions posed by the term "denial." Let me quickly say that my paper
will not settle any of these questions. My aim will be much more
modest: it will be to raise some issues and, I hope, to stimulate dis-

cussions by going over mostly old ground from the literature. (I had intended to present a review of the more recent empirical studies, but I quickly found that, except for two or three studies to which I refer, denial is a neglected topic for systematic research—a surprising fact in view of its seeming popularity.) I shall be concerned primarily with the question of definition and underlying mechanisms, and the adaptive versus the maladaptive consequences of denial.

Denial is, and always has been, a fuzzy and complex concept which has acquired many meanings and connotations, depending upon the context in which it has been invoked as an explanation. In trying to propose an all-purpose definition, one is immediately confronted with a host of theoretical issues that relate to the underlying processes.

In addition to the simple dictionary definition, namely, "denial is the act of saying no," or "denial is refusal to acknowledge; a disowning or disavowal (*Verleugnung*)"—which incidentally was Freud's favorite word for denial—the term in its strict psychoanalytic application involves the notion of an *unconscious defense mechanism*, that is, a defense against painful stimuli originating in the external world, as contrasted with inner or instinctual demands, which characterize *repression*. Stated succinctly, denial is a term for almost all defensive endeavors which are assumed to be directed against stimuli originating in the outside world, specifically some painful aspect of reality. Perhaps even more succinctly, one might define it as a refusal to recognize the reality of a traumatic perception. Though denial can be direct, because of its unconscious status it is more often than not *inferred* by indirect evidence through behavior that is said to mask, bolster or maintain denial. For example, euphoria and elation under inappropriate circumstances, minimization, disregard or delay in confronting real external problems through various forms of attention deployment (e.g., engaging in denying fantasies), and substitute activities and so-called "screen affects" are a few indirect signs of denial.

Denial is frequently said to be an elemental component of all outer-directed defenses, such as projection, displacement, isolation and undoing. Denial has generally been viewed as a very *primitive* mental mechanism. In fact, for this reason Anna Freud (1936) has termed it a *pre-stage* of the defenses; it occurs in the earliest period of life, the narcissistic stage, in which the child rejects (or as the analyst's metaphor would have it, "spits out") anything unpleasurable, even before the internal/external distinction is achieved. The closing of the child's eyelids in sleep has been posited as another prototypical antecedent. Sleep, especially, seems an apt model insofar as one can conceive the wishful dreams as the parallel of denying fantasy. Denial, then, may itself be seen as undergoing development from its very primitive operation to the more complex one implied by the notion of a defense mechanism in the adult.

In the adult, the ego may be said to have at its disposal a screening apparatus which can reduce a percept to a signal. Should the signal evoke pain or anxiety (beyond a certain threshold) the percept does not achieve conscious awareness—it is denied or somehow blocked. That is the basic proposition. What specifically is denied? The total impact of the percept, that is, both the cognitive *and* its inseparable intensity components, the affects. One might ask, what is the fate of the warded-off percept, the cognition and associated affect? I'll come back to these important issues later, but for now I want to round out my discussion of the denial construct by noting that it is generally considered by clinicians as the defense *par excellence* of psychosis, for it of course directly implicates faulty reality testing.

Nevertheless, denial is said to occur in nonpsychotic persons as well. It is true that in Freud's earliest discussions of *disavowal* or denial he characterized this defense as specifically characterizing the psychotic's relation to reality. He spoke of the psychotic as "turning away from reality," by which Freud meant a rather massive rejection, repudiation, or disavowal of external reality. It represented a more or less complete detachment from the outside world, which had lost its meaning for the person. In a similar vein, Freud frequently spoke of the psychotic's "loss of reality." Yet it is also true that Freud viewed the *neurotic* as "fleeing from reality," and at least "distorting" reality to some extent; but here he was clear in maintaining that it was only in certain limited, conflictual areas in which there was distortion. In fact Freud (1924) seemed rather careful to use the term "disavowal" when referring to the psychotic's relation to reality, and terms like "ignoring" or "avoiding" for the neurotic's stance.

Freud (1927) elaborated his understanding of the nonpsychotic's use of denial by addressing himself to the perversion of fetishism. Here he introduced the rather intriguing notion of "splitting within the ego"—the idea that a person may entertain two mutually contradictory beliefs without apparent dissonance or tension resolution. The fact that Freud's (1938, 1940) model of consciousness included a conscious and a preconscious system allowed for the postulation of a protective screen between these two levels of awareness, both, it should be noted, *within the ego.*

Denial is not an all-or-none affair. It can be massive, covering a large area of external reality as in the psychotic, or operate within a fairly specific conflictual or painful situation, as in the case of the fetishist or of the death of a loved one, respectively. Denial within the neurotic or normal level of adaptation is perhaps best captured in the colloquial language that uses such expressions as "putting one's head into the sand" or "whistling past the graveyard" or "If you don't look it will go away," and the like (Watzlawick, Weakland, and Fish, 1974). Unless supported by the environment, such denial will not be successfully maintained for more than brief periods at a time. Without reinforcement from physicians, family, friends, and others, denial within the normal range probably could not be sustained. Similarly, but on a group, cultural or national scale, the strategy of denial may be sustained or even encouraged by more impersonal social units, like the government, the press or the church.

It is important to distinguish between psychotic denial and denial that is socially engendered and reinforced. Although it may seem paradoxical, one might even argue that adequate or optimal reality contact requires a good deal of denial. What I have in mind here is the often overlooked fact that the "very process of socialization in any society consists of teaching the young what they must *not* see, *not* hear, *not* think or say. Without definite rules about what should remain outside of one's awareness, an orderly society would be as unthinkable as one that fails to teach its members what they *must* be aware of and communicate about" (Watzlawick et al., 1974). Of course, here I am obviously treading on the basic philosophical question, what do we mean by "reality"?

To evaluate and properly place denial on the psychotic-normal continuum, one would need to characterize that which is being denied on a number of dimensions, such as its massiveness or scope, its centrality to the person's survival (in both the psychological and biological senses), the degree of potential control the person has through other more active coping efforts, that is, the degree of inevitability in relation to the fear of harm or the degree of imminence, to name a few.

The consequences of denial are of great clinical significance, that is, the determination of the fate of the denied percept and affect. Stated differently and more functionally, does denial of the nonpsychotic kind inevitably lead to negative effects, such as psychosomatic disorders; or may it in fact be adaptive, and if so, under what conditions? The literature is by no means clear on these questions; it is most often anecdotal and, if experimental, rarely captures the real-life intensities of the relevant variables. The evaluation of denial by means of the subincision film paradigm, for example, is of quite a different order than denial of an actual incurable illness. To put these findings on the same yardstick is at best only suggestive. Certain general conclusions do, however, seem to emerge that do not do serious violence to the contextual embeddedness of denial.

Before proceeding, let me address the question of the fate of the denied percept/affect (or "cognition"). Here the psychoanalytic literature is fairly clear in proposing that despite the absence of conscious awareness in successful denial, registration—however distorted—nevertheless is achieved at some level. (This occurs on the model of subliminal registration [cf. Fisher, 1960].) What is denied may under certain conditions be recovered, for example, through dreams, imagery, hypnosis, and the like. Another interesting model is that of Horowitz (1975), who postulates the assignment of warded-off information to prolonged but active memory storage, with phasic intrusions into consciousness. In other words, there is a mixed phase of oscillation between denial and "emotional numbness," an intrusive repetition into thought and/or compulsive behaviors. These models imply that one subscribes to the assumption of non-transparency and non-unity of consciousness, assumptions that inhere in the psychoanalytic notion of unconscious defense mechanisms. (A very useful overview of these issues may be found in Sackeim and Gur's [1978] "Self-deception, Self-confrontation and Consciousness." In it, self-deception is posited as a superordinate conceptual category, with denial and other defense mechanisms as special instances.)

In discussing the discrepancies found between the many indicators of stress—the verbal, the physiological, the behavioral—Lazarus et al. (1974) posed the question, "Which of these indicators is the correct one—is it the verbal report of denial of distress, or is it the underlying autonomic arousal?" Their answer that stress is a "multidimensional concept with components of physiological arousal and various organ systems, subjective phenomenology and behavioral reactions" is at least compatible with, if not an expression of the non-transparency, non-unity assumptions. If we agree that the denied material (i.e., external stimuli, percepts, cognitions and affective dispositions) is not lost but is stored and processed at *some* level, we still wish to know much more about its mechanisms, the vicissitudes that the denied material may undergo, and under what conditions. The contemporary work suggesting that mental events in the right hemisphere can be disconnected functionally from the left (the left being the locus for normal verbal consciousness) offers some exciting leads for understanding Freud's notion of *splitting*, and may indeed be a central mechanism for denial (Galin, 1974).

That denial takes its toll is certainly a common observation. In fact, the psychoanalytic literature is replete with the clinical observation involving denial, be it of anger or anxiety, as a major determinant in the development of psychosomatic disorders. A recent sophisticated discussion of the underlying processes involved, notably in hypertension, may be found in Schwartz (1977), whose comprehensive psychobiological model of disregulation couched in information-processing and feedback-system terms is most impressive.

Denial may take its toll, but it may also serve very important adaptive functions by conserving energy and postponing action. This observation is becoming more and more frequent, especially when reference is made to seriously ill patients such as those afflicted with cancer or myocardial infarction. Among such patients, even extreme denial is used by otherwise normal and stable people as part of coping with the illness. Aitken-Swan and Easson (1959) found that about 20% of 231 cancer patients denied the presence of a malignancy. The same percentage was found by Gilbertson and Wangensteen (1962), even after the patients had been specifically told that their condition was malignant. Denial among male heart patients was also found to be approximately 20% (Croog, Shapiro, and Levine, 1971), when patients were interviewed three weeks post-hospitalization and denied they had had a heart attack. That denial in these patients may have served adaptive ends is strongly suggested by Hackett, Cassem, and Wishnie (1968), who found a relationship between degree of denial and acute mortality; the high-denier patients had better survival records in the coronary care unit.

Since this is one of the rare studies with a special focus on denial, the methodology is of interest. They classified the patients into three types based on extensive interviews after discharge from the hospital. The term "major denial" was used to describe patients who stated unequivocally that they felt no fear at any time throughout their hospital stay or earlier in their lives. "Partial denial" designated those who initially denied being frightened, but who eventually admitted at least some fear. "Minimal denial" described patients who either complained of anxiety or readily admitted feeling frightened. The clinical judgment was based not only on the patient's fear responses during his present hospitalization, but his past was examined as well, making it difficult to separate denial as a state from a general personality disposition. In some later work by Hackett and Cassem (1974), in which they report on the development of a more systematic 31-item denial scale, the authors claim that their coronary patients' "denial behavior" appeared reasonably stable and consistently reflected past behavior, particularly for the "major deniers."

It seems that as a group the "major deniers" shared certain personality characteristics:

In addition to denying fear verbally the patients also tended to minimize or displace symptoms to other organ symptoms. They downplayed danger, displaced threat to other objects, *for example*, finances, or projected their fear; *for example*, "my wife was scared but I wasn't." The patients displayed a jovial, hearty manner, they regularly debunked worry, *for example*, "what good does it do you?" And they used clichés whenever they were asked about death, *for example*, "if your number is up, it's up, so what?" or "if your name is on the ticket you've got to buy it." Occasionally the patients described a history of risk taking or reckless behavior which they pursued not only with relish but with a sense of invulnerability and unfailing luck. Some of the patients reported nicknames given them by others denoting strength and vigor such as "the bull" or "iron man" [p. 97].

(Incidentally, these were in fact some of the clinical observations that were used to construct the rating scale.)

In light of previous work on depressed patients by Sachar, MacKenzie, Binstock, and Mack (1968) showing lowering of physiological stress as a function of successful denial, and similar earlier findings by Wolff, Friedman, Hofer, and Mason (1964) with parents of children dying of leukemia, one would have to conclude that denial *can* effectively reduce, not just psychic distress as gauged through verbal report, but also physiological indices of stress. To determine the conditions that constitute successful versus unsuccessful denial would require a complex design involving both situation-specific and personality-dispositional features interactionally. An issue that has for good reason been neglected in the empirical literature is the degree to which the denial is, in fact, out of awareness; this is certainly central in determining whether it is to be called "successful," or whether "denial" was involved in the first place. (Perhaps the less precise term "denial-like behavior" suggested by Janis [see Chapter 2] may have to suffice unless one is privy to in-depth information about a patient or subject.)

A few words about individual differences. Personality predisposition is obviously a vast territory, frequently muddied by the use of unimaginative personality trait batteries. At least based on my own experience, I would still favor some of the less psychometrically well-established metrics of such constructs as "ego strength" and certain cognitive styles. In an interesting recent study, Wilson, Waid, and Orne (1978) found ego strength to be related to intentional control over autonomic responsivity. (Subjects were motivated to prevent physiological responses in a lie-detection paradigm. They denied knowledge of six memorized words.) In discussing their findings, the authors combine their data with Roessler's findings (1973) that high ego strength is associated with larger autonomic responses to stimuli, and suggest that high ego strength may be "associated with the ability to reduce as well as enhance autonomic responsivity to psychological stress, depending on situational requirements" (p. 91).

Another promising and fairly recent finding by Sandman (1972) has demonstrated that field-independent subjects display greater physiological differentiation in different conditions as well as responding with wide variation to stress and non-stress stimuli. (This was seen by the author as being more in line with the James-Lange theory.) Whereas field-dependent subjects seemed to respond more in terms of unidimensional arousal, as suggested by Cannon's theory, and were described as diminishing the threat value of the stimulus by filtering it at the external level, through rejection of (Lacey, 1967) or orientation away from (Glad and Glad, 1963) the environment. This is not a far cry from the construct of denial. The leveling-sharpening cognitive style dimension (Israel, 1969) is yet another promising one that has borne some fruit in several studies.

Possibly because it is the most novel, in conclusion I will refer back to some of the work of Sackeim and Gur (1978) and others in the area of cerebral specialization and coping strategies. A network of empirical relationships cutting across a number of conceptual domains—field dependence, subliminal stimulation, self-deception, emotional expressiveness, left-right eye movement tendencies, and defensiveness—is gradually being formed in the literature. For example, it was recently discovered by Schwartz, Davidson, and Maer (1975) that in response to emotional questions, the average person tends to move his eyes to the left (indicating relative activation of the right hemisphere). To nonemotional questions the eyes tend to move toward the right (i.e., left hemisphere dominance). Gur and Gur (1975) have extended this observation to denial in psychosomatic disorders; they found that people who consistently move their eyes to the left regardless of type of question, score higher on scales of denial *and* report higher incidence of psychosomatic complaints. As Schwartz (1977) points out in his discussion of these and similar data, this "suggests the intriguing hypothesis that the brain can, under certain conditions, learn to cope with negative affective physiological states by functionally severing communications across the two hemispheres. The conscious brain would then perceive a reduction in the affective process." I find his diagrammatic scaffolds most intriguing for our understanding of the multiple interlocking processes that may provide both a positive and a negative role to the presence of awareness in the total self-regulation of the brain. His model may open the way for the much needed systematic research into the mechanisms and individual differences underlying denial.

REFERENCES

Aitken-Swan, J. & Easson, E. C. (1959), Reactions of cancer patients on being told their diagnosis. *Brit. Med. J.*, 1:779–783.

Becker, E. (1973), *The Denial of Death.* New York: Free Press.

Croog, S. H., Shapiro, D. C. & Levine, S. (1971), Denial among male heart patients. *Psychosom. Med.*, 33:385–397.

Fisher, C. (1960), Introduction. In: *Preconscious Stimulation in Dreams, Associations, and Images. Psychological Issues,* Monogr. No. 7, ed. O. Pötzl, R. Allers, & J. Teller. New York: International Universities Press.

Freud, A. (1936), *The Ego and the Mechanisms of Defense.* New York: International Universities Press, 1946.

Freud, S. (1924), The loss of reality in neurosis and psychosis. *Standard Edition,* 19:183–187. London: Hogarth Press, 1961.

———— (1927), Fetishism. *Standard Edition,* 21:149–157. London: Hogarth Press, 1961.

———— (1938), Splitting of the ego in the process of defense. *Standard Edition,* 23:271–278. London: Hogarth Press, 1964.

———— (1940), An outline of psycho-analysis. *Standard Edition,* 23: 141–207. London: Hogarth Press, 1964.

Galin, D. (1974), Implications of left-right cerebral lateralization for psychiatry. *Arch. Gen. Psychiat.*, 9:412–418.

Gilbertson, V. A. & Wangensteen, O. H. (1962), Should the doctor tell the patient that the disease is cancer? In: *The Physician and the Total Care of the Cancer Patient.* New York: American Cancer Society, pp. 80–85.

Glad, D. D. & Glad, V. B. (1963), *Interpersonality Synopsis.* New York: Libra.

Gur, R. E. & Gur, R. C. (1975), Defense mechanisms, psychosomatic symptomatology, and conjugate lateral eye movements. *J. Consult. Clin. Psychol.*, 43:416–420.

Hackett, T. P. & Cassem, N. H. (1974), Development of a quantitative rating scale to assess denial. *J. Psychosom. Res.*, 18:93–100.

———— ———— & Wishnie, H. A. (1968), The coronary care unit: An appraisal of its psychological hazards. *New England J. Med.*, 279: 1365–1370.

94

LEO GOLDBERGER

Horowitz, M. (1975), Intrusive and repetitive thoughts after experimental stress: A summary. *Arch. Gen. Psychiat.*, 32:1457-1463.
Israel, N. R. (1969), Leveling-sharpening and anticipatory cardiac response. *Psychosom. Med.*, 31:499-509.
Jacobson, E. (1957), Denial and repression. *J. Amer. Psychoanal. Assn.*, 5:61-92.
Janis, I. L. (1958), *Psychological Stress.* New York: Wiley.
Kübler-Ross, E. (1969), *On Death and Dying.* London: Macmillan.
Lacey, J. I. (1967), Somatic response patterning and stress: Some revisions of activation theory. In: *Psychological Stress*, ed. M. H. Appley & R. Trumbull. New York: Appleton-Century-Crofts, pp. 14-42.
Lazarus, R. S., Averill, J. R. & Opton, Jr., E. M. (1974), The psychology of coping: Issues of research and assessment. In: *Coping and Adaptation,* ed. G. V. Coelho, D. A. Hamburg & J. E. Adams. New York: Basic Books, pp. 249-315.
Lewin, B. D. (1950), *The Psychoanalysis of Elation.* New York: Norton.
Lifton, R. (1968), *Death in Life: Survivors of Hiroshima.* New York: Random House.
Maddocks, M. (1979), Coping with an age of stress. *Christian Science Monitor,* May 12.
Moore, B. E. & Rubinfine, D. L. (1969), *The Mechanism of Denial.* Monograph Series, Kris Study Group of the New York Psychoanalytic Institute. New York: International Universities Press.
Roessler, R. (1973), Presidential address, 1972: Personality, psychophysiology, and performance. *Psychophysiology,* 10:315-327.
Sachar, E. J. MacKenzie, J. M., Binstock, W. A. & Mack, J. E. (1968), Corticosteroid responses to the psychotherapy of reactive depressions: II. Further clinical and physiological implications. *Psychosom. Med.*, 30:23-44.
Sackeim, H. A. & Gur, R. C. (1978), Self-deception, self-confrontation, and consciousness. In: *Consciousness and Self-Regulation: Advances in Research.* Vol. II, ed. G. E. Schwartz & D. Shapiro. New York: Plenum Press, pp. 139-197.
Sandman, C. C. (1972), Psychophysiological parameters of emotional expression. *Diss. Abstr. Internat.*, 33:2356-2357.
Schwartz, G. E. (1977), Psychosomatic disorders and biofeedback: A psychobiological model of disregulation. In: *Psychopathology: Experimental Models*, ed. J. D. Maser & M. E. P. Seligman. San Francisco: Freeman, pp. 270-307.
―――, Davidson, R. J. & Maer, F. (1975), Right-hemisphere lateralization for emotion in the human brain: Interactions with cognition. *Science*, 190:286-288.
Sjöbäck, H. (1973), *The Psychoanalytic Theory of Defensive Processes.* New York: Wiley.
Waelder, R. (1951), The structure of paranoid ideas. *Internat. J. Psycho-Anal.*, 32:167-177.

Watzlawick, P., Weakland, J. & Fish, R. (1974), *Principles of Problem Formation and Problem Solution.* New York: Norton.
Weinstein, E. A. & Kahn, R. L. (1955), *Denial of Illness.* Springfield, Ill.: Thomas.
Weisman, A. D. (1972), *On Dying and Denying: A Psychiatric Study of Terminality.* New York: Behavioral Publications.
Wilson, S. K., Waid, W. M. & Orne, M. T. (1978), Ego strength and the intentional control of autonomic responsivity. *Psychosom. Med.,* 40:91. (Abstract.)
Wolff, C. T., Friedman, S. B., Hofer, M. A. & Mason, J. W. (1964), Relationship between psychological defenses and mean urinary 17-hydroxycorticosteroid excretion rates: I. A predictive study of parents of totally ill children. *Psychosom. Med.,* 26:576–591.

DISCUSSION

DEFINITIONAL PROBLEMS

Dr. Goldberger's presentation provided the opportunity to discuss certain definitional problems of the concept of denial. No attempt was made to reach agreement on a particular definition, nor was there any systematic analysis of the various components. The participants appeared to regard this as a rather time-consuming, intellectual exercise, and preferred to concentrate on those aspects which have substantive implications. Some of the issues were as follows:

NEGATIVE CONNOTATIONS OF "DENIAL"

Dr. Milgram: Part of the problem with the word "denial" is that it inherently has negative connotations. Freud stated that a man should have total insight and understanding of himself and learn to live with it. This is a very incomplete, if not erroneous, message. Insight is not that important, and denial is not that bad. Denial is not the absence of something; it is the substitution of something for something else. When a person says, "I am not sad,

I will not give in to sadness," he is in fact saying, "I will be happy." The statement "I will not die" implies "I will live." In effect, *denial is the affirmation of the opposite of that which is denied,* and we need a new word along these positive lines. This is very similar to the definition of health. It is not the absence of the illnesses one doesn't have; all the sicknesses I don't have don't mean a thing to me; the question is which are the things that I am doing to promote health. It is an active concept. Preventive mental health means that one is doing positive things, and in this context denial can be seen as a very positive act.

The Need for Definition

*Following a brief discussion of the dictionary definition of denial, e.g., "The asserting (of anything) to be untrue or untenable; also, the denying of the existence or reality of a thing" (*The Oxford English Dictionary*), the advantage of a clear example over the exact definition was noted.*

Dr. Lazarus: When one takes clear examples of the phenomenon, the precise definition becomes less necessary. In a course called "The Psychological Core of Medicine," we try to teach medical students that denial is an important mental operation which is found in a variety of normal and abnormal expressions. This is very difficult for them to comprehend. One of the students made some videotapes of his experience on the wards, and the following experience demonstrated to him the phenomenon of denial: It concerned a patient with malignant melanoma in terminal care following amputation of the leg, with great pain and all the signs of a very advanced disease. The doctor came in on rounds, and in front of the students discussed with the patient and his wife the nature of the terminal care, and that there was nothing further to be done. The husband and wife asked various questions about pain medication and hospitalization procedures, which were all answered by the Chief Surgeon and the Assistant Surgeon, who then left with their entire entourage, leaving only the medical student at the bedside. The wife turned to him and said: "Yes, but will my husband go back to work?" That was denial par excellence, and the student came back and said, "Oh, now I get it."

Even if we had a good new definition of denial, I don't think this would help much. We should have *many names,* differentiating varieties of the process, for which "denial" is not always the best word. However, if we go too far in this direction, we will lose track of the fact that there are environmental constraints to which we have to respond. The concept of denial has the advantage of indicating that there really is something to which one needs to respond. I think it would not be fruitful to give that up.

There are two things to be considered. Firstly, conditions are different, i.e., the adaptational demands vary, and make the process differentially successful or unsuccessful. Secondly, there are varieties of cognitive processes that have all been encompassed within the one term, and we should be differentiating them because they each describe separate mental acts; we need to be very precise and careful in making these differentiations when doing research or working with a patient.

THE ROLE OF AWARENESS IN DENIAL

The role of awareness in denial, while brought up on several occasions, has a direct relevance to the problem of definition. Is a person who is aware *of his denial, in fact, denying?*

Dr. Horowitz: There is a clinical phenomenon which is very common in impending disaster situations; it consists of cognitive calculation in which the person says, "I know I understand the situation, so I should pay more attention to the appraisal of it as threatening." It is not just lip-service; it leads to effective decision-making. This is a common situation which people can report as a separate conscious experience. In the absence of such awareness a person says, "Oh, I am not denying anything here. I have a correct appraisal of the situation." This is, in fact, the denial of denial.

Dr. Breznitz: Isn't a certain amount of such "denial of denial" inherent in all denials? Isn't the fact that a person is unaware of what he is doing an important ingredient of the denial process itself? In the same way that in the context of intrapsychic defense mechanisms a certain amount of repression (i.e., lack of awareness of the defending process and its function) is essential, so when dealing with defenses against external information, their defensive nature must be hidden from the person utilizing them. *Although the termination of an unsuccessful attempt of denial may lead to awareness, this is not the case while the defense is still operative.* The awareness of personal biases in threatening situations, as pointed out by Dr. Horowitz, is an interesting phenomenon in its own right, but should not be viewed as denial proper.

DENIAL AS AN ACTIVE PROCESS

When the suggestion was made to consider the possibility of viewing "denial" as the absence of "reality testing," this was quickly rejected on the grounds that "reality testing" implies that one is going out of his or her way in order to find out whether something which was true in the past is still true in the present. There can be lack of purposeful reality testing without necessarily implying the operation of denial. Denial cannot just be the absence of something, since it requires an active rather than a passive mode of defense. The selective screening, non-attending or inhibiting of threatening information in the service of some pleasure principle cannot be achieved without some energy expenditure.

Dr. Lazarus urged the adoption of a process view of denial,, i.e., a cognitive manipulation which is in constant flux. To illustrate his point, he cited the following: One of the professional workers in the hospital spent an hour with a terminal cancer patient discussing his illness. During the entire discussion the patient manifested such extreme denial that when he left, the professional worker remarked, "This man is a perfect, a beautiful example of a denier." Thereupon, the "denier" left the office, turned the corner of the hospital, chanced upon a social worker and burst into tears, crying: "I am dying."

Where is the denier? What has happened? There are a number of scenarios which one can write for this, including the possibility that the denial was encouraged by the interaction between the patient and the person first seen. He might have been rather severe, or he might have been pushing, as many professionals and relatives do, to maintain a positive aura about the situation. Another perfectly reasonable possibility is that the patient tried very hard to construct a denial interpretation of the situation, and although he carried it through during the entire interview, left convinced that it was impossible to maintain.

There is a difficult methodological problem here, since what we think is denial is often not at all denial, but simply an attempt encouraged by other people to make some construction about what is happening.

Dr. Gal: Denial and its opposite, vigilance, may actually occur in some people at the same time. This further complicates the issue.

Dr. Lazarus: This is an important comment in view of the fact that we are constantly speaking of these as though they were discrete opposites. The information from our research suggests that they can happen simultaneously: that is, not necessarily from moment to moment, but certainly within the same encounter. It is time that we recognize that we are not doing *either* this *or* that, but are doing many things at the same time.

Dr. Breznitz: It might be worthwhile to distinguish between ambiguity as a distinct state on the one hand, and rapid oscillation on the other. Ambiguity implies that the conflicting bits of information are not sufficiently clear to posit a simultaneous confrontation. In the case of rapid transition from one state to another, there is no ambiguity involved, only quick temporal changes. While we often think of those two phenomena as belonging to essentially the same category, they differ in many respects, the level of tolerance of ambiguity being just one of them. A relatively steady state of ambiguity may in fact be conducive to entirely different denial-like behaviors than oscillation.

4

THE PARADOX OF DENIAL

DONALD P. SPENCE

The paradox of denial stems from the fact that denial is never complete. For denial to function as a defense mechanism, it can only be partially effective; only by allowing some threatening information to register can it orient the person where *not* to look. Because it functions in this partial manner, denial allows some information to register; variously elaborated and transformed, it can be mixed with the subject's own fantasies, and can often produce a supposed reality which is more terrifying than the actual reality. It is this very "leakage" which keeps the mechanism in operation. If all input were blocked—if denial were complete—the mechanism would probably cease operating. What seems to happen is that a finely adjusted feedback loop is created which determines just how much negative information is permitted to slip through. If too much leakage is allowed, the person becomes anxious and denial is increased; with too little leakage, denial is discontinued and the person is exposed to threats which he cannot tolerate, at which point the denial comes back into operation.

This model can be clarified by looking at two recent experiments on leakage. In the first, a study of eye fixation and defense by Luborsky, Blinder, and Schimek (1965), subjects were classified from their Rorschach responses as Repressors or Isolators. Next, they were exposed to a variety of threatening pictures, with their eye movements recorded with a Mackworth eye-movement camera. Consider the differences in pattern of looking at a bare-breasted woman: The Isolator looked equally at the breast in the foreground and the man reading the newspaper in the background; the Repressor studiously avoided the breast and looked only at the man. When asked about the picture in later questions, he forgot that he had seen it.

When we study the pattern of the Repressors' fixations, we find that they systematically skirt the forbidden area of the breast without *once* straying into it. We are tempted to conclude that the avoidance is not random but highly efficient — the person knows just where *not* to look. We must postulate the existence of a well-functioning input channel that provides the person with the information (1) to trigger the defense; and (2) modulate and coordinate its enactment. Some part of the visual system, presumably non-foveal, is sensing the exposed breast and keeps central foveal vision restricted to only the safe areas of the picture. Because of the non-foveal, fragmentary nature of this initial input, it does not reach awareness directly. And because of its fragmentary nature, it can also, as we mentioned earlier, more easily combine with other partial fantasies and image fragments.

In the second study (Spence and Feinberg, 1967), we set up a situation in which subjects were exposed to personal information about themselves that was partially visible and partially concealed. If their curiosity got the better of them, they would want to look further, but the looking was tinged with danger because the new information might be upsetting. (Suppose you are applying to college and see a letter from Harvard in your mail box; do you open it or remain in doubt? The situation is somewhat similar.) The subjects were observed to see how far they would act on their curiosity.

When the subject came into the lab, he saw a table covered with blue books. In the middle of the table was a blue book with his name attached and the following note:

Regarding JOHN DOE [subject's name in capital letters]. Here is the subject's booklet with the traits we discussed earlier. The Personal Reaction Inventory shows that this subject has certain of these traits. I have gone through the booklet and written his name under the traits that apply to him. If you have further comments on any trait, put them on the bottom of the page. See you next week.

The subject's name was written under the following traits: bossy, rude, dull, afraid, lonely, and ashamed. He had to open the book to discover this information.

The subjects were divided into three groups on the basis of their reaction to the blue books (all reactions were observed by an experimenter looking through a one-way mirror). *Lookers* would read the note and look through the booklet; *Peekers* would read the note but not open the book; and *Avoiders* would not open the book and apparently not notice the note. There were roughly 10 persons in each group.

When the subject was brought into the room, he was told to make a figure-drawing, and to expect further instructions when the drawing was finished. We expected that the figure-drawing would provide a handy measure of the extent to which he wanted not to become curious; to this end, we scored the drawings for detail and elaboration, reasoning that the more the subject wanted to avoid the blue books, the more time he would spend on the figure-drawing. We also (in a separate session) rated each subject on the Crown-Marlow Social Desirability Scale, and the Byrne Repression-Sensitization Scale.

The findings were as follows: First, we found that looking behavior is correlated significantly with both scales. Subjects high on social desirability tend to be Avoiders rather than Lookers; this makes sense because high scores are indicative of a need to appear blameless and conscientious. Subjects on the Repressive end of the Byrne Scale also tend to be Avoiders rather than Lookers. Both correlations are significant at the .05 level. Although the two scales are intercorrelated, the correlation is not terribly high ($r = .46$).

Of particular interest is the relation between looking behavior and elaboration on the figure-drawing. We had two judges rate each figure-drawing on a seven-point scale, ranging from extreme overelaboration (7) to extreme lack of detailing (1). Correlation between judges was .84; the few disparities were resolved through discussion and a consensus was used as the final score. The more elaborated figures tended to be drawn by the Avoiders, and the correlation between looking style and degree of elaboration was significant at the .02 level. We tend to think that elaboration was protective; in other words, the subject drew a detailed figure to avoid noticing the note. Thus, it makes sense to find that Avoiders tend to draw the more elaborate figures; compulsive detail gives them an excuse *not to look* at the booklets or confront the question of whether to open the booklet which might contain negative information. Particularly striking is the fact that many in this group apparently did not notice the note on the booklet until the experimenter came in to take away the figure-drawing, and even then (in the case of one subject) the discovery was not immediate. She looked through the other booklets but did not seem to notice her own, even though it was placed in the middle of the desk. We had the strong impression that some information about her own book was registering all the time and guiding her involvement in the figure-drawing, just as peripheral information about the breast, in the study by Luborsky et al. (1965), was guiding subjects' foveal eye movements.

What are the implications of these two studies? First, we find that denial can be *shaped* by cognitive style. Persons high on the Crown-Marlow, the Byrne, and on other measures not yet determined, are more likely to choose this mechanism as a way of coping with a dangerous reality. Second, we find that denial is *mediated* by a variety of different mechanisms, of which the most obvious are:

1. *Fragmentary registration.* Selection of important details is partial, incomplete and impressionistic, guided by feeling more than intellect.

2. *Preoccupation with trivial detail.* This preoccupation, illustrated most clearly by the figure-drawing in the second experiment, complements the fact that registration is only fragmentary; it provides a convenient refuge from the suspected danger and prevents careful and systematic study of the danger.

3. *Rationalization.* If we had asked some of the Avoiders why they behaved as they did, they might have told us, "We weren't supposed to know what's in the booklet, so we didn't look closely." Similar statements were made by Germans during the Holocaust—

they weren't supposed to know. Assertions of learned helplessness enable them to avoid looking directly at the danger.

4. *Unwitting incorporation of the target stimulus.* Because of the fact that denial is only partial, some information is getting through. In the second study, a careful examination of the figure-drawings might have revealed how fragments of the danger stimulus (i.e., the blue book and the note) might have been unwittingly incorporated by the subject, transformed and worked into the final product. But we have no direct evidence. For that, we turn to the third study. In this study, we looked at patients who were at risk for cervical cancer and asked how the use of denial would mediate the expression of cancer derivatives in their speech.

In laying out the background for his theory of dreams, Freud (1900) raises the question of whether dreams can be understood in terms of their somatic source. He lists three kinds of sources: external sensory stimuli, such as bright lights or noise; internal sensory stimuli, such as retinal excitation from outside light; and internal, organic somatic stimuli, such as hunger pangs, local symptoms, and the like. The theory of somatic sources has a long history, and complicated theories had been developed, long before Freud, to identify a specific organ as the source of a specific type of dream. Thus heart trouble was supposed to trigger dreams of short duration with terrifying endings—the analogue of a heart attack; lung problems were supposed to trigger dreams of suffocation and crowding; and GI problems, dreams of food and nausea. You can see the kind of metaphorical reasoning that took place, and we have reason to be skeptical of such neat theories.

Nevertheless, Freud was quite willing to admit that somatic sources can often be identified in dreams; however, he tended to minimize their importance because he saw them as a special class of a more general law. Somatic sources were simply an example of a day residue; furthermore, somatic sources, although necessary for the formations of a dream, were not sufficient, he argued, without a related infantile wish. Thus it would be wrong to concentrate on them alone, and they receive only brief mention in his *Interpretation of Dreams.* But even though he tended to minimize their importance, Freud was willing to admit that a certain proportion of dreams could be explained entirely by somatic sources; one study cited a figure of 13%.

Some recent supporting data is provided by Bokert (1967) in a doctoral study at New York University. Eighteen subjects spent three nights in a sleep lab; in a counter-balanced design, the subjects were made thirsty on two of the nights and were sated on the third. Thirst was produced by eating a spicy meal of spaghetti and peppers before bedtime. During one of the thirst nights, the words "a cool delicious drink of water" were whispered while the subject was asleep. All dreams were monitored by eye movements, and the subject was awakened for a full dream report at the end of the eye-movement period. These reports were then transcribed and content-analyzed for thirst words and thirst derivatives.

The main finding was that more thirst words appeared in dreams following the spicy meal than following the sated condition. There was also a significant increase in the rate of thirst words over time—more appeared in later dreams in any given night. There was no increase in thirst words in the auditory condition; the priming stimulus did not seem to potentiate the effect. The fact that Bokert found a main effect of thirst without the need to take into account its specific dynamic meaning for each subject suggests that under certain conditions, a somatic stimulus may have a sufficient influence on dream content.

The following experiment may be seen as an extension of this general model by substituting ongoing disease process for somatic stimuli; and substituting natural language for dreams. Can an ongoing disease process affect choice of language, even when the disease process is still latent and not in the patient's awareness? And can defensive style, in particular the use of denial, influence the pattern of derivatives?

Some fifteen years ago, Schmale and Iker (1971) had interviewed a sample of 68 women at risk for cervical cancer. These women were coming to the hospital for cone biopsy after a series of positive Pap smears, and the interview took place under double-blind conditions, before biopsy results were returned from the lab. Schmale (who did all but one of the interviews) made an assessment of hopelessness by noting such criteria as a history of long-standing devotion to causes with little or no feeling of success or pleasure; lack of correlation between actual accomplishment and subjective feelings; and feelings of doom or depression in connection with the subject's behavior. He made the assumption that feelings of hopelessness, so defined, would be correlated with the outcome of the biopsy.

The original study strongly supported the hopelessness/illness paradigm. Of the 68 women in the original sample, 50 were correctly identified on the basis of the hopelessness criteria, giving a chi square of 12.18, p < .001. Of the 28 women who carried a positive diagnosis from the biopsy, 68% were predicted correctly; of the 40 women who carried a negative diagnosis, 77% were predicted correctly. Thus it would seem as if patients who project hopelessness at the time of the interview would tend to be those harboring an ongoing cancer process.

Notice that Schmale and Iker did not concern themselves with defensive style. Nor did they study how the ongoing disease process would be reflected in choice of words, and how this choice would interact with defensive style. These are the questions we asked of the same data. What expectations can be generated from our model of denial?

First, we would expect fragmentary registration of the danger. Patients from this sample who used denial would be expected to be partially aware of the risk (because of our assumption that denial can never be complete), but rather selective in their assessment of the situation and integration of all known facts. Second, we would expect some preoccupation with irrelevant issues, combined with one or more rationalizations about why they were in the hospital. I don't have time to go into these in detail, but many of the defended patients were convinced that their doctor had made a mistake, that they were in the hospital only to humor him, etc.; in fact, we used extensive rationalization as one of the criteria for putting patients into this group. Finally, more important for this study, we looked for an unwitting incorporation of part or parts of the ongoing disease process. We call this process "lexical leakage."

We hypothesized that a person's choice of words is "influenced not only by the semantic and syntactic constraints within a particular speech context, but also by unconscious mental processes and states" (Spence, Scarborough, and Ginsberg, 1978). Thus we expected that derivatives of the disease process would appear more often in the speech of patients carrying a positive biopsy than in patients carrying a negative biopsy. We also expected that the distribution pattern of these marker words would be related to denial; that patients who used denial and carried a positive biopsy would produce their marker words in a way that would make them more difficult to detect (I'll define this pattern in more detail below).

METHODOLOGY

We rated 62 patients on denial by giving the interviews, stripped of all reference to diagnosis, to two judges. Each judge used a seven-point scale which ranged from complete denial ("There's nothing wrong with me") to open worry and concern ("I'm sure I have cancer"). Each of the seven scale points was defined by a set of key words or phrases to give the judge a clear sense of its referent and to make sure that both judges used the scale in the same way. Reliability between judges was .94; they agreed on all but 8 of the 62 cases, and in no instance did the judges differ by more than two scale points. Disagreements were resolved through discussion.

Ratings of denial were uncorrelated with outcome of the cone biopsy (r = − .02) or with the interviewer's prediction of cancer (r = − .07). The first finding indicates that the patient's style of reaction to the current risk had nothing to do with how sick she actually was; we seem to be measuring a style of coping, as intended, and not a sensitivity to the ongoing cancer process. The second finding suggests that the interviewer's prediction of cancer (drawn from the original study) was not influenced by defensive style.

Because of the zero correlation between defensive style and diagnosis, it was possible to set up a two-by-two table with roughly 15 patients in each cell. Patients who scored above the median on the denial scale I called "concerned" patients. (Some carried a positive and some carried a negative diagnosis.) Patients who scored below the median I called "defended" patients; they were about equally split between positive and negative biopsy.

Marker words. We developed two clusters of marker words to measure hopelessness and hope. The hopelessness cluster was derived from an interview by Kübler-Ross (1969) in her book *Death and Dying* (an interview with a patient in the terminal stages of cancer). Two judges independently read through the interview and listed all words which were synonyms of hopelessness (e.g., fail, fear, grief, sad, worthlessness, etc.). Thirty words were chosen by *both* judges; two additional words were selected by *only* the first, and 17 by only the second. The two lists were combined (because we wanted to exhaust all possible references to hopelessness) and then further expanded by representing each verb in all possible tenses (e.g., fail, fails, failed, failing) and each noun in both singular and plural endings. The final cluster contained 89 words (see Table 1)..

The hope cluster (which consisted of 81 words) was derived from three content analysis dictionaries; it contained such words as hope, want, wish, yearn, etc., and once again, verbs and nouns were represented in all possible forms (see Table 2). (There is a chapter titled "Hope" in Kübler-Ross, but it contains a mixture of hope, anger, and despair.)

If hopelessness was present in the surface structure of the patient's speech, we would expect to find more markers from the hopeless cluster and fewer from the hope cluster than we would in

TABLE 1
HOPELESS CLUSTER

Bad	Dizzy	Impact	Sad
Bitter	Down	Leaving	Scare
Blame	Dropped	Loss	Sick
Blow	End	Low	Slow
Cancer	Fail	Miss	Tired
Cessation	Fear	Morgue	Trouble
Collapse	Finish	Never	Unfortunate
Concern	Grief	Nothing	Wait
Cruel	Hard	Pain	Worse
Death	Hopeless	Problem	Worthless
Die	Illness	Rid	Wrong

Note—Both singular and plural forms of each noun and all declensions of each root verb (e.g., blame) are included in the clusters on Tables 1 and 2.

TABLE 2
HOPE CLUSTER

Ambition	Eager	Intend	Urge
Aspire	Envy	Longing	Want
Crave	Expect	Motive	Wish
Dare	Hope	Need	Yearn
Desire	Incentive	Prefer	Zeal
Dream	Inspire	Strive	

a comparison subject. The number of words found for a given cluster was divided by the total number of words in the speech sample to arrive at a rate; this score was multiplied by 1000 to give a rate per 1000 words. To normalize for proportions, we took the square root of this fraction.

Language analysis. Each interview was keypunched, proofread, and stored on computer tape. All identifying information (place names, proper names, etc.) was replaced by codes. A specially designed computer program sorted all words spoken by each patient and listed them alphabetically, by frequency and by case, on a second tape. All words used by the interviewer were sorted on another tape; they were also cross-indexed by case. Another program searched the sorted output and counted matches between the patient's or interviewer's speech and the two predetermined clusters of words, hopelessness and hope. The program returned the rate each cluster was used by either patient or interviewer in each of the 62 interviews; it also computed t's between cancer patients (positive biopsy; N = 27) and controls (negative biopsy; N = 35).

RESULTS

PATIENTS' LANGUAGE

Concerned patients. Mean scores for the two sets of marker words for the cancer and control patients in the concerned group are presented in Table 3. Cancer patients have a significantly higher frequency of words from the Hopeless cluster ($t = 2.13$, $p < .05$) than do control patients, although their rate still falls below the rate shown by Kübler-Ross' terminal patient. In other words, cancer patients, as compared to controls, use more of the same words spoken by the terminal patient even though they are not explicitly aware of their own diagnosis. They also use significantly fewer words from the Hope cluster ($t = -2.81$, $p < .01$). These findings are independent of context (later in the paper, we will look more closely at the way in which one of the significant markers is used in the course of the interview).

When Hopeless and Hope cluster scores are used together to predict diagnosis, the multiple correlation with the criterion is .55, $p < .01$. Going back to the original study by Schmale and Iker (1971), we find that the interviewer's assessment of hopelessness correlated .44 with the criterion. If we add his assessment of deep

TABLE 3
MEAN RATES FOR MARKER CLUSTERS IN PATIENTS' SPEECH

		Cluster	
Diagnosis	Hope		Hopeless

	Concerned Patients *(N = 32)*		
Cancer	1.82		3.94
		(t = − 2.81)***	(t = 2.13)*
Control	2.23		3.63
	Defended Patients *(N = 30)*		
Cancer	2.25		3.60
Control	2.33		3.71
	Total Sample *(N = 62)*		
Cancer	2.01		3.79
		(t = − 2.57)**	
Control	2.28		3.67
	Kübler-Ross Patient *(N = 1)*		
Terminal	2.04		5.33

***p < .01
**p < .02
*p < .05

structure to the two measures of surface structure, we can raise the correlation to .62, p < .01. When all three predictors are entered in a multiple regression analysis, the Hope cluster is selected first as the strongest predictor, the Hopeless cluster second, and the judge's rating third; in other words, the two sets of marker words account for more diagnostic information than the judge's prediction.

The correlations among all variables and the criterion are presented in Table 4, top section. Note first that the two verbal clusters are essentially independent (r = − .11); thus a patient who uses a high number of hope words will not necessarily use a low number of hopeless words, and the fact that both clusters correlate significantly with the criterion is not a matter of saying the same thing in two different ways. Second, the judge's estimate of hopelessness is not correlated with the verbal cluster of hopeless words (r = .10), which suggests that he is not sensitive to the subtle language changes in the cancer patients.

Defended patients. No differences appear between cancer and control clusters on either cluster of marker words (see Table 3), and there are no significant correlations between clusters and judges' predictions (Table 4). Patients who deny the risk of cancer are apparently more guarded in their use of specific words; the cluster of words used by the Kübler-Ross patient is not significantly elevated in the cancer patients in this group, and their rate is no higher than the control patients in the concerned group. Nevertheless, the judge was able to discriminate significantly between cancer patients and controls (r = .44, Table 4). This finding, coupled with the fact that his prediction did not correlate with the Hopeless cluster, suggests that he must have been using other kinds of information to form his prediction.

Can the language of these patients be decoded in some other way? Their heavy use of denial suggests that displacement might be an important mechanism, and that a count of the number of *different* markers used might discriminate between cancer patients and controls. Thus, a defended cancer patient might express her hopelessness by using a wide range of Kübler-Ross markers, but no one marker very often; thus the aggregate rate would not be higher than normal, but the number of different words used would be significantly larger than controls.

Table 5 presents the mean range scores for the different groups of patients, where range means the number of different words used within any one cluster. Our expectations are correct for the Hopeless cluster. Cancer patients in the defended group use a significantly larger number of marker words from the Hopeless cluster than do controls (t = 2.58, p < .02). This difference does not appear among patients in the concerned group; here rate discriminates but range does not. It is tempting to speculate that patients who are concerned about the risk of cancer, use at an unconscious level some kind of displacement mechanism which distributes the reference to hopelessness over a wide range of words, thereby keeping this theme well disguised. On the other hand, patients who are more concerned about the risk of cancer are less in need of such a

TABLE 4
CORRELATION MATRICES FOR PATIENTS' SPEECH

	Prediction	Hope Cluster	Hopeless Cluster
	Concerned Patients (N=32)		
Diagnosis	.44**	−.46***	.36*
Prediction		−.34	.10
Hope Cluster			−.11
	Defended Patients (N=30)		
Diagnosis	.44**	−.11	−.13
Prediction		.06	.00
Hope Cluster			−.02

***p<.01
**p<.02
*p<.05

TABLE 5
MEAN RANGES FOR MARKER CLUSTERS IN PATIENTS' SPEECH

	Cluster	
Sample	Hope	Hopeless
	Concerned Patients (N=32)	
Cancer	6.67	19.40
Control	7.24	19.76
	Defended Patients (N=30)	
Cancer	8.75	21.75
		(t=2.58)**
Control	7.28	17.67
	Kübler-Ross Patient (N=1)	
	7	50

**p<.02

displacement mechanism; as a result, their feelings can be concentrated in a limited number of markers, frequently used, and the overall rate is a better index than range.

As another way of looking at this phenomenon of displacement in the defended patients, we inverted the matrix and searched for all words from an initial subset of 181 which discriminated between positive and negative cases. We rejected any word whose discrimination level (Student's t) fell below 1.5, i.e., significant for 30 cases at slightly better than the 20% level. (We set our cutoff purposely low to allow us to look at a wide range of markers.) To simplify the analysis, we used only positive markers, that is, words which appeared more often among the positive cases. Twelve markers met this double criterion for the concerned patients and 20 for the defended patients. In all comparisons, we are referring to the rate of occurrence per 1000 words, enabling us to compare patients with different amounts of verbal output.

The two sets of words are presented in Tables 6 and 7, along with the discriminant level for each word and a rating of Relatedness. The two lists are arranged in decreasing order of significance, and the line shows where the level changes from significant to nonsignificant. There are significantly more words above the line in the patients who use denial (p < .02, Fisher exact test). This difference does not reflect a difference in the number of words spoken by the two groups of patients nor a difference in the number of different words.

I think we have here another example of the use of displacement. The defended patients use a greater number of discriminating marker words because of the greater need to disguise the emerging theme. Rather than use two words like *cancer* and *death* over and over again and run the risk of leaking too much information, they use a number of different marker words to carry the effect. There is a further disguise: when we look at the two sets of words above the line, we see that the words used by concerned patients are clearly denotative, clearly related to the illness, and show a minimum degree of transformation or displacement. By comparison, the marker words used by the defended patients are primarily connotative. One might conclude that these words are transformations of the original cancer theme; even though they are markers in the statistical sense, they are so well disguised that they make no

TABLE 6
SIGNIFICANT MARKER WORDS FOR DEFENDED GROUP

Word	Discriminant Level (t)	Relatedness (1 = none; 7 = most)
Dark	3.35	4.0
Disgusted	2.85	5.2
Screaming	2.84	5.2
Difficulty	2.68	5.7
Conflict	2.36	5.3
Depend	2.35	4.6
Drop	2.35	3.2
Tense	2.35	5.7
Accept	2.15	5.0
Strain	2.10	5.4
Black	2.04	(score missing)
Death	2.01	6.9
(All words above this line are each significant, p < .05, two-tailed t test)		
Fractured	1.83	3.0
Complains	1.83	5.4
Confused	1.80	5.0
Infections	1.76	4.8
Crying	1.71	5.8
Winter	1.70	2.5
Finish	1.55	5.1
Unhappy	1.53	6.3

Correlation between Discriminant Level and Relatedness: r = − 1.06, n.s.

TABLE 7
SIGNIFICANT MARKER WORDS FOR CONCERNED GROUP

Word	Discriminant Level (t)	Relatedness (1 = none; 7 = most)
Cancer	2.74	6.8
Death	2.40	6.9
(All words above this line are each significant, p < .05, two-tailed t test)		
Painful	1.98	6.3
Worried	1.89	6.2
Fall	1.82	3.5
Black	1.74	(score missing)
Bitter	1.57	5.8
Ached	1.57	6.0
Bled	1.55	5.3
Complains	1.54	5.4
Infections	1.54	4.8
Alcoholic	1.51	4.0

Correlation between Discriminant Level and Relatedness: r = .61, p < .05.

obvious reference to the likelihood of cancer or the fear of death. Thus they can be uttered with no risk of violating the patient's defensive style.

Ratings of Relatedness are also summarized in Tables 6 and 7. We asked a group of judges to scale each of our marker words on a seven-point scale, ranging from highly related to terminal illness (7) to unrelated (1). In our concerned patients, the extent to which a marker word discriminates between positive and negative patients is highly correlated with the extent to which it is judged to relate to terminal illness. Thus the markers *death* and *cancer* are the two best markers for this group of patients and they are scaled 6.8 and 6.9 by our panel of judges. Less significant markers are judged less related to terminal illness; overall, the correlation between level of discrimination (t) and judges' estimate of relatedness is .61, $p < .05$. In other words, the judges' estimate is a fairly good predictor of the likelihood that the word will be a successful marker.

When we go to the defended patients, the relationship disappears; the correlation between marker discrimination and judges' rating falls to near zero. Again, one might suspect that additional transformations are set in motion by the patient's defense, and that the highly defended patients censor the appearance of clearly related markers because they are too directly threatening; they use more ambiguous indicators instead.

Let me summarize these two sets of findings for the defended patients. When we look at the closed set of Kübler-Ross markers (i.e., the words used by a specific terminal cancer patient) we find that the positive defended patients use a greater number of *different* words than do the negative defended patients; by using displacement in this manner, they dilute the theme of hopelessness and minimize the impact of the leakage. When we look at a less restricted set of words and ask which of these are discriminating between positive and negative cases in the defended group, the results are essentially the same — more different words are used. In addition, their relation to the theme of terminal illness tends to be more disguised and bears no relation to their use as a marker word. Both sets of data give us the feeling that the defended patient is buffering the impact of leakage by (a) distributing the words over different forms; and (b) using many more transformations. In short, the defended patient is using a much more complex code.

Discussion

Let me return now to the argument that denial, by definition, must be incomplete. We have argued that some kind of "leakage" must take place in order to keep the mechanism in operation. What have we learned about the different forms that leakage can take?

In the first study—patterns of looking at a barebreasted woman—we had only presumptive evidence for leakage. We concluded from the pattern of eye-movements that some kind of non-foveal information was being registered which warned the subject where not to look, but we could say nothing about the precise content of this leakage. In the second study—forms of defensive looking—we found a correlation between figure-drawing elaboration and avoidance of the blue book, and made the assumption that some kind of information was being picked up by the Avoiders which committed them to work more industriously on their drawings. But again, we had no specific information about leakage.

In the third study—the analysis of language in women at risk for cervical cancer—we found clear evidence for leakage, and we could begin to draw some conclusions about patterns of expression. Consider the use of Kübler-Ross markers, i.e., the Hopeless cluster. Patients who tended to deny the danger and who also carried a positive biopsy used a wider range of these markers than did patients who denied the danger but who carried a negative biopsy. Some information about an ongoing process was apparently getting through to the positive patients, but it was being distributed in such a way as to minimize the concentration of negative information at any one place. If I use the two words *cancer* and *death* in one sentence my meaning is quite clear; but if I separate these words by 15 minutes of speech, then it would take an acute listener to pick up the connection.

How is this distribution carried out? We can hypothesize two kinds of thresholds—one for repetition of themes, and one of repetition of specific words. Markers referring to hopelessness are not allowed to exceed a certain density of concentration per unit time; as a result, they are distributed over the full scope of the interview. The second mechanism controls the use of repetition. When the time has come to use another word from the Kübler-Ross cluster, a check is made to see whether it has been used before; if it has, a replacement will be used instead.

Both of these procedures, i.e., distributing the marker words over time and minimizing the repetition of single words, serve the function of disguising the theme of hopelessness from both the speaker and the listener. We can see that this kind of disguise is a particular way of putting denial into effect. It also gives us a clue to the problem of how leakage and denial interact. The emission of a marker word (i.e., low-level leakage) seems to trigger some mechanism which (a) delays the next marker word for a fixed period of time; and (b) eliminates the just-emitted marker word from the cluster. Notice that it is the leakage which triggers the denial, just as the non-foveal information in the first study guided the avoidance of the breast.

A similar leakage of death-related marker words can be found in the transcript of a psychoanalytic session with a woman anticipating surgery on her leg (Janis, 1958). The majority of these references were apparently unnoticed by both patient and therapist, often because the surrounding context helped to minimize the significance of the "leakage." Let me list the more striking examples (critical words are italicized):

    p. 65 — "It would *kill* me if I had to give up those things [smoking and high heels]"

    p. 66 — "Before, I would have been *scared to death* to stand up in front of them"

    p. 67 — "*Nothing* to live for"

    p. 67 — "I would rather be *dead* than to be like that [referring to a friend]"

    p. 67 — "...when mother almost *drowned*"

    p. 68 — "To *disarm* him would be to *de-leg* him, to make him helpless"

    p. 69 — "He [father] was very *hurt* and he just looked at me with a *hurt* expression and said, 'You say the most *cutting* things! Some day someone will *cut* you down. Someone will take you down a *peg* or two.'...Why don't you *cut* me down?"

The session ended with the patient crying, terrified of the upcoming operation, and openly afraid of dying. The disguised emergence of the marker words gave preliminary inklings of this final breakdown which was very likely facilitated by the uncovering and interpretations of the analyst. It is worth noting, however, that the majority of the marker words went undetected, attesting to the security of the patient's defense. As with our cancer patients, she was able to distribute them over time and over word choice in such a way that the underlying theme did not attract attention. Had this been an ordinary interview, we might assume that her denial would remain unchallenged. Instead of setting in motion the work of worrying, the alerting information merely strengthened the denial —which further reduced the work of worrying.

How does this come about? One possibility has to do with a serious failure to understand the sense of what is being said during the preparatory period. For reasons not entirely clear, I have the impression that patients who depend heavily on denial switch their attention from the meaning of the sentence to the individual words, from the deep structure of the informational material to the surface structure. Registered as so many words, the warnings become meaningless and do nothing to change the patient's overall estimation of the danger. The isolated words, on the other hand, registered out of context may reinforce the vague fantasy of danger that keeps the denial in operation.

If our model is right, we should expect to find a correlation, in our positive patients who use denial, between use of marker words and rationalization and other clinical signs of defense. We would expect that as the marker words are "leaked" into their speech, they trigger one or more of these clinical manifestations. Something of this kind seems to happen with Janis' patient. In the first example, she makes the statement (noted above) that "It would kill me if I had to give up those things," referring to smoking and high-heeled shoes, and we interpreted *kill* as a marker word. In the very next sentence, she reasserts her denial: "But now I know that I don't need to worry about those things anymore." A similar pattern appears in the following sequences: "I know that I had been worried about my leg getting worse and having to be *amputated*" (undisguised leakage) followed by "But now I know there's no danger of that at all." "I don't feel any particular *fear* of the operation" (disguised leakage) followed by "I'm really looking forward to it."

In a recent article (Fiore, 1979), a man in remission from cancer described his experience with doctors during the early phases of his illness. He placed particular stress on the language used to convey certain kinds of warnings, and made frequent suggestions as to how the wording could be changed. For example, the physician might say, "You will have a lot of pain but we have the drugs to help you" or "Chemotherapy is highly toxic and you will lose your hair and become nauseated." Both of these sentences emphasize the negative and lend themselves to misinterpretation. Alternatives might be the following: "You will be receiving some very powerful medicine capable of killing rapidly producing cells," or (even better), "You will be receiving some very powerful medicine that has worked wonders with other patients."

We can hypothesize that he found the doctors' language unpleasant because he tended to break it down into its constituent parts. If a negative word was surrounded by qualifiers, the qualifiers disappeared; if he heard the phrase "chemotherapy is highly toxic" he was left with "toxic" and all of its unpleasant implications. As the negative markers accumulated, they reinforced the denial, and we might assume that they interfered even further with adequate understanding of subsequent sentences, further increasing attention to surface structure and discrete words. After a certain point, it may no longer be possible to frame any kind of effective reassurance. But if we translate the same information into more positive language, we can effectively eliminate the subtle leakage of frightening marker words; as a consequence, the denial is no longer reinforced and we actually improve the chances for effective communication.

Because denial is never complete, it can never do more than operate as a highly selective filter. We can hypothesize that a certain amount of negative information slips by the filter; therefore it becomes very important how we talk to people at risk. Just as patients in ICUs were frequently traumatized by bits and pieces of conversations they overheard when they were supposedly asleep or unconscious, so it would be foolish to assume that denial will protect a person from unpleasant information. As I have tried to point out, we have a paradox here—the use of denial actually puts the person even more at risk. Incoming language is picked over to search for potential negative markers; these are registered out of context with a resultant loss of information and an increase in terror.

REFERENCES

Bokert, E. G. (1967), The effects of thirst and a related verbal stimulus on dream reports. Unpublished doctoral dissertation, New York University.

Fiore, N. (1979), Fighting cancer—one patient's perspective. *New England J. Med.*, 300:284–289.

Freud, S. (1900), The interpretation of dreams. *Standard Edition*, 4 & 5. London: Hogarth Press, 1958, pp. 220–240.

Janis, I. (1958), *Psychological Stress*. New York: Wiley.

Kübler-Ross, E. (1969), *On Death and Dying*. New York: Macmillan.

Luborsky, L., Blinder, B. & Schimek, J. (1965), Looking, recalling, and GSR as a function of defense. *J. Abnorm. Psychol.*, 70:270–280.

Schmale, A. H. & Iker, H. (1971), Hopelessness as a predictor of cervical cancer. *Soc. Sci. & Med.*, 5:95–100.

Spence, D. P. & Feinberg, C. (1967), Forms of defensive looking: A naturalistic experiment. *J. Nerv. Ment. Dis.*, 145:261–271.

_____ , Scarborough, H. & Ginsberg, E. (1978), Lexical correlates of cervical cancer. *Soc. Sci. & Med.*, 12:141–145.

DISCUSSION

IMPLICATIONS OF RESEARCH FINDINGS

IMPLICATIONS FOR DIAGNOSIS

Dr. Breznitz: The most dramatic finding, in my judgment, was that it was possible to actually predict the outcome of the biopsy in the non-denier. Although Dr. Spence was very cautious in suggesting that this finding might have been mediated by the physician's differential behavior which was somehow picked up by the patient, another alternative explanation ought to be considered. It is a far-fetched explanation that I wish to propose; but if true, it has such tremendous potentialities that it is worthwhile mentioning — *the patients themselves may know more about their physical condition than they can articulate.* Maybe they can read certain cues about their health which they are unable to verbalize. Might the traffic of information between the conceptual realm and the biological realm be indeed a two-way traffic which can be used for diagnostic purposes?

Dr. Safer: I think this hypothesis is far from crazy because the physicians were not in a position to know who had cancer; the

125

women themselves must have been in intimate contact with what was happening in their bodies.

Dr. Spence: That is certainly a reasonable suggestion. It reminds me of a comment someone made when she first heard the data and said: "Oh, is there a connection between the way you talk and whether you have cancer? I have to watch my language from now on."

Dr. Giora: A book by Buss on dreams mentions diagnostic dreams in which the patient diagnoses his condition before his environment can do so.

Dr. Werblowsky: I recall Carl Jung telling me many times of cases of patients who had dreams that made not only a correct diagnosis, but also a correct prognosis of the development of a certain disease, long before it was properly diagnosed and subjected to treatment. At that time I didn't inquire how many dreams were there and what percentage of those was correct, but this kind of phenomenon apparently exists in considerable numbers.

Implications for Stress Inoculation and Information Management

Dr. Janis: Because of selective attention, selective listening, and so on, the very words that are being used in any inoculation attempt can be distorted, and a wrong message can be arrived at. To reasonably ensure that the message was properly obtained, one needs more than just the input. The subjects should be able to reproduce the message in their output, not unlike the Rapaport debating technique that is used in dealing with intergroup conflicts.

Dr. Breznitz: Concerning the issue of what to tell terminally ill patients, I have reached the conclusion that the patient himself must tell the physician how much he is willing to know. This, of course, is easier said than done. The present study points, however, to some initial steps in that direction, by mentioning the clues leaking through a patient's verbal behavior. The context-free aspect of these markers is particularly important because it makes them relatively easy to recognize.

The operation of denial-like mechanisms in institutional settings such as hospitals can sometimes be seen in norms about the particular choice of words, such as words concerning terminal disease. In Israel the word "cancer" is almost a taboo word on some wards, and is altogether very rarely used. People prefer a variety of different names, referring to it as "the disease," or other such more neutral terms. Is there a similar phenomenon in the United States?

Dr. Horowitz: There used to be a parade of terms on the wards from CA to malignancy, back to CA, to four or five new words coined frequently so that the patient wouldn't know; then the patients started knowing, and now everyone says, "cancer."

5

PSYCHOLOGICAL RESPONSE TO SERIOUS LIFE EVENTS

MARDI J. HOROWITZ

One of the great paradoxes of the mind is that it must use existing inner models to interpret new events; models based on the past must interpret the present and be revised to meet the future. Evolution and development have favored the best balance between retention of earlier forms and the acceptance of new stimuli. The equilibrium between old forms and new information is not easily or quickly balanced, however, when present events are those of loss. This chapter discusses psychological responses to those serious life events that involve loss, either of a part of the self, or of others — of a world as it once was.

An ideal adjustment to loss (having done what one can to prevent it) is to accept it, replace that which is lost, and go on living. But there is an important, painful interval between the first pangs of recognition of loss and adaptation to circumstances as they must be. During that interval, there are states characterized by unusual levels of both intrusion of ideas and feelings, and denial of ideas and numbing of emotions. Underlying these shifts in state are changes in inner models of the self, others, and the world; some are due to alterations in dominance among models and others to the formation of new models. Such changes are based on a gradual processing of new information.

These aspects of psychological response can be systematically studied in any group of persons who experience major life events. The resulting theory may help in planning the most humane support and treatment for those who experience intense responses to stress.

STATES THAT FOLLOW SERIOUS LIFE EVENTS

Considering the general disparities of psychological research, a relatively remarkable concordance is found in the clinical, field, and experimental studies of response to the stress of serious events or to vicarious simulations of events. The frequency of two broadly defined states increases after such occurrences; one epitomized by intrusive experiences, the other by denial and numbing. These seemingly paradoxical, but inextricably interrelated states have been given various names in the extensive literature on stress (Breuer and Freud, 1895; Freud, 1920; Lazarus, 1966; Janis, 1958, 1969; Parkes, 1972; Coelho, Hamburg, and Adams, 1974; Parad, Resnick, and Parad, 1976). The contents of these state and phase labels are usually specific to each individual. The terms, however, point to the general form of the experience, whatever the particular content (Horowitz, 1976).

PHASES

States of intrusion and of denial or avoidance do not occur in any prescribed pattern, but appear to oscillate in ways particular to each person. Nonetheless, there is phasic tendency. An initial period of outcry may occur and be followed by either denial or intrusive states, possibly in oscillation with each other. Then, in a period labeled "working through," the frequency and intensity of each of these states is reduced. When a relative baseline is reached, a period of completion is said to occur. This general sequence is diagrammed in Figure 1. It is also useful to consider the intensification of these phases as diagrammed in Figure 2.

SIGNS AND SYMPTOMS DURING DENIAL STATES

In a special clinic for the evaluation and treatment of persons with stress response syndromes after serious life events (Center for the Study of Neuroses, University of California, San Francisco), we have attempted to sequentially clarify these signs and symptoms. An overview of the denial phase is provided in Table 1 (p. 133). In order to understand the frequency of such symptoms in a relevant group, data from 66 patients seen consecutively at our stress clinic were assembled. Based on the operational definitions for signs and symptoms of denial given in Table 2 (p. 134), clinician reports produced the numerical scores described in Table 3 (p. 135).

The 66 patients all sought help for problem states that had occurred after a recent serious life event. Half had experienced the loss of a loved one by death or separation, half had personally undergone a physical loss caused by accident, violence, medical or surgical procedures. There were 50 women and 16 men; the mean age was 34 (with a range of 20 to 75). Selection criteria excluded persons with psychotic states, turbulent personality styles, severe ongoing stress and complicated psychiatric syndromes. Additional data on these 66 people and explanation of methods used in the study are reported in more detail elsewhere (Horowitz, Wilner, and Alvarez, 1979; Horowitz, Wilner, Kaltreider, and Alvarez, 1980).

SIGNS AND SYMPTOMS DURING INTRUSION STATES

Intrusive experiences commonly alternate with denial or avoidance states and are the essential elements of post-traumatic disorders (Freud, 1920). They can be found after every type of serious life event, and in laboratory analogies to such events, where a variety of emotional responses are evoked (Horowitz, 1975a; Horowitz and Wilner, 1976). In Table 4 (p. 135), the overall pattern of such signs and symptoms is organized by the same descriptive sets used in the classification of denial experiences.

Table 5 (p. 136) lists the operational definitions used by our clinicians for the assessment of intrusive states in persons with stress response syndromes.

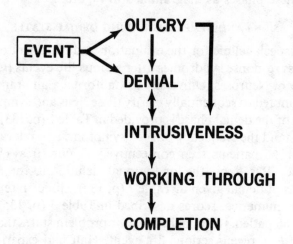

FIGURE 1

Phasic Organization of Denial and Intrusion States

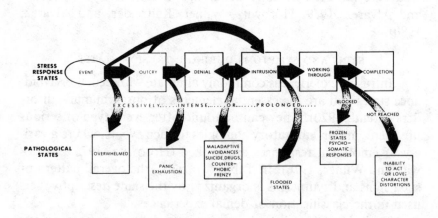

FIGURE 2

Pathological Intensification of Stress Response Phases

TABLE 1
SIGNS AND SYMPTOMS OF DENIAL PHASE OF STRESS RESPONSE SYNDROMES

Perception and Attention	Daze
	Selective inattention
	Inability to appreciate significance of stimuli
Consciousness	Amnesia (complete or partial)
	Non-experience
Ideational Processing	Disavowal of meanings of stimuli
	Loss of reality appropriacy
	Constriction of associational width
	Inflexibility of organization of thought
	Fantasies to counteract reality
Emotional	Numbness
Somatic	Tension-inhibition type symptoms
Actions	Frantic overactivity to withdrawal

We have found that it is very important to query the patient in a particular way after such experiences. Those who are articulate, intelligent, open and self-confident will of course report such experiences spontaneously, but many persons have no experience in communicating the form of their ideas and feelings, and usually describe only the contents. The frequency and means of clinicians' ratings for the signs and symptoms of intrusion are reported in Table 6 (p. 137).

COMMON INTRUSIVE CONTENTS

The advantage of the state descriptions given so far lies in their focus on the *form* of the experiences, which facilitates the examination of response tendencies across a variety of stressful events. There are, however, some contents of response that are also generally prevalent across stressful life events. These contents are the themes that may enter consciousness intrusively, or be warded off during periods of denial or avoidance. They have been described in detail elsewhere (Horowitz, 1976), and are briefly listed in Table 7 (p. 137) as concepts that frequently take an intrusive form in conscious experience.

Awareness of the frequency and multiplicity of such concerns is particularly useful to those who help others to master these experiences. No person has only one response to an event, and the idea

TABLE 2
OPERATIONAL DEFINITIONS OF SIGNS AND SYMPTOMS OF DENIAL

AVOIDANCE OF ASSOCIATIONAL CONNECTIONS — inhibiting expectable and fairly obvious personal or general continuations of meaning, implications, contingencies.

NUMBNESS — a present subjective sense of not having feelings, or feeling "benumbed," including a sense that one is *not* having potential emotions when it *is* a sense, however intuitive, rather than a pure intellectualization.

REDUCED LEVEL OF FEELING RESPONSES TO OUTER STIMULI — includes flatness of expectable emotional responses; constriction.

RIGIDLY ROLE-ADHERENT OR STEREOTYPED — carrying on by playing a part; socially automatic response sets.

LOSS OF REALITY APPROPRIATENESS OF THOUGHT BY SWITCHING ATTITUDES — going from strong to weak, good to bad, active to passive, liking to disliking, or other changes to the degree that thought about any one meaning or implication is blunted and confused.

UNREALISTIC NARROWING OF ATTENTION, VAGUENESS, OR DISAVOWAL OF STIMULI — includes flexibility of attention deployment, lack of centering on a focus, and avoidance of certain otherwise likely perceptual information; includes insensitivity to changes in body.

INATTENTION, DAZE — includes staring off into space, failure to determine significance of stimuli, clouding of alertness.

INFLEXIBILITY OR CONSTRICTION OF THOUGHT — failure to explore relatively obvious or likely avenues of meaning other than the given theme under contemplation.

LOSS OF TRAIN OF THOUGHT — temporary or micromomentary lapses in continuation of a communicative experience, or reports of similar inability to concentrate on a line of inner processing of information.

LOSS OF REALITY APPROPRIATENESS OF THOUGHT BY SLIDING MEANINGS — distorting, minimizing, or exaggerating to the point where real meanings are clouded over.

MEMORY FAILURE — inability to recall expected details or sequences of events, amnestic areas, inability to remember in usually expected manner.

LOSS OF REALITY APPROPRIATENESS OF THOUGHT BY USE OF DISAVOWAL — saying to oneself or others that some meanings, which are or would be fairly obvious, are not so.

WARDING OFF TRAINS OF REALITY-ORIENTED THOUGHT BY USE OF FANTASY — excessive focus on what might have been, what could be, or imaginative stories as a way of not facing realistic consequences or implications.

TABLE 3
FREQUENCY AND MEANS OF SIGNS AND SYMPTOMS OF DENIAL REPORTED
BY CLINICIANS FOR 66 PATIENTS WITH STRESS RESPONSE SYNDROMES
AFTER A RECENT LIFE EVENT

	Percent	Group Mean*
Numbness	69	1.8
Avoidance of Associational Connections	69	1.7
Reduced Level of Feeling Responses to Outer Stimuli	67	1.7
Rigidly Role-Adherent or Stereotyped	62	1.5
Loss of Reality Appropriateness of Thought by Switching Attitudes	64	1.4
Unrealistic Narrowing of Attention, Vagueness or Disavowal of Stimuli	52	1.2
Inattention, Daze	48	1.2
Inflexibility or Constriction of Thought	46	1.0
Loss of Train of Thoughts	44	0.9
Loss of Reality Appropriateness of Thought by Sliding Meanings	41	0.8
Memory Failure	34	0.8
Loss of Reality Appropriateness of Thought by Use of Disavowal	25	0.6
Warding Off Trains of Reality-Oriented Thought by Use of Fantasy	15	0.3

*On a scale in which not present = 0, minor = 1, moderate = 3 and major = 5 for intensity of the experience within the past 7 days

TABLE 4
SIGNS AND SYMPTOMS OF THE INTRUSIVENESS PHASE
OF STRESS RESPONSE SYNDROMES

Perception and Attention	Hypervigilance, startle reactions Sleep and dream disturbance
Consciousness	Intrusive-repetitive thoughts and behaviors (illusions, pseudohallucinations, nightmares, ruminations and repetitions)
Ideational Processing	Overgeneralization Inability to concentrate on other topics, preoccupation Confusion and disorganization
Emotional	Emotional attacks or "pangs"
Somatic	Symptomatic sequelae of chronic fight or flight readiness (or of exhaustion)
Actions	Search for lost persons and situations, compulsive repetitions

TABLE 5

OPERATIONAL DEFINITIONS OF SIGNS AND SYMPTOMS OF INTRUSION

PANGS OF EMOTION — a "spell," episode or wave of feeling that has a quality of increasing and then decreasing, rather than being a prevailing mood or subjective tone.

RUMINATION OR PREOCCUPATION — continuous conscious awareness about the event and associations to the event beyond that involved in ordinary thinking through a problem or situation to a point of decision or completion. It has a sense of uncontrolled repetition to it.

FEAR OF LOSING BODILY CONTROL, OR HYPERACTIVITY IN ANY BODILY SYSTEM — includes subjective sensations of urinating, defecating without will; fears of being unable to control vocalization; arm movements, hiding, running; obvious somatic responses such as excessive sweating, diarrhea, tachycardia.

INTRUSIVE IDEAS IN WORD FORM — thoughts that pop into the mind, and are sudden and unbidden.

DIFFICULTY IN DISPELLING IDEAS — inability to stop awareness of an idea or topic once it has come to mind, even if thinking about it were deliberate; also includes emotions and moods that cannot be stopped.

HYPERVIGILANCE — excessive alertness, excessive scanning of the surrounding environment, too aroused in the sense of perceptual search, tensely expectant, or more driven towards obtaining stimuli than normal.

REENACTMENTS — any behavior that repeats any aspect of the serious life event, from minor ticlike movements and gestures to acting-out in major movements and sequences. Includes enactments of personal responses to the life event, whether or not they were part of the real action surrounding the event.

BAD DREAMS — any dream with an unpleasant subjective experience, not just the classical nightmare with anxious awakenings.

INTRUSIVE THOUGHTS OR IMAGES WHILE TRYING TO SLEEP — (see intrusive ideas and intrusive images)

INTRUSIVE IMAGES — unbidden sensations in any modality. Any hallucination or pseudohallucination would be scored here as well, if it came to mind in a nonvolitional manner. The emphasis here is on sensory quality, which, however similar to that of ordinary thought images, may be more intense, and occur as a sudden, unwanted entry into awareness.

STARTLE REACTIONS — flinching after noises, unusual orienting reactions, blanching or otherwise reacting to stimuli that usually do not warrant such responses.

ILLUSIONS — a misperception in which a person, object, or scene is misappraised as something else; for example, a bush is seen for a moment as a person, or a person is misrecognized as someone else.

TABLE 5—*Continued*

HALLUCINATIONS, PSEUDOHALLUCINATIONS—imaginary or fantasy-based emotional reactions as if they were real, whether or not the person intellectually thinks so. Includes "felt presences" of others in the room. Smell, taste, touch, movement, auditory, and visual sensations, as well as out of the body experiences are included.

TABLE 6

FREQUENCY AND MEANS OF SIGNS AND SYMPTOMS OF INTRUSION REPORTED BY CLINICIANS FOR 66 PATIENTS WITH STRESS RESPONSE SYNDROMES AFTER A RECENT SERIOUS LIFE EVENT

	Percent	Group Mean*
Pangs of Emotion	95	3.1
Rumination or Preoccupation	90	2.9
Fear of Losing Bodily Control or Hyperactivity in any Bodily System	82	2.6
Intrusive Ideas (in Word Form)	77	2.3
Difficulty in Dispelling Ideas	74	2.1
Hypervigilance	69	1.6
Bad Dreams	54	1.6
Intrusive Thoughts or Images when Trying to Sleep	51	1.6
Reenactments	57	1.5
Intrusive Images	51	1.4
Startle Reactions	34	0.6
Illusions	26	0.6
Hallucinations, Pseudohallucinations	8	0.2

*On a scale in which not present = 0, minor = 1, moderate = 3 and major = 5 for intensity of the experience within the past 7 days

TABLE 7

COMMON THEMES AFTER LOSS OR INJURY

Fear of repetition.
Fear of merger with victims.
Shame and rage over vulnerability.
Rage at the source.
Rage at those exempted.
Fear of loss of control of aggressive impulses.
Guilt or shame over aggressive impulses.
Guilt or shame over surviving.
Sadness over losses.

of workingthrough one constellation may be used as a resistance to further assimilation. Some themes are avoided at the same time that others are intrusively present, adding further complexity to the general ordering of response states over time. Working through each concern to a point of completion requires differentiation of reality from fantasy, and continued restructuring of the real world and one's place in it.

To summarize, certain common stress response tendencies can be abstracted from clinical, field, and experimental studies among populations reacting to different life events. Simple knowledge of such states helps a person know what to expect and how to assess responses when they occur. Beyond the classification of states of experience, however, understanding why experiences occur may be even more helpful in planning a working-through process. States of mind, and transitions from one state to another, can be usefully explained from two points of view: (1) the cognitive schemata or models used to organize information, and (2) the processes of information transformation.

EXPLANATION OF STATES: THE EFFECTS OF SERIOUS LIFE EVENTS ON COGNITIVE SCHEMATA

A serious, stress-inducing life event is defined as such because it changes homeostasis. Negative stress stems from experience of loss or injury, psychological or material, real or fantasied. If action cannot alter the situation, then inner models or schemata must be revised so that they conform to the new reality.

As already mentioned, no one has just one fully integrated self-image, or just one model of role relationships for his attachments to others. Each person will have several important models that were developed in childhood and change throughout adult life (Erikson, 1958). Early schemata have been revised, but are also retained in their earlier forms and can be reactivated during any regression. As a result of a serious life change, the hierarchical importance of existing schemata may be altered, and schemata may be revised (Piaget, 1937).

The slow revision of models will be discussed later. The rapid changes are conceptualized as a shift induced by initial interpretations of the event and its implications, where models of self and relationships to others function to organize conscious experience and patterns of action.

Bereavement provides one well-studied example. As reviewed elsewhere (Parkes, 1972; Horowitz, 1980), the loss of the loved one sets in motion a quick shift from previous self-images of mutual attachment and support, to self-images as bereft or abandoned. These self-images may originally have been established as a consequence of earlier life experience with real or fantasied separations, however momentary, if not with the actual experience of death. This shift in self-image and role relationship model is one cause of a change in state, as diagrammed in Figure 3.

Each of the universal themes described earlier in Table 7, as well as other individually important themes based on personal history, will contain relevant versions of the person's self-images and role relationships. If a person has an accident with subsequent loss of his arm, or if he is fired from his work, there may be a rapid shift from a competent self-image to an already existing but previously dormant one as worthless and defective. Similarly, if a person experiences the death of a loved one who functioned to stabilize a competent self-image, then among the first effects of the loss may be a shift to usually latent models in which the self is defective and worthless. An example of this type of shift is diagrammed in Figure 4. The intrusive state is associated with unbidden thoughts of worthlessness and uncontrolled pangs of shame. A defensive shift in self-image can alter the state of mind to one that is blank, numb, and insulated.

The news of any serious life event, and responsive associations to it will be matched against the person's current dominant self-image and relationship models as well as those that are important, but less dominant. The outcome of this matching of news to inner models will depend on the goodness of fit and the importance of each model. Suppose, as a simplified example, that a person has a dominant self-image as competent that is relatively stable and usually serves as the primary organizer of mental processes. Suppose also that this person has a dormant, inactive self-image as incompetent, a residual from previous life experiences. When that person sustains a loss or insult, the event will be matched against two self-images: competent and incompetent. For a time the incompetent self-image may dominate thought, leading to a temporary reaction of increased vulnerability. Such experiences, how-

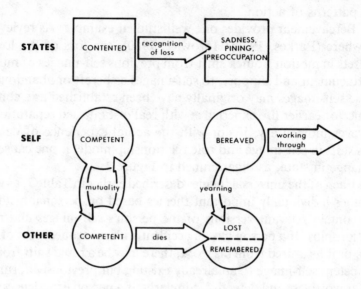

FIGURE 3
Effects of Normal Mourning on Self-Images and Role Relationships

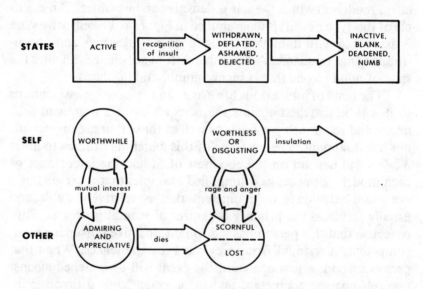

FIGURE 4
Effects of Bereavement: Defective Self-Images and Role Relationships

ever, will be brief, partial, or peripheral to central conscious awareness.

In contrast, suppose that the person has a dominant self-image of competence that is brittle or unstable, and a usually inactive but important self-image as incompetent based on previous traumas. The newly sustained losses are more likely, in this instance, to cause a shift so that the latter dominates. Reactions resulting from this incompetent self-image are likely to be more extended in time, more intense, or more central to experience.

Issues of self-image and role relationship models, and the shifts between them, have been discussed in detail elsewhere as important components in the theoretical explanation of various states of mind in a particular person (Horowitz, 1979). The main point here is that one component of stress reaction is due to the shift in dominant models of self and other that can occur as part of the internalization of news about serious life events. Working through the news involves relating to it according to several models. Processes interact through shifts in the models evoked by the news, and changes to meet the new reality. In the short run, ideation and control determine *which* of a person's models are dominant organizers of experience. In the long run, ideation and control determine *if* and *how* models are changed. The remainder of this discussion will deal with ideation and control, based on a central assertion that variations in controls account for much of the variation in stress response states across persons and in each person over time.

EXPLANATION OF STATE CHANGES: PROCESSING THE MEANINGS OF SERIOUS LIFE EVENTS

It takes time for a person to assimilate a serious life event. If the event is of sufficient power, there will be signs and symptoms of deflection from normal states to the intrusiveness, denial, or combined intrusion/denial states described. Some persons will enter a stress response state, even when a mild but personally significant event occurs. Information-processing alters these states and we need to know how this is done. If we know, we can facilitate the natural, healing, adaptive processes when help is requested.

BACKGROUND

Before Freud's time, psychological traumas such as these were explained by neurologists as altered information-processing and regulatory capacities, which were induced as a combination of shock resulting from hypnotic states of consciousness, hereditary weakness of the nervous system, and the hope of secondary gains such as compensation after railway accidents (Charcot, 1877). Breuer and Freud (1895) rejected hereditary weakness of the nervous system as an explanation, and replaced it with a theory of psychological conflict. Freud (1920) also attempted to base his theory of neurotic conflict on biological factors, deflections of drive and energy systems caused by conflict. He explained traumatization as a sudden overload of both information and physical energy. The information-processing aspect of this theory continues to be developed; the energic and instinctual components of his theory remain speculative.

In Freud's explanation of intrusiveness and denial states after serious life events, excessive stimulation was seen as the inciting cause. Perhaps building on what was then a new concept of physiological homeostasis, he developed a model that included defensive controls — one of the first psychological models to include unconscious information-processing and feedback concepts.

Freud theorized along the following lines. When novel perceptions combined with inner meanings to form ideas that evoked strong emotional responses such as fear, controls were activated to regulate levels of tension. A hypothetical "stimulus barrier" attenuated sensory input; repression and other defense mechanisms attenuated emergent ideas and feelings. Traumatization occurred as controls failed in the face of powerful evocative events. A tension state of high drive characteristics resulted, and the intensification of secondary defenses then produced denial states. Episodic defensive failures led to intrusion. Conflict explained these stress states.

Freud then attempted to relate traumatization to libido theory. He puzzled over what drives might be activated by devastating life events. Desires for pleasure seemed out of the question. The horrible combat nightmares that haunted World War I veterans drove some to suicide; they could not be seen as the end-product of wishfulfillment. Hypothesizing another level of drives more primitive than the pleasure principle, which he called the "repetition compulsion," Freud (1920) speculated on these as a derivative of the death instinct, with aggressive drives seen as another derivative.

It is a well-validated observation that compulsive repetition follows stressful life events, but observations are not explanations. The explanatory principle of a drive for repetition was reexamined by later theorists. Hartmann (1939), Bibring (1943), and Waelder (1964), each thinking separately, divided the repetition compulsion into two components: ego functions and id functions. The ego function of repetition was seen as an automatic, unconscious effort at mastery of an event previously appraised as overwhelming. The id functions were viewed as aggressive drives, or as innate tendencies for reproduction of certain types of stimuli. A superego function of self-punishment by retraumatization was also suggested.

More recently, Schur (1966) reviewed this effort to retain Freud's concepts. He questioned the energic and drive components, and suggested efforts to see if the theory of conceptual and emotional mastery could not be expanded to explain the data derived from observations. Rangell (1967) reviewed the theories for explaining trauma from the various metapsychological points of view, and arrived at the following summation of the psychoanalytic theory:

> A traumatic occurrence is characterized by the intrusion into the psychic apparatus of a stimulus or series of stimuli (the *traumatic event*), varying in their qualitative manifest contents, in their quantitative characteristics, and in their time relationships, which set off an unconscious train of intrapsychic events (the *traumatic process*) beyond the capacity of the ego to master at that particular time. The dynamics of the traumatic intrapsychic process which ensues leads to the rupture, partial or complete, of the ego's barrier or defensive capacities against stimuli, without a corresponding subsequent ability of the ego to adequately repair the damage in sufficient time to maintain mastery and a state of security. The resulting state (the *traumatic state*) is a feeling of psychic helplessness, in a series of gradations from brief, transitory, and relative, to more complete and long-lasting. As a result of insufficient resources on the part of the ego, there is a feeling of lack of control and a vulnerability to further stimuli, without the expectation of adequate containment, mastery, and adaptation [p. 80].

The goal of the present attempt is to examine one level of explanation in more detail: mental functions that alter the traumatic state to a state of greater stability. This level of explanation falls within the cognitive point of view. It examines the information-processing operations that can lead to coping, defense, or defensive failures.

COGNITIVE PROCESSES AND COGNITIVE CONTROLS

In the section on structure, the mind was described as operating to maintain inner models of self and the world. These inner models are used to interpret new information and are revised to remain true to current reality. Serious life events such as a loss or injury present news that will eventually change the inner models. But change is slow; time is essential for review of the implications of the news and available options for response. The mind continues to process important new information until the situation or the models change and reality and their models reach accord. This important tendency to integrate reality and schemata can be called a *completion tendency.*

COMPLETION TENDENCY AND ACTIVE MEMORY STORAGE

Until completion occurs, the new information and reactions to it are stored in active memory. According to this theory, active memory contents will be transformed into representations wherever that process is not actively inhibited (Horowitz and Becker, 1972). This tendency for repeated representation will end only when these are no longer stored in active memory. In the instance of very important contents, termination in active memory will not occur with decay, but only when information-processing is complete. At that point, the news will be a part of long-term models and revised inner schemata.

As ideas related to the stress event are represented, there will be a very natural comparison of the news with relevant schemata. Because a stress event is, by definition, an important change, there will be a discrepancy between the implications of the news, and these schemata. This discrepancy evokes emotion. Serious life events, and the repetition of information related to them, are so different from inner models of attachment that very painful emotional responses occur — emotional states of such power that controls are activated to prevent the threat of unendurable anguish or flooding. This interaction of ideas, emotions, and controls is diagrammed in Figure 5.

News and immediate responses to serious life events remain stored in active memory because on first encounter the meanings seem to have great personal importance. Since the contents are strongly coded in active memory, they tend to be represented intensely and frequently. With each recurrence of the information, comparisons are made again, and emotional activation increases. Emotional responses are also represented, and so become part of the constellation stored in active memory. When other tasks are more immediately relevant, or when emotional responses such as fear, guilt, rage, or sorrow are a threat, controls are initiated. This feedback modulates the flow of information and reduces emotional response.

CONTROLS

Excessive controls interrupt the process, change the state of the person to some form of denial, and may prevent complete processing of the event. Failures of control lead to excessive levels of emotion, flooding, and retraumatization, causing entry into intrusive states. Optimal controls slow down recognition processes and so provide tolerable doses of new information and emotional responses. They lead to working states or less intense oscillations between denial and intrusive states. In this optimal condition, some intrusiveness will occur with repeated representation, some denial will occur when controls operate more pervasively, but the overall result will be adaptive, in that completion will eventually occur. Inner models will eventually conform to the new reality, as in the process of completion of mourning. When this happens, information storage in active memory will terminate, as shown in Figure 6.

At any given time, different sets of meanings of a stress event will exist in different stages. For example, fear of repetition, or fear of merger with a victim might be a recurrent intrusive experience, while survivor guilt themes might be completely inhibited and, for the moment, avoided in experience. Later, in situations of greater safety, the latter theme might be allowed to enter awareness and be represented as an intrusive experience.

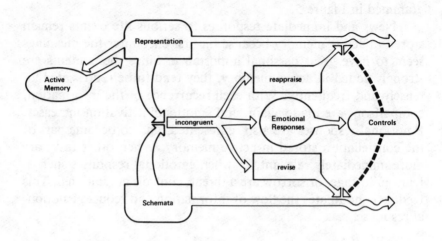

FIGURE 5
Interaction of Ideas, Emotions and Controls

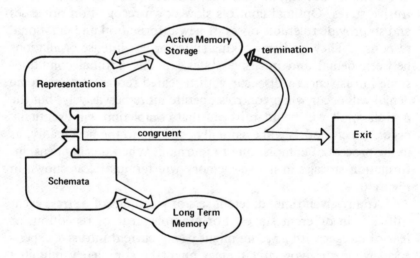

FIGURE 6
Termination of Active Memory

This model accounts for compulsive repetition, phasic states of intrusion and denial or numbing, variation in the level of experience between different constellations of response, and eventual resolution of stress response syndromes. While general stress response tendencies can be abstracted in this way, persons also respond uniquely. This is due in part to how their developmental history colors personal meanings of an event and how current life tasks and environment are affected by the event. Individual variation in response to the same type of life event is also partly due to variations in the habitual style and capacity for control.

Controls of Information-Processing: A More Detailed Look

An alteration in control functions will lead to change in the ideas and feelings experienced by the person, to a possible change in the dominant schemata for organization of information at a given time, and sometimes to a change in overall state. Persons under stress vary in their use of controls over time, according to specific events and personality differences. Since controls are operations rather than outcomes, they must be inferred from outcomes. That is why there has been no agreement on a general psychological theory of control. Variations account for many differences in the patterning of states, but some classification of controls is necessary for the development of a theory related to observations in a given sector of psychological study. From our work observing and treating stress response syndromes, we have developed tentative classifications of control operations, presented here and related briefly to the psychoanalytic theory of defense mechanisms.

BACKGROUND

In the topographic model that is part of psychoanalytic theory, control is described as the degree of censorship between unconscious, preconscious, and conscious expressions of concepts. In the tripartite structural model of id, ego and superego, control is described as one of many ego functions. Defenses are one variety of controls, usually operative without conscious awareness of their function. The names for these defense mechanisms state *what* they accomplish (e.g., undoing), rather than how this is accomplished; the cognitive operations are not stipulated. Wallerstein

(1967) pointed out this hiatus in the existing theory of defense. He defined "defense mechanism" as a theoretical construct used to denote a function, "defense" as the outcome, and "defensive maneuvers" as complex configurations.

The term "control" is used here instead of "defense mechanism," in order to avoid imparting value judgments to the process as adaptive or maladaptive, developmentally conservative or progressive, or consciously or unconsciously operative. Controls can be discussed in terms of psychological or biological systems. Here discussion is strictly psychological, although no inference drawn is inconsistent with what is known about neurobiological regulatory processes. Since many controls can be postulated at various levels of psychological systems, the focus is on controls inferred from the observation of change processes in persons passing through periods of response to serious life events.

VARIETIES OF CONTROL

Controls serve to maintain a state and determine transition from one state to another. The basic controls are inhibition and facilitation, but it is helpful to be more specific about what is inhibited or facilitated. To do so, controls are separated into three levels of abstraction: (1) the selection of the overall topic and mode of thinking about it; (2) the selection of those self-images and role relationship models that will organize interpretations of information; and (3) the selection of information to form sequences of thought. As controls are discussed within these categories, the common results during stress response syndromes will be described. This will connect the observations of signs and symptoms summarized in earlier tables to the explanatory theory of a completion tendency. Any end-results, such as the recurrent and intrusive image of a dead body seen during an automobile accident weeks before, will be a consequence of the operation of many controls. For simple illustration, the tables that follow show each control listed separately along with typical end-results of the operation, or failure of operation, of that control.

The most extensive recent review and formulation of the controls that may lead to coping, defense, or failures to successfully cope or defend has been provided by Haan (1977). She calls these failures "fragmentation." In analysis of the development and resolution of stress response syndromes in the clinical context, it has been useful to think of controls as resulting in coping, defense, or relative failure. The particular control processes listed by Haan, however, are not entirely cohesive with our clinical observations.

This is not the appropriate place for a detailed analysis of her system, but, since one is always wary of newly developed lists, especially lists of defense mechanisms, some salient points ought to be mentioned. Many of her examples of fragmentation occur frequently in psychotic states, and less frequently in the neurotic states that characterize stress response syndromes. For example, tangential concretisms, neologisms, confabulation, delusional ideation and the like were seldom noted in the clinical sample we described earlier; other failures of control have been noted, and lead to the type of signs and symptoms listed in earlier tables.

Haan's list of defensive processes is worded in terms of classical theory (A. Freud, 1936), and I tend to see these more as the outcome of cognitive processes than as the processes themselves. For example, under the cognitive function of "Delayed Response" Haan lists tolerance of ambiguity as coping, doubt as defense, and immobilization as fragmentation or failure. I, on the other hand, would regard tolerance of ambiguity as the result of a variety of cognitive processes, and would instead see dosing of information-processing by episodic inhibition as the appropriate coping function under "Delayed Response." Comparably, I would view maladaptive extensions of inhibitions as the defensive level of Delayed Response, and doubt as the result of cognitive switching between alternative premises on a given topic. Sliding meanings, observed as a frequent operation to avoid emotional responses, is hard to find in her classification, as are some other maneuvers believed to be important.

Haan divides processes into three other kinds of classifications: cognitive functions, attention-focusing functions, and affective-impulse regulations. Here I am in essential, but not complete, agreement. It does seem most useful to group several control operations under cognitive functions; this is where I begin with an overlapping, but somewhat different, set. While I agree with her classification of affective-impulse regulations, her formulations do not contain sufficient recognition of contemporary ego psychology (e.g., Kohut, 1971; Blanck and Blanck, 1974; Kernberg, 1975), and the importance of mental sets for self-image and role relationship schemata (Horowitz, 1980). What I believe she means by affective-impulse regulations is subsumed here under the heading of controls that select self-images and role relationships, since the cognitive structures include issues of controlling and selecting particular aims, impulses, and drive derivatives. Attention-focusing functions are also seen here as format selection controls. I believe that several different entries are indicated, not just the set, as listed by Haan, of concentration as coping, denial as defense, and fixation or distraction as fragmentation. Once again, I see concentration as the result of several control operations that set the topic for sequential organization of thought.

This too brief exposition and comparison of the theory of controls espoused here and that of Haan is not meant to indicate sharp disagreement, but rather joint construction with some discord. We are still far from a general theory of psychological controls; the field has been as complex as that of personality research, with as many pitfalls. For the time being, it seems that controls, defenses, and the like have to be defined as patterns relevant to the particular context of observation. What follows is the working model of controls, which is reflected in the processing of information about serious life events by persons who have shown some difficulty in mastering their reactions to these experiences.

CONTROLS THAT SELECT INFORMATION

The main controls of the flow of simultaneous and sequential arrangements of information are varieties of inhibition and facilitation. These operations lead to such commonly described defenses as denial, repression, undoing, and reaction formation. It is helpful to define several levels of these basic controls by listing them in an ideal order, one followed when there is adaptive, if idealized, working through. This list (as shown in Table 8) begins with facilitation, i.e., the control operation used to choose from recorded impressions those ideas that have the most important and relevant personal implications. Active inhibition of representations is a control that may be used adaptively to dampen ideas and feelings that might distract a person from immediate needs for action. As shown in Table 8, these controls can have adaptive, defensive, or maladaptive consequences. These outcomes, however, are only

TABLE 8
CONTROLS OF INFORMATION FLOW

Information Flow Selection Process	Common Results* During Stress Response States		
	Coping	Defense	Control Failure
Facilitating	Contemplation	Rumination	Inability to think clearly or concentrate
Inhibiting	Dosing	Denial, repression, suppression, isolation, numbing, dissociation, use of drugs, flight, or suicide as avoidances	Intrusions and emotional flooding
Switching attitudes, premises, or schemata	Emotional balancing or counterweighting	Undoing, reaction formation, doubt, indecisiveness, compulsions	Intrusions and emotional flooding
Sliding meanings and valuations	Humor, wisdom	Rationalizations, distortions, exaggerations or minimization of threats and responses	Intrusions and emotional flooding
Shifting locus of meanings	Useful identifications, acceptance of the nature of life	Externalizations, displacements, inappropriate identifications, self-preoccupations, hypochondriasis	Hallucinosis
Rearranging information	Problem appraisal, problem-solving, planning, creative expressions	Comforting illusions and delusions	Confusions
Seeking information	Understanding, learning new skills, hypotheses on future	Intellectualization, searching frenzy	Apathy
Revising inner models of self and expectations	Adaptation, altruism, sublimation, anticipation	Counterphobic self-images, illusional role relationships, inappropriate role reversals	Giving up and hopeless states
Practicing new modes	De-automatization and desensitization of outmoded elements and linkages, automatization of new ways	Counterphobic rehearsals	Lack of preparedness

*All results are multiply determined and are simply examples where operation of the particular process makes an important contribution.

illustrative; any result is the product of multiple processes, not just a single set of controls.

Switching between sets of information is a higher level of abstraction, a control maneuver that requires a subordinate level of inhibition and facilitation. Sliding meanings, including augmentation and reduction of value, is also a complex process, as is shifting the locus of meaning. These controls permit the mind to contemplate and gain perspective on the various implications of a serious life event and responses to it. When switching sets of information is effective, it facilitates emotional balancing and broad appraisals. Sliding meanings along various scales of value enables estimation of the degree of danger and the relative weight of counteractions. Shifting the locus of meaning can differentiate fantasy from reality, a function that is especially important when we consider the universal tendency toward magical thinking about causality.

After the extension and organization of associations selected as most pertinent and realistic, information is rearranged to arrive at various "position statements" about the implications of the serious event. Problem-solving occurs and involves choices between alternative implications and possible routes of response. Seeking new information where it is needed is an effective control that requires attention to gathering knowledge of threat or response tactics.

Of a still higher order are those controls based on information-processing that revise preexisting schemata so that new plans can be practiced until they become as automatic as those they replace. In Table 8 such adaptive use of controls is described as outcome, as are sample results when the outcome is defensive and the controls are weak in relation to the tendency toward representation of ideas and feelings that are not worked through.

CONTROLS THAT SELECT SELF-IMAGES
AND ROLE RELATIONSHIP MODELS

The processes of control just described are those that accomplish the more familiar coping and defensive operations. There are also controls that set not only the sequential flow of information, but the organizing schemata that will be used to pattern that information. The assumption here is that multiple self-images and role relationship models are available to every person and that these change in terms of dominance as organizers. A speculative attempt

TABLE 9
CONTROLS OF SCHEMATA

| | Common Results During Stress Responses | | |
Selection	Coping	Defense	Control Failure
Membership Set (individual importance vs. group or unity	Increased ideological conviction, oceanic feelings	Altruistic surrender, self-centered preoccupation and hypochondriasis	Annihilation, dread
Self-Schemata Set Choice of available self-images	Progressions and regressions in self-concept	Dissociation	Chaotic lapse of identity
Viewing self subjectively or objectively	Heightened sense of identity	Depersonalization	Confusion
Other (Role Relationship) Schemata Set Choice of available self-actions — other role schemata	Seeking help from others, pining for attachments, searching behavior, progressions and regressions in interpersonal patterns	Splitting, introjective experiences	Helplessness, panic

is made in Table 9 to specify the controls, at this level of abstraction, that are most prominent during the states that tend to follow serious life events. The three classifications mentioned are setting of controls for schemata of membership, self-images, and role relationships.

As for membership set, any person can view himself as belonging or independent. After a serious life event, he may modulate emotional reactions to a loss of self by increasing use of schemata in which he is less independent and more unified with a group. This control can lead to coping, as when group coherence reduces combat stress (Borus, 1973). Also, feelings of humanitarian, oceanic or mystical unity may help a person accept his knowledge of impending death. With failures of such controls, the person may experience catastrophic dread with ideas of global annihilation.

Controls also select which of several possible self-images will organize a series of ideas. End-results include the various progressions and regressions of identity that commonly occur after serious life events, such as the death of a loved one. Failure to select or stabilize a self-image can lead to chaotic lapses in identity. In a similar manner, one can choose to experience a given self-image as either subject or object, leading to a variety of common stress responses, such as unusually heightened states of self-actualization or depersonalization.

When implications of a serious life event are examined, another way to reduce emotional response levels is to alter the governing model of role relationship between self and others. A common coping response is to see the self as more than usually in need, and to seek help and support or become dependent on others. Common defensive responses are to adopt illusions of self-sufficiency, to split relationships into those that are all good or all bad, or to heighten introjective experiences in order to maintain an illusion of attachment. When these controls fail, a panic state of helplessness may result.

FORMAT SELECTION

Format selection is a broad level of abstraction that refers to choice of topic, mode of thinking about that topic, and in a general way, level of activation. Within this highest level of abstraction, the control operations most relevant to modulating responses to stress are summarized in Table 10. Listed first is conceptual area selection, an operation that determines what will be thought about next. In the course of working through the news of a serious event, the event or an aspect of it may be inhibited or facilitated; the news is either avoided or confronted. This operation can lead to coping experiences, as when a person doses recognition of a threat by allowing himself time for avoiding unpleasant realities in order to regain composure. A defensive (rather than coping) end-result might be total inhibition, with no time spent facing any aspect of the topic. An inability to inhibit and keep from being overwhelmed by the stress event can lead to flooding or dazed states, episodes that could be considered defensive or adaptive failures.

Another set of controls involves selection of the mode of organization of information. One such operation involves considera-

TABLE 10
CONTROLS OF FORMAT

| | Common Results During Stress Responses | | |
Selection	Coping	Defense	Control Failure
Conceptual Area (time on and off threats)	Dosing; periods of activity and passivity	Preoccupation and counter-occupation	Dazed state and flooding
Mode of Organization:			
Temporal set (viewing by short or long time periods)	Looking at only one step at a time; relating the event to the infinity of time and space	Avoidance of present demands for action	Overwhelmed
Sequential set (problem-solving vs. experiential or fantasy modes)	Thinking only about what to do next; fantasy about restoration of lost object	Fantasy preoccupation, unrealistic plans	Confusion, freezing, or intrusion
Representational set (words, images, enacting)	Problem-solving lexically because images evoke too many emotions; intellectualization	Isolation	Intrusive images
Locus set (external or internal sources of information)	Restorative changes between activity and contemplation	Compulsive action to avoid thought	Flooding, illusions, hallucinations
Activation Level (excitation of various systems)	Healthy cycles of alertness and repose	Hyperalertness, semi-stuporous, dulling, altered states of consciousness, physiological reactions	Shock

tion of the event in relationship to varied temporal contexts, that is, in terms of long or short segments of time. Extremes of such controls are common during response to stressful life events. One frequent end-result is concentration on experiencing time in extremely brief intervals; a person handles a seemingly overwhelming situation by breaking it down into a series of micro-intervals to be taken one at a time, and thinks only about what should be done in the next minute or two. A second common response is to scan unusually long sweeps of time in order to place a bitter moment of suffering into the longer perspective so that it either loses significance, or is meaningful in terms of some larger, even cosmic, plan.

Another control for organizing stress-related information is to select sequential sets. This determines the kind of flow from one bit of information to another. For example, problem-solving is a mode in which information is arranged into sets by principles of logic and fidelity to real probabilities. A quite different set is used in fantasy or experiential flows, in which information sets may be associatively linked by sensory similarities and congruencies of wish or fear, rather than by probability or accuracy.

Heightening such controls after a serious life event leads to common responses. After being raped, for instance, a woman might find herself thinking only of what to do next, whom to call, or what to say, and would rigorously avoid reexperiencing and remembering the terrifying event or any similar past experience. Another result of such control can occur when the woman fantasizes unlikely revenge stories and avoids thinking about what she has to do next, such as reporting what has happened. Similarly, after a death a person may fantasize restoration of the lost person, and avoid thinking of life functions he must now assume. The results of failures in control may be intrusion of fantasy during problem-solving thought, or intrusion of awareness of real problems, with either one leading to emotional flooding.

Control of representational sets is another way to modulate expression of thought (Horowitz, 1972, 1978). These controls determine whether the flow of information will proceed in lexical, image, or enactive (motoric) forms. With the use of such controls, some persons remember a serious event only in words, damping out images to avoid emotional arousal from quasi-perceptual thought. Such operations help coping; they also may accomplish defenses such as isolation and intellectualization. The episodes of intensive images of a bloodied body that might occur weeks after an accident, for example, are seen as a combination of the impetus of active memory, other motives, and relative failure of these control operations.

In a similar manner, other controls set the locus on search for or relative acceptance of internal or external sources of information. End-results may be a useful search for relevant external information that also wards off the feelings that emerge when personal implications are contemplated. Levels of activation of various systems can also be controlled. This leads to various altered states of consciousness and to physiological responses, ranging from hyperarousal to hypoarousal (Fischer, 1971).

CHARACTER VARIATION

This chapter has focused on the signs and symptoms commonly found in persons having either unusually intense or ordinary responses to serious life events. It has dealt at some length with how these signs and symptoms are formed as the result of information-processing attempts to integrate life events with pre-existent schemata. The past history of the person and revision of inner models according to the new meanings have been described briefly; a fuller discussion is beyond the scope of this chapter. While past history would account for considerable individual variation or typological variations, some variance in responsivity is based on differences in habitual controls.

Most persons blend controls in flexible diverse fashions; but, in response to stressful life events, the prototypical hysterical personality may tend to inhibit; the prototypical obsessional may habitually switch meanings; the narcissistic personality may tend toward sliding meanings (Horowitz, 1974, 1975b). That is why, since therapeutic intervention often has to do with modification of controls, a focus on controls as well as meanings is of importance.

SUMMARY

Serious life events may lead to stress response syndromes characterized by states of intrusion and of denial. Working through the meanings of the stressful event is part of a general completion tendency aimed at keeping inner models as congruent with reality as possible. Emotional responses to recognition of the discrepancy between an inner model and the implications of serious news tends to activate control operations that may, in the long run, either abet or interrupt the completion tendency. Understanding the effect of these controls on the processing of information is an essential precursor to a general theory of traumatization, and an eventual rational strategy for the treatment of such disorders.

REFERENCES

Bibring, E. (1943), The conception of the repetition compulsion. *Psychoanal. Quart.*, 12:486–519.

Blanck, G. & Blanck, R. (1974), *Ego Psychology*. New York: International Universities Press.

Borus, J. F. (1973), Adjustment issues facing the Vietnam returnee. *Arch. Gen. Psychiat.*, 28:501–506.

Breuer, J. & Freud, S. (1895), Studies on hysteria. *Standard Edition*, 2: 1–323. London: Hogarth Press, 1955.

Charcot, J. M. (1877), *Lectures on Diseases of the Nervous System*. London: New Sydenham Society.

Coelho, G. V., Hamburg, D. A. & Adams, J. E., Eds. (1974), *Coping and Adaptation*. New York: Basic Books.

Erikson, E. (1958), The problem of ego identity. *J. Amer. Psychiat. Assn.*, 4:56–121.

Fischer, R. (1971), A cartography of the ecstatic and meditative states: The experimental and experiential features of a perception-hallucination continuum are considered. *Science*, 174:897–904.

Freud, A. (1936), *The Ego and the Mechanisms of Defense*. New York: International Universities Press, 1946.

Freud, S. (1920), Beyond the pleasure principle. *Standard Edition*, 18: 7–64. London: Hogarth Press, 1953.

Haan, N. (1977), *Coping and Defending*. New York: Academic Press.

Hartmann, H. (1939), *Ego Psychology and the Problem of Adaptation*. New York: International Universities Press, 1958.

Horowitz, M. J. (1972), Modes of representation of thought. *J. Amer. Psychoanal. Assn.*, 20:793–819.

———— (1974), Stress response syndromes: Character style and brief psychotherapy. *Arch. Gen. Psychiat.*, 31:768–781.

———— (1975a), Intrusive and repetitive thoughts after experimental stress: A summary. *Arch. Gen. Psychiat.*, 32:1457–1463.

———— (1975b), Sliding meanings: A defense against threat in narcissistic personalities. *Internat. J. Psychoanal. Psychother.*, 4:167–180.

———— (1976), *Stress Response Syndromes*. New York: Aronson.

———— (1978), *Image Formation and Cognition*, 2nd edition. New York: Appleton-Century-Crofts.

———— (1979), *States of Mind*. New York: Plenum.

———— (1980), Depressive responses after loss. In: *Stress and Anxiety*, ed. I. G. Sarason & C. S. Spielberger. New York: Hemisphere, pp. 235–264.

———— & Becker, S. (1972), Cognitive response to stress: Experimental studies of a "compulsion to repeat trauma." In: *Psychoanalysis and Contemporary Science*, ed. R. Holt & E. Peterfreund. New York: Macmillan, pp. 258–305.

———— & Wilner, N. (1976), Stress films, emotion and cognitive response. *Arch. Gen. Psychiat.*, 30:1339–1344.

———— ———— & Alvarez, W. (1979), Impact of event scale: A measure of presumptive stress. *Psychosom. Med.*, 41:209–218.

———— ————, Kaltreider, N. & Alvaroz, W. (1980), Signs and symptoms of post traumatic stress and adjustment disorders. *Arch. Gen. Psychiat.*, 37:85–92.

Janis, I. (1958), *Psychological Stress*. New York: Wiley.

_____ (1969), *Stress and Frustration.* New York: Harcourt Brace Jovanovich.

Kernberg, O. (1975), *The Borderline Conditions and Pathological Narcissism.* New York: Aronson.

Kohut, H. (1971), *The Analysis of the Self.* New York: International Universities Press.

Lazarus, R. (1966), *Psychological Stress and the Coping Process.* New York: McGraw-Hill.

Parad, H., Resnick, H. & Parad, L. (1976), *Emergency Mental Health Services and Disaster Management.* New York: Prentice-Hall.

Parkes, C. M. (1972), *Bereavement.* New York: International Universities Press.

Piaget, J. (1937), *The Construction of Reality in the Child.* New York: Basic Books.

Rangell, L. (1967), The metapsychology of psychic trauma. In: *Psychic Trauma,* ed. S. S. Furst. New York: Basic Books.

Schur, M. (1966), *The Id and the Regulatory Principles of Mental Functioning.* New York: International Universities Press.

Waelder, L. (1964), Statements as reported by S. Gifford in Repetition Compulsion. *J. Amer. Psychoanal. Assn.,* 12:632–649.

Wallerstein, R. S. (1967), Development and metapsychology of the defensive organization of the ego. *J. Amer. Psychoanal. Assn.,* 15:130–149.

DISCUSSION

"WORKING THROUGH" AS A PROCESS

Dr. Horowitz stated his interest in psychological microanalysis of the post-traumatic sequence, rather than in its outcomes — the centrality of the question "how" rather than "what." The following discussion concentrated on the transition process, and particularly the oscillation between denial and intrusion.

Dr. Nagler: I view the fact that Dr. Horowitz' formulations are process-oriented rather than outcome-oriented, among their main advantages. This leads us to focus on the control system that is activated; differential outcomes may be due to different ways of information-processing.

Dr. Lazarus: In recent years there is a movement away from purely intrapsychic concern to concerns which actually deal with the environment. In the model regarding transitions from one state to another, I miss the role of the environment. For example, when a depressed patient affects his family, they now react to him in a certain way which may further reinforce his feelings of inadequacy and loneliness, and so on. Such an analysis of the patient's envi-

161

ronment offers therapeutic opportunities to deal with the counter-productive behavior of the family or friends, rather than concentrating entirely upon the patient.

Dr. Horowitz: The state analysis concept includes articulation with the environment, that is, the context of environmental events which are being represented by the person. The environment leads to certain states, which lead to behaviors that affect other people, which in turn lead to new events that the person represents, which lead to new states, and so on. It is an open system approach including both the intrapsychic representation and a transactional matrix. In fact, that is how we analyze the therapy. The therapist is producing events in response to the patient producing events in response to everyone else producing events. We divide a period into episodes, but instead of using units like hours, days, or weeks, our units are states. We are segmenting a period according to the changeability of the person's states.

Dr. Lazarus: Why do the oscillations between denial and intrusion occur? Is it because of something happening in the environment?

Dr. Horowitz: There are many reasons why states are unstable. One is interaction with the environment, which does not stay stable so that reminders or provocations can occur gradually. Another reason relates to the person's safety. Since any stress event will arouse a variety of associational meanings, all of which have to be processed, and since there is probably unconscious monitoring of what it is safe to contemplate, any change that modifies safety may lead to change in one's state. If the person is in danger, he may initially damp down all processing in order not to feel too frighteningly lonely; yet other influences may disrupt the process and allow more distressing thoughts to be aroused. It is like the interaction of hope and worry. Give a person hope and he will be able to worry about it. It's very common in patients with leukemia. When they are told by their physician that there are no more chemical remedies, they not infrequently report a certain serenity; time has no meaning. And then if they are told that there is a new drug, they get worried and upset about it and its possible effects.

In terms of the dynamics of controls, this is analogous to general systems theory; assuming the controls are competent, oscillation should follow. Similarly, when people are anxious, they institute controls, their anxiety goes down, their motive for controls is reduced, the controls begin to lessen, out comes an intrusive plot, up goes the anxiety, up goes control, and so on.

Dr. Janis: In some instances both intrusion and denial may serve an adaptive function. I recall the case of a courageous young woman on our faculty, who used to walk home late at night taking routes considered unsafe, until she was attacked and wounded. She wanted to continue behaving as before, but was now automatically afraid of using the same route. One could see that there is an adaptive value to that kind of worrying process. She was taken out of the realm of her denial by an automatic decision rule to "stay away from routes that are dangerous, that are like the one where you experienced the trauma." Maybe there is a functional value to these intrusions; they facilitate an emotional learning process that allows the person to develop a new script very rapidly, and to apply the lessons even against one's own will. In her case, however, I could also see the struggle against the overgeneralization of this script because she was experiencing problems of timidity in other spheres. Here one could also see the functional value of certain aspects of her denial-like behavior; she was trying to confine that script to some place where it was going to function adequately and not overgeneralize, as emotional responses tend to do. Maybe this constant interaction, the fluctuation between intrusion and denial, represents some aspect of this adaptive learning process. Maybe there is a kind of survival value in this (if you will excuse a very crude Darwinian metaphor here), and the struggle between denial and intrusion is a by-product of the way in which we are programmed to learn from traumas.

Dr. Breznitz: When trying to analyze the impact of a particular traumatic event, it is not sufficient to be concerned with the actual intensity of the loss. A potentially more important question is: *How much reminding is going to take place in the person's environment?* It is not reminders based necessarily on memories, but on actual external provocation. If, for instance, following bereavement one continues to live in a house where every single item reminds one of the loss, this is dramatically different from the person in a more "neutral" environment. While the important aspect of the loss is clearly internal and cannot be escaped, the objective environment has certain properties which serve as cues to evoke images and memories again and again. *The stronger these cues are, the greater the effort needed to deny their eliciting function.*

Remindability or relevance is often unrelated to the intensity of the original trauma. Thus, death from a disease which has an obvious strong genetic component reminds one of the constant threat that the same will be repeated on self or other blood relatives. *It is such relevance to the present that keeps a past trauma from settling into the recesses of the past.*

The following illustrates some of the more paradoxical implications of this thesis. Consider a person who has lost one parent as compared with someone who has lost both. If my argument is correct, it may be more difficult to work through the loss of one parent, since the fact that there is another parent who can die keeps the trauma continuously relevant. Clinical experience often indicates the difficulty of persons who have experienced traumatic loss in establishing new emotional bonds. I submit that this is partially due to the fact that the establishment of new bonds will increase the relevance value of the traumatic loss which is now in danger of recurring. It is as if the working-through process were continuously being monitored by present relevancies.

At the same time, deliberate reminders, such as having the picture of the dead person conspicuously visible, listening to a particular song, or other such cues, may constitute attempts to habituate and extinguish the intensity of their emotional impact.

Dr. Goldberger: Is it not the case that the completion of the post-traumatic process, the manner in which the active memory is laid to rest, depends on the patient's ability to find a new interpretation of the event — one that he can accept freely without feeling fatalistically or passively struck with, as if rewriting a script? I am referring not just to a small bit of a new script such as "How do I feel about being lonely?" or "How do I feel about suffering?" but a reinterpretation in the holistic sense, providing a new frame of reference.

Dr. Horowitz: The most dramatic changes can occur following a remark by the therapist that allows the person to shift his or her interpretation of the situation. An inadvertent metaphor can lead to a change in the person's self-image. Let me give an example that Laurence Frank always uses: In a medical school where the behavior of terminally ill patients was being demonstrated, there was a depressed and morose woman patient expressing a great deal of strain and worry. When he said to her, "At least we can show all these young medical students how a brave person dies," her behavior changed dramatically. She brightened up and became courageous. He didn't say, "You are going to live"; he didn't say, "There is hope for your illness"; he didn't alter any of the premises about the terminal nature of the illness, but he gave her a concept around which she could change her self-image to one of being worthwhile and competent.

THERAPEUTIC CONSIDERATIONS

Dr. Elkes: I would like Dr. Horowitz to explain to us how he uses the psychoanalytic approach to therapy, considering his statement that patients are seen only for about twelve hours. This seems to me to be particularly difficult in view of my own experiences in helping clients in need of assistance following a life-crisis. Commitment to some time-consuming work is important, and I have found it useful to first convince the clients that they received a signal which warrants taking time out. This can range roughly from nine days to three weeks. It is preceded by three days during which they are encouraged to be totally by themselves spending their time writing an autobiography. The writing is guided by some questions and statements of problems, encouraging honesty. This seems necessary as the opening for the therapeutic procedure which involves training of awareness and imagery control, relearning a different way of viewing themselves, training in self-monitoring a few times a day, and a partial reentry into contacts with their usual environment.

Dr. Horowitz: Our treatment is psychoanalytic in that it is guided by the psychoanalytic understanding that there are unconscious as well as conscious processes; that the materials are to be understood in terms of relationships as well as the processing of ideas; and that the reason people are not healing is not ignorance, but rather that there is some conflict involved. The therapy of twelve hours may deal with any kind of mental content, but it is always anchored to their immediate reaction to the series of states associated with the trauma. The event gives the process a current immediacy which in a way allows the therapy to be brief.

6

INFORMATION-PROCESSING ASPECTS OF DENIAL: SOME TENTATIVE FORMULATIONS

VERNON HAMILTON

I suspect that the principal features of this paper will be controversial. It will be postulated that by far the most significant components of emotionality, feeling, mood, personality and motivation are cognitive or semantic structures in long-term memory. The theoretical direction I have taken is substantially due to my conviction that to become scientifically more respectable, psychology and psychologists must try to objectify and quantify what is not directly observable. There seems to be no better time than the present era in which the potency, the number, and the severity of stressors are increasing and the spurious oversimplifications of behavioristic dogma are being discarded. It is unlikely that the latter particular loss or existential threat will generate denial processes in many behavioral scientists!

While elevating cognitive/information-processing events to a position of primary importance, I do not intend to abolish the role of psychophysiological or hormonal events in experiences or control of emotionality. There is no doubt at all that peripheral and electrocortical arousal and the release of corticosteroids affect the perception of danger as well as loss. Without these mechanisms, neither could be experienced fleetingly, chronically, or at virtually intolerable levels; nor would it be possible to *generate* coping processes without this energy source. The facts are, however, that the recognition or anticipation of aversive experience *precedes* the physiological or neuropharmacological response; furthermore, this response and its subsequent function as a stimulus contains only gross and low-grade information which has no elaborated cognitive content as such (Hamilton, 1976b, 1979a, b, c).

For once, I find myself in agreement with a dictionary definition of a word with psychological implications — *Oxford* defines "denial" as a *"statement that a thing is not true or existent."* For our purposes this definition is acceptable with the addition of a number of specifications of the terms "statement" and "thing." In general I would argue that there are *types* of negating statements and *levels* of negation. Furthermore, "things" are defined by objects, situations or persons, or by representational stimuli. The representational stimuli may be explicitly or implicitly verbal, pictorial, postural, or hormonal, or any combination of these. They may be objective and concrete, or subjectively inferential, or a mixture of both. In any of these events we are not dealing with purely sensory quanta of energy; stimuli have immediate meaning by virtue of the informational data which a complex but efficient internal scanning and recognizing process attaches to them. Because of the fine-grain nature of human conceptual differentiation, this recognition of meaning — in my view — employs the structures of semantic networks for its task. For these reasons, I will argue that the processes of denial are based on an internal cognitive analysis of statements, referring to "things" which superordinate processes have recognized as potentially or actually harmful. Some twenty years ago these processes were termed "cognitive controls" by Jerome Bruner, George Klein, Riley Gardner, Hermann Witkin and others; after a period of unpopularity for this concept, they have been revived by Erdelyi (1974), Neisser (1976) and myself (Hamilton, 1976a, 1979b, c), as information-processing operations concerned with self-protective, hedonistic anticipations and outcomes of behavior.

TYPES AND LEVELS OF DENIAL

I intend to show that the many types and instances of behavior which deserve the term "denial"—because they involve negating statements applied to objects, events or persons—may be adequately conceptualized and possibly explained by a single set of processes which only differ quantitatively. It may be useful to examine briefly a number of conditions which fit the earlier definition of denial. Since imposing a rank order is clearly premature, it will not be attempted.

Let us start with motivated perception. In Allport and Postman's (1948) celebrated study of rumor, there is a cartoon of a New York subway scene depicting a well-dressed, unaggressive black man, and a white person in overalls adopting an aggressive posture, holding an open razor in his left hand, threatening the black man. It is well known that high-prejudiced subjects more frequently than others produced perceptual and mnemonic responses that reflected their stereotyped hostile attitudes toward blacks. In order to maintain stable cognitive and behavioral structures, the objective evidence had to be suppressed, modified or rationalized by these subjects so that the responses reflected subjectively rather than objectively oriented cognitive processes. If informational data favoring blacks were ever allowed into a hierarchy of concepts, this was suppressed, repressed, inhibited, scotomized or denied. A well-organized existing set of cognitive/semantic structures favored the selection of prejudiced long-term memory information, which would not generate discomfort, conflict or emotionally arousing cognitive work.

In the study of prejudice, objective knowledge of the stimulus array usually is not available to introspection or consciousness. Studies by Lazarus and his colleagues (Koriat, Melkman, Averill, and Lazarus, 1972; Lazarus, 1974), however, refer to situations in which denial is only partial, and relatively superficial, for example, the crude humor of some new medical students when first taking part in dissection of the human body. The German word *Galgenhumor* describes a similar type and level of coping with knowledge that is intrinsically and extrinsically frightening, aversive or dangerous. This type of denial usually describes some people's behavior before an important test or examination, or in wartime before going into action, or when faced with knowledge of a terminal

illness. Lazarus has used the term "conscious detachment" to label
the coping process which enables the person to perform optimally
in any situation without interference from aversive or threatening
cognitive intrusions. These, however, are not excluded from awareness.

In a similar position on a gradient of awareness or consciousness, we may place the evidence of denial processes from the subincision film studies carried out by Lazarus and his colleagues
(Lazarus, 1966), as well as the evidence of Walter Fenz' work with
sport parachutists (Fenz, 1964, 1975). Much of the latter has been
confirmed more recently by Ursin, Baade, and Levine (1978) with
tests on Norwegian army parachutists in training. Ursin and his
colleagues place somewhat greater emphasis, however, on the primary role of cognitive processes in the elevation and changes in
peripheral and electrocortical arousal than does Fenz.

Although the effects of denial orientation or film commentary
in the Lazarus studies were demonstrated in skin conductance and
heart rate attenuation, in my opinion the role of arousal was not
fully clarified in the studies of the 1960s. For my purposes, differences in skin conductance between "high deniers" and "low deniers" (on a paper and pencil test) is of particular relevance. Here the
"high deniers" show significantly greater skin conductance. This
implies, it can be argued, that: (1) denial, like other types of inhibition, is an energy-demanding activity; (2) arousal in denial is
similar to arousal required for cognitive work (Kahneman, 1973);
(3) it is plausible to infer, therefore, that denial is an ongoing cognitive activity; and (4) it should be possible to demonstrate that the
greater the evidence of denial operations and strategies, the more
pronounced the deficits in complex information-processing tasks
in a setting conceptually relatable to the foci of denial. To the
above extent, denial or anxiety makes a similar contribution to the
information-processing capacity of the person as does a conscious
preoccupation with the anticipation and implication of threats and
dangers.

It may be argued that other explanations are more plausible
when considering Fenz' (1964, 1975) results on stressors and strain
associated with parachuting. Fenz' data are always very complex
and not always easily amenable to a set of fully balanced deduc-
tions. The evidence that "deniers" have lower skin conductance

levels and changes compared with "non-deniers" in response to *pictures* of parachuting, must be offset by two other findings. The first is that novice parachutists, compared with experienced jumpers, have a significantly higher arousal level during the jump sequence as well as during exposure to verbal material of systematically increasing parachuting relevance. This makes the subjects of Fenz' study comparable to those of Lazarus (1966) who were also novices with respect to the subincision and factory-accident films.

The second piece of evidence, not necessarily supporting the link of lowered arousal with denial, comes from experienced parachutists who show this relationship only with the *most* relevant stimulus material, but not with stimuli of intermediate relevance. Similarly, their arousal level is high at a safe distance from the actual jump, but within normal range at the point of jumping. Fear of failure is here displaced by anticipation of success by focusing closely on the most relevant responses—the jumping routine. What emerges, therefore, is the dominant role of information-processing events in the control of emotionality. This must be the case, too, however temporarily, if denial is associated with a reduction in adrenocorticotrophic hormone (Warburton, 1979).

Still within the range of partial or full insight or awareness are the negating statements which one finds with skepticism, or with George Orwell's "double-think," and even in many instances of "double-bind" (Bateson, Jackson, Haley, and Weakland, 1956). Of interest here are not only the personal goals of the individuals exhibiting this behavior, but the information-processing strategies which they reflect. Cynicism, however, as elaborated by reference to Jewish anti-Semitism (Sarnoff, 1971), for example, contains cognitive processes and operations of the more complex psychodynamic type which I will discuss presently.

Although war widows and orphans, the war injured, or Holocaust survivors generally show an apparently adequate level of adaptive coping, I believe that this is basically more apparent than real. We cannot carry out controlled experiments here, but the prediction ought to be made that lower thresholds of strain vulnerability are endemic in a system, which, often confronted with the results of similar experiences, has to expend controlling energy to raise the retrieval threshold of exceedingly aversive and/or melancholic events in memory. I will try to elaborate on this point a little later on.

An extreme level of denial, that is, of rejecting information or knowledge that *must* be available at some point or stage of the cognitive processing system, is present in amnesias, in hysteric fugues, and in states of multiple personalities, where neurological trauma is assumed to have been excluded. It is plausible to suggest that these states of limited consciousness are self-induced, whereas the denial statements made to justify behavior following post-hypnotic suggestion, for example, are externally induced. Although it is possible to overgeneralize, we ought to remind ourselves that the types of denial mentioned are the result of interactions between selective attention and long-term memory operations and processes. These are concerned at their highest level with the expression of each person's dominant and characteristic modes of action and experience, and with the attainment of hierarchically ordered goals.

ATTENTIONAL AND MEMORY PROCESSES IN DENIAL

Some of the most telling evidence for the critical role of attention and memory in denial comes from laboratory experiments in which emotionally loaded stressors are deliberately excluded. An affectively neutral situation is often used in recognition experiments to which signal detection methodology is applied. The number of so-called "false negative" or "false positive" responses accompanied by certainty judgments defines the measures of sensitivity to stimuli (d') and the rigidity or looseness of the criteria (β) applied to stimulus identification. While it is relatively straightforward to suggest that "false negatives" represent a rejection of a correct piece of information, it is less obvious in the case of "false positives," except by extending one's definition of denial to compensatory, non-negating, but irrelevant processes. Denial of knowledge of information with a variety of social connotations has been available for a long time from the serial and repeated reproduction experiments conducted by F. C. Bartlett 50 years ago (Bartlett, 1932), and from eyewitnessing or testimony experiments. A recent symposium edited by Gruneberg, Morris, and Sykes (1978) presents an excellent survey of this particular field. The reason for relating denial processes to this kind of work is the well-supported proposition that recognition is better than recall, and that recall under hypnosis can be substantially better than self-induced recall.

Enough has been said to lay the basis for a cognitive/semantic/ informational analysis of denial. My selection of examples should indicate that there appears to be a possibility of bridging the conceptual gap between psychiatric and psychodynamic orientations, and those of cognitive psychological orientations toward human behavior characterized by the negation of experience and knowledge encoded in memory. Let me briefly restate the essentials of these two orientations before I proceed to the tentative integration which I believe is possible.

The cognitive orientation states that stimuli pass through a closely related series of sequential as well as simultaneous steps in which holding, analyzing, focusing and refocusing, recognizing, and labeling processes and operations alternate and terminate. It is customary to conceptualize these events by one or another of a number of box diagrams, as illustrated in Figure 1. Failure to remember, or the negation of a particular stimulation, is held to be a function of inadequacy of the memory and attention components and the specific information input situation. Of particular importance are the complexity, physical intensity and speed of stimulation, the task instructions, and therefore, selective attentional set.

This box diagram can be modified, while retaining its chief components, to indicate the *functional* properties of long-term memory and selective attention, as shown in Figure 2. In doing so, we are relating concepts derived from cognitive style and control theory to the more analytic operations which must underlie them. A second modification of Figure 1 concerns the introduction in Figure 2 of the term "semantic memory" in the context of personality and motivational dispositions. The justification for this modification lies in the modern approach to concept formation by reference to the semantic basis of concepts.

An early, but no longer fully accepted, attempt to demonstrate a partial conceptual structure is shown in Figure 3. Combining the concepts of Figures 2 and 3 has led me to propose that the essential aspects of individual personality and motivation are the availability of schematically organized cognitive/semantic structures in the form of networks. I will return to this concept later.

The general psychiatric and the psychodynamic orientation toward denial hitherto has employed a different level of discourse of definition and specification. Its central concept is repression,

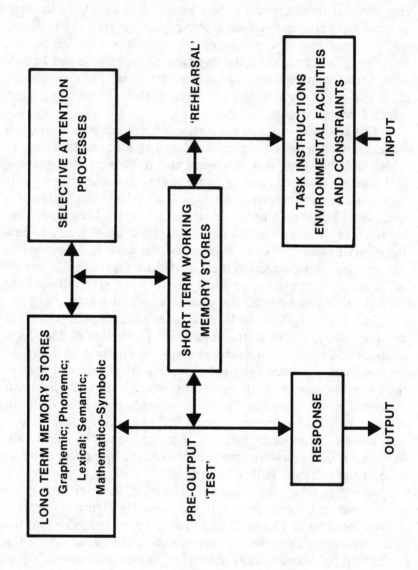

FIGURE 1
General Model of Human Information-Processing

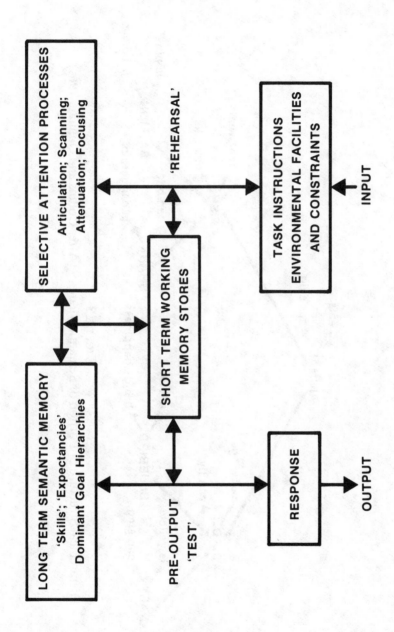

FIGURE 2
Model of Cognitive/Semantic Processing System

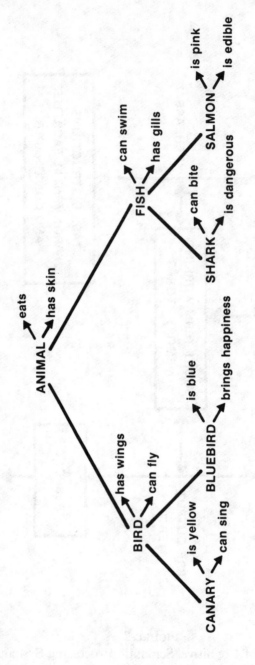

FIGURE 3

Hierarchical Structure of Portion of Semantic Memory (After Collins and Quillian, 1969)

which has the function of defending the person against knowledge that is unacceptable to other areas of knowledge, insight or consciousness. The process is not amenable to control or introspection, and according to Anna Freud (1966), fundamentally serves the mastery of anxiety. Classical psychoanalytic theory and some of its more recent modifications must be considered prescientific statements, despite their internal coherence and often unanswerable logic (see also Peterfreund's [1971] cogent comments). This must be said for two reasons: (1) it excludes the kind of knowledge now available from information-processing theories; and (2) it maintains a 19th-century categorical division between cognition, conation and affect.

Even Arieti (1967) maintains the distinction between the repression of emotions and the repression of aversive "cognitive ramification" (p. 166). Later on he writes, "It is mostly the accompanying unconscious or physiological emotion which will determine whether the stage becomes conscious or not. These unconscious emotions operate like extremely complicated servo-mechanisms of cybernetic systems. Only gross motivational trends, conscious or unconscious, can be discerned" (p. 169). The reference to servo-mechanisms is important, even though the logical follow-up, that these mechanisms respond to information, is absent. Arieti also argues that the mechanism of the "censor" explains very little, and that it is not possible to say what mechanisms outside the realm of consciousness decide whether a person is capable of coping with unpleasantness or aversiveness. These views reflect, of course, the difference between the data and concepts of empirical psychology and clinically oriented psychopathologists. It should be possible, however, to bridge this gap by offering cognitive explanatory constructs for repression, censorship, and decision-making processes outside awareness.

The bridging process is helped by Horowitz' views of the participation of schematic models of the self and others in coping with traumatization (Horowitz, 1976, 1979). Horowitz views denial as a common cognitive process, particularly in response to serious life events, which leads to symptom formation in the absence of a "completion tendency," and which itself depends on cognitive restructuring of the models of the self and critical others. Denial is seen here as a defense against excessive stimulation, and the rever-

sal of symptoms is logically and cognitively related to a gradual inoculation against the unacceptable emotions. This is termed "dosing" by Horowitz. In a theory of stress vulnerability, denial as well
as "dosing" are seen as attempts at avoiding aversiveness and
strain. The former occurs by preventing conceptual completion or
restructuring of the critical experience schema, the latter by gradu-
ating this process, a sequence which is not unlike desensitization.

What is missing from this and similar approaches is an objectifiable identification and specification of what cognitive/semantic/
informational processes and operations are involved in denial, or
in the gradual integration of the aversive content that is initially
denied. In light of the earlier arguments, there seems to be ample
grounds for considering these processes and operations as instances
of ordinary problem-solving. A complex set of stimuli has to be
held in working memory; it has to be identified by articulating and
attenuating attentional processes working with long-term memory
structures, until a recognition match has been achieved. Then the
input is coded on the basis of these subjective personal dispositions. If the resultant code fits the outcome expectancies and ac-
ceptability criteria of existing schematic structures, the stimuli can
begin to be integrated with these, and a stimulus-appropriate response can be made. If the identification triggers accessible long-
term memory (LTM) structures with low retrieval thresholds which
encode sensitivity to and rejection of aversive informational data,
then the content will be rejected, i.e., negated by dominant, self-
protecting structures. We may speak here of misperception, of
"false negatives," of cognitive distortion or problem-solving failure. The difference between "neutral" and "personally relevant"
problem-solving processes lies in conditioned peripheral and electrocortical arousal associations, and in the complex lifespan setting of the affectively loaded information.

On the basis of my own research (Hamilton, 1979c), I must
argue that the massive so-called "emotional response" is a function
of the overpowering amount of information made accessible in
LTM by the aversive event. This is an augmenting, positive feedback process that is a dual function of: (1) low threshold peripheral and central arousal; and (2) of an existing, elaborated reservoir
of LTM structures concerned with the anticipation and avoidance
of strain from aversive information input. Buchsbaum (1976) has

shown that a homeostatic system is available to enable a stimulus-intensity-control mechanism to reduce evoked cortical potentials. Whereas limbic system mechanisms are capable of reducing stimulus intensity at a sensory level, higher-order systems are required to deal with stimulus intensity control when the stimuli are conceptually complex and when they are analyzable into highly differentiated meaning. Higher-order systems are also required when complex processes and operations are available for relating high intensity stimulus *meaning* to an existing system of achieving hierarchically organized goals, by response and behavior preferences which are characteristic of the person.

A COGNITIVE/SEMANTIC MODEL OF PERSONALITY AND MOTIVATION

In 1972 I first suggested (Hamilton, 1972a, b, c) that the real explanation for the impairment of complex cognitive tasks by high anxiety may be that anxiety is itself information. In later publications (Hamilton, 1975, 1976a, b), I argued in greater detail that anxiety, as task-irrelevant information, could be thought of as competing for processing space and time in short-term memory (STM) and selective attention components of the processing system, while it was fully utilized with complex processes and operations directed by a primary task. Research data available thus far have not disconfirmed this formulation, and noncognitive arousal could be relegated to a secondary, though necessary, causal factor (Hamilton, 1979c, 1981).

The cognitive reconceptualization of anxiety has led to an overall reassessment of my conceptions of personality and motivation, more rapidly than may be justified. This cannot be discussed in any meaningful detail here, except insofar as it has a bearing on an information-processing analysis of denial. The central thesis of the model is that there is no basic distinction between the neurophysiological language of the cognitive/semantic/informational LTM codes and the method of their participation in decision-making, choice of behavior and conflict resolution, whether the stimulus situation is neutrally intellectual or has important implications for the self-image and its social goals. In addition, just as there are hierarchical semantic structures for the word "animal" or animal species, as was shown in Figure 3, so are there semantic structures encoding the individual's goals and self-concepts. Just as the collective "animal" represents the content of *one* cognitive/semantic schematic structure, so are there cognitive/semantic structures reflecting personal characteristics and their goals. Figure 4 attempts to illustrate this conceptualization by reference to the structures that may be subsumed by an affirmative response to an item from an introversion-extroversion or social anxiety questionnaire. Each semantic/conceptual identifier depends on subsidiary, additional defining terms and concepts, and there are complex superordinate schematic relationships among the experience, response and behavior categories shown in this illustration. The cognitive/semantic redefinition of personality and motivation may be said to go well beyond the interesting neo-behaviorist analysis by Mischel (1973) of social learning theory. Its implications are also more general than Martindale's (1975) reinterpretation of some Freudian processes on the basis of changes in semantic structures, although this suggestion fits quite well with the present propositions. These were independently developed, and are fully consistent with Pylyshyn's (1973) statement that LTM retrieval (which also means storage), must be in terms of symbols for objects, situations, people and their relationships, representing finite amounts of propositional information.

APPLICATION OF THE COGNITIVE/SEMANTIC MODEL OF PERSONALITY AND MOTIVATION TO THE ANALYSIS OF DENIAL

Whether one adopts a neurophysiological approach, or a developmental-genetic model of the kind proposed by Piaget or Heinz Werner, or a behavior differentiation model derived from psycholinguistics, it is difficult to avoid a hierarchical conception of the nature of the cognitive schema. The explanatory direction adopted here originated from Donald Hebb's (1949) concept of organizations of cell assemblies with their reverberatory circuits operating in phase sequences. Figure 5 reminds us of the essential features of this model. Functional relationships between discrete informational data become established through contiguity and joint participation in making responses which are experienced as goal-directed and rewarding. Hebb was the first modern psychologist to suggest that "insight" and motivation may require similar structures and processes. This suggestion can now be expanded by

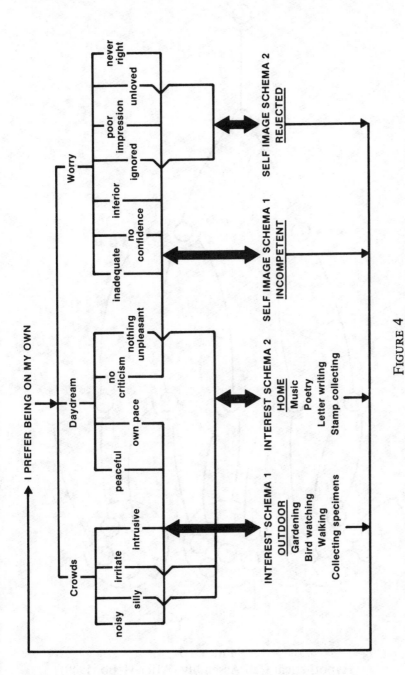

FIGURE 4

Interest and Self-Image Schemata Implied by Introversion Questionnaire Item

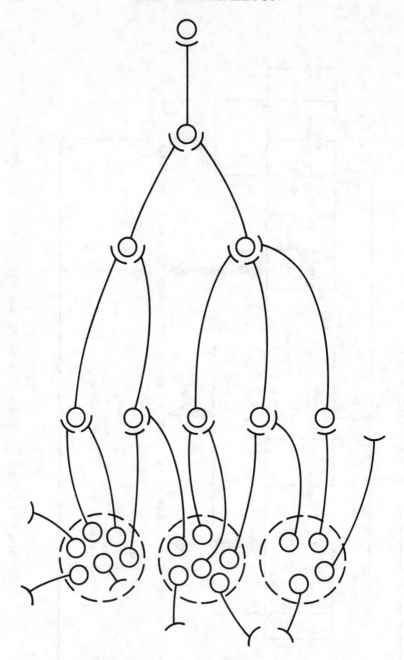

FIGURE 5
Hypothetical Cell Assembly (After Hebb, 1949)

postulating that interactions and integrations between functionally related stimuli, subjective or objective goals, and combinations of habits for carrying out a successful response can be achieved only if the basic informational data from all behavior structures are coded in a single language employing common symbols.

Let me proceed to supply some content for this hypothetical model by examining the possible cognitive/semantic structure of the self-image component "inferior," which figured earlier in the semantic network analysis of social introversion. Figure 6 schematizes the functional integration and differentiation of five behavioral goals. It suggests one possible method by which the economy of the human processing system can be achieved through the encoding of a superordinate lexicon of semantic terms, each of which can represent the individual's idiosyncratic use of a subordinate lexicon. In Figure 7 one particular subassembly has been further analyzed with respect to its hypothetical cognitive/semantic content. Combining the hypothetical information from Figures 6 and 7, some conceptualizations may be obtained of the actual content of the human LTM stores.

At this point it is necessary to be reminded of how the information-processing system is actually thought to generate a response. One of the earlier diagrams (Figure 1) may now be filled in with the hypothetical content of a "neutral" word recognition task as in Figure 8. A relatively low probability stimulus word presented at subthreshold speed generates a series of attempted matches, approximations and mismatches. The word "hidden" has been entered into the long- and short-term working memory stages to indicate the *possibility* that a *semantic* identification was partially achieved at one stage of the analysis. However, because "unobtrusive" is less common and means more as well as less than "hidden," and because approximations to "hidden" did not match with graphemic and phonemic LTM store analyses, both words remained unavailable. Significantly, the probability of "hidden" was fully negated, although it had clearly a fairly low retrieval threshold. Its presence, even in a functionally related sense, was denied.

Although this particular example of recognition processes is entirely hypothetical, some of the suggested processes and operations are already supported by cognitive/semantic research data (Norman, 1976; Seymour, 1976). There is some justification, there-

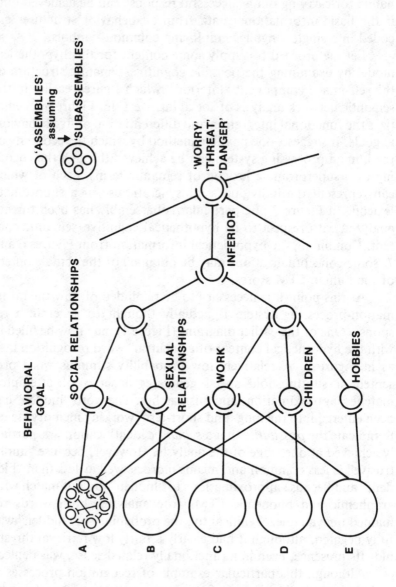

FIGURE 6
Hypothethical Conceptual Structure of "Inferior"

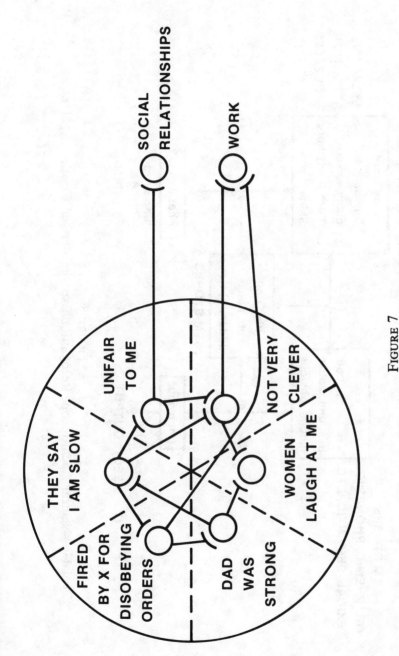

FIGURE 7

Hypothetical Information Content of Conceptual Subassembly "A" in Figure 6
Serving Conceptual Structures "Work" and "Social" Relationships

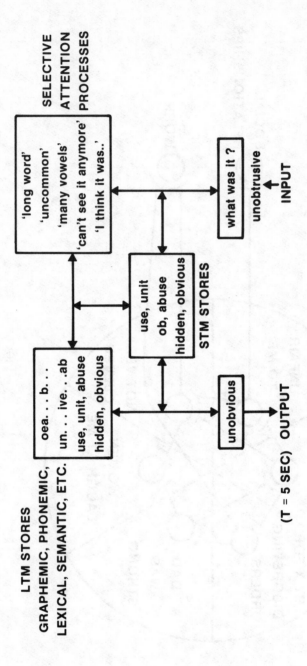

FIGURE 8

Denial in "Neutral" Tachistocope Recognition Experiment ("False Positive"), Unpaced

fore, for attempting a similar analysis of the processes and operations which might be initiated with an aversively toned stimulus word in an ego-threat experiment. Figure 9 suggests what may happen, in information-processing terms, by presenting the word "failure" to a subject scoring high on Test, Trait or State Anxiety, as well as on "sensitization." The processing stages here deal with larger semantic units than those shown in Figure 8 because the matching and retrieval processes are guided by superordinate LTM content and strategies. These were specified earlier in Figure 2, and are concerned with selective articulation and attenuation strategies driven by goal expectancies, goal hierarchies and subjectively acceptable skills for achieving maximal gratification, quiescence and personal stability. With these goals and this type of subject, a common word like "failure" may be misperceived, but not before it has been correctly identified in all processing systems. The operation of response inhibition, suppression, repression, negation or denial is indicated by the heavy lines in Figure 9. Again, the hypothetical nature of the illustration needs to be stressed, especially the distribution of cognitive data between the major processing components. At the same time, I wish to draw attention to one particular feature of Figure 9—the number of cognitive/semantic steps, that is, the amount of basically irrelevant information-processing of an anxious subject, engendered by stimulation with a "threat" word.

It is indisputable that LTM content has a developmental history, and Figure 9 primarily demonstrates the application of the informational model of anxiety which I have advocated in the last few years. The more anxious the person, the greater the number of cognitive/semantic structures encoding the subjectively experienced objects of threat, danger or aversiveness; the greater the degree of their conceptual elaboration and differentiation in semantic network; and, of particular relevance to the present discussion, the greater the number of available stimulus identifiers with the function of meeting, overcoming and denying knowledge of threats, dangers and aversiveness. The informational load of anxiety will reach similar proportions with a *single*, dominant threatening object event or situation which occupies the nucleus of an aversive cognitive/semantic network. In this case, it may be proposed that we have a possible modern analogue of the Freudian "fixation" point, of an Adlerian "complex," or of the colloquial psychiatric

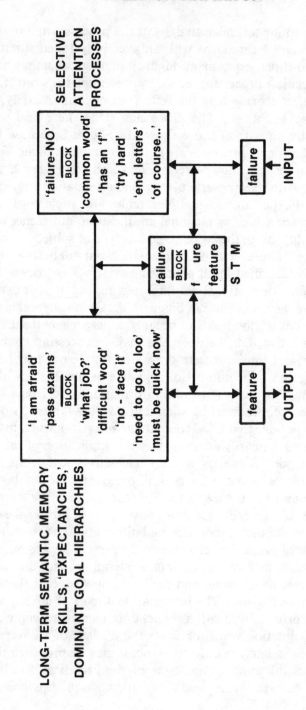

FIGURE 9

Denial in "Affective Tachistocopic Recognition Experiment ("False Positive"), Unpaced

"trauma." All of these alternative conceptualizations depend on the participation of firmly conditioned biological arousal processes. These energize the behavioral responses and facilitate the elaborative cognitive/semantic operations as well as the maintenance of a subjectively acceptable temporary or permanent endstate. Although the relationship between anxiety and depression has not been fully worked through yet, I have already proposed that the cognitive/semantic processes and operations in the experience and handling of actual or imagined loss are not categorically different from those of anxiety, and that it is possible to conceive of depression as a defense against anxiety, by denying that it is any longer a relevant reaction to the person's evaluation of stimulus events.

TOWARD A MATHEMATICAL DESCRIPTION OF THE INFORMATION-PROCESSING APPROACH TO DENIAL

Until such time as other evidence becomes available, a materialistic and physicalistic approach to human behavior must be the most parsimonious. Therefore, model building, quantification and analogues derived from other sciences are entirely appropriate procedures for our attempts to understand and visualize the hidden processes of human thinking. One glance at the complexity of a section of an RNA or DNA molecule will convince us, however, of the enormity of this task. Any present attempts, therefore, to try to offer a systematic description of even one class of human self-protective thought processes, must be primitive and short-lived.

Three general propositions may be stated which at least are consistent with present knowledge, from which they are deduced:

1. Denial processes are informational processes, which handle particular classes of data coded in cognitive/semantic structures.

2. These processes contribute to the information-processing load of the responding cognitive system by adding irrelevant, subsidiary or alternative goal-seeking operations which include the *active inhibition* of unwanted LTM structures.

3. In the presence of excessive response- and decision-making needs, the information-processing efficiency of the cognitive system will be reduced in some sphere of activity because its processing space and time are limited at any given phase of operations.

The last two propositions may be written in symbolic form by an adaptation of a statement which I offered some time ago (Hamilton, 1975); this is written out in Figure 10. The quantification of the terms I_{eps} and $I_{(C_i eps)}$ is not excessively difficult, as I have shown on previous occasions (Hamilton, 1979c), and the amount of informational encoding of $I_{(A_i)}$ and $I_{(L_i)}$, that is, anxiety and depression, can be grossly inferred already from questionnaire scores. Earlier comments and illustrations suggest, however, that questionnaire assessments may have to be superseded by semantic network analyses or something similar in order to obtain a better approximation of the full extent of aversive cognitive LTM content. Some preliminary work in this direction commenced last year at Reading. If the statement shown in Figure 10 is useful, it should be possible to demonstrate that subjects who employ denial strategies will show cognitive performance inefficiency if these strategies are appropriately stimulated. This evidence is available in at least one study cited by Silverman (1972). Here an *inverse* relationship was demonstrated between instructions to inhibit aggressive/hostile thoughts and cognitive performance.

The first proposition now requires restating because anxiety and loss are not denial in themselves, but rather what may need to be denied. The restructuring strategies and operations—RSO_i in Figure 10—consist of a number of components, such as those shown in Figure 11. The principal feature of this statement is the "non-processing instructions." This stage of cognitive work has a meaningful analogue in computer programming, but must be conceived here as having complex feedback loops to other stages and components of the restructuring strategies and operations, as well as to the primary LTM data sources of anxiety and experiences of loss. These are too numerous and complex to illustrate for the present.

Fundamentally, however, denial needs to be seen as the effect of the operation of forces of energy. If, as it appears, denial has discontinuous properties, that is to say, if it diverges from the customary stimulus evaluation strategies of the person, and if it appears that a *gradual* process has led to this, then normal mathematical procedures are unable to contribute to a quantification of the forces. For this reason, too, neo-Lewinian topology is inappropriate.

Mathematicians, like Zeeman at Warwick University in the United Kingdom, who has interests in the biological and social sci-

FOR MAXIMUM ADAPTIVE CAPACITY

$$APC + SPC > I_{eps} + I_{(C_i eps)} + I_{(D_i)}$$

where

$$I_{(D_i)} = I_{(A_i)} + I_{(L_i)} + I_{(RSO_i)}$$

APC	Average processing capacity	i	internally generated information
SPC	Spare processing capacity	e	Externally generated information
I	Information	p	Primary information
C	Competing responses	s	Secondary information
D	Denial		
A	Anxiety		
L	Loss		
RSO	Restructuring strategies and operations		

FIGURE 10

Types and Sources of Information-Processing Demand
with Anxiety, Loss, and Denial of Aversiveness

$$I_{RSO_i} = \left(\begin{array}{c} \text{Distorted} \\ \text{Recognition} \end{array} \; \frac{AND}{OR} \; \text{Negation} \; \frac{AND}{OR} \; \begin{array}{c} \text{Selection} \\ \text{Recognition} \end{array} \; \frac{AND}{OR} \; \begin{array}{c} \text{Retrieval of} \\ \text{Substitute} \\ \text{Structures} \end{array} \right)$$

\+

NON-PROCESSING 'INSTRUCTIONS'

FIGURE 11

Hypothetical Information Processes Operating
in Achieving Denial of Stimulus Meaning

ences, believe that "catastrophe theory," invented by the French mathematician Thom (1975), may be a new tool for the quantification of human behavior and behavior changes. The theory involves topology because the underlying forces in nature can be described as smooth surfaces of equilibrium (Zeeman, 1976). When equilibrium breaks down, "catastrophes" occur. One type of breakdown of equilibrium occurs when gradually changing forces or motivations lead to abrupt changes in behavior. Zeeman's applications of the new method to psychology have been largely confined so far to bimodal and opposite distributions of behavior, like fight and flight, fear and rage, or anger and self-pity. This is one type and level of conflict. Another type and level is the one that interests us here: the conflict between recognition-nonrecognition, affirming-negating, or accepting-denying information.

It may be argued that once we have accepted the notion of a unitary symbolic language for the coding, integration and retrieval of information that embraces knowledge of the external objective world as well as its subjective interpretation and systematic elaboration by a person, and if the actions of that person depend on a choice of responses with different anticipated outcomes and degrees of satisfying expectancies which are coded in the same language with comparable grammatical rules, then we have a system of forces which can be summated with many variations in its constituents, as required by "catastrophe theory." If this is a logical deduction from previous propositions, then a method of quantifying the force and direction of internal cognitive/semantic processes and their effects may be available. This would lead to more precise predictions of vulnerability to stressors, and a more precise choice of therapeutic strategies for the relief of disabling strain symptoms.

The special utility of the application of differential calculus to disturbances of a system in equilibrium seems to be its capacity to predict the choice of one particular symptomatic resolution of conflict, and that point in the balance of forces when coping gives way to an unadaptive solution. This would require a series of measurements of information-processing strategies, goals and capacities at the reductionist level of number of conceptual categories, size of categories, goal-approach and goal-avoidance categories, as well as the level of adaptive or coping strain at which task-irrelevant data and responses begin to intrude.

It is a formidable task. If it succeeds, Freud will survive in an even more illustrious light; behavioral science will achieve the status it deserves; and the tools will become available to help us to cope more effectively, more painlessly, and more rationally with the mountainous ecological dangers of the future, which are in part the results of our own ignorance.

REFERENCES

Allport, G. W. & Postman, L. (1948), *The Psychology of Rumor.* New York: Holt.

Arieti, S. (1967), *The Intrapsychic Self.* New York: Basic Books.

Bartlett, F. C. (1932), *Remembering.* Cambridge, Eng.: Cambridge University Press.

Bateson, G., Jackson, D., Haley, J. & Weakland, J. (1956), Toward a theory of schizophrenia. *Behav. Sci.,* 1:251-264.

Buchsbaum, M. (1976), Self-regulation of stimulus intensity: Augmenting/reducing and the average evoked response. In: *Consciousness and Self-Regulation: Advances in Research.* Vol. 1, ed. G. E. Schwartz & D. Shapiro. London: Wiley.

Collins, A. M. & Quillian, M. R. (1969), Retrieval time from semantic memory. *J. Verbal Learning & Verbal Behav.,* 8:240-247.

Erdelyi, M. H. (1974), A new look at the New Look: Perceptual defense and vigilance. *Psychol. Rev.,* 81:1-25.

Fenz, W. (1964), Conflict and stress as related to physiological activation and sensory, perceptual and cognitive functioning. *Psychol. Monogr.,* 78:1-33 (Whole No. 585).

_____ (1975), Strategies for coping with stress. In: *Stress and Anxiety,* Vol. 2, ed. I. G. Sarason & C. D. Spielberger. Washington, D.C.: Hemisphere.

Freud, A. (1966), *Normality and Pathology in Childhood.* New York: International Universities Press.

Gruneberg, M. M., Morris, P. E. & Sykes, R. N. (1978), *Practical Aspects of Memory.* London: Academic Press.

Hamilton, V. (1972a), The size constancy problem in schizophrenia: A cognitive skill analysis. *Brit. J. Psychol.,* 63:73-84.

_____ (1972b), Continuities and individual differences in conservation. *Brit. J. Psychol.,* 63:429-440.

_____ (1972c), Conservation and maternal attitude: An analysis of suboptimal cognition. *J. Child Psychol. Psychiat.,* 13:147-166.

_____ (1975), Socialization anxiety and information processing: A capacity model of anxiety-induced performance deficits. In: *Stress and Anxiety,* Vol. 2, ed. I. G. Sarason & C. D. Spielberger. Washington,

D.C.: Hemisphere.

_____ (1976a), Motivation and personality in cognitive development. In: *The Development of Cognitive Processes*, ed. V. Hamilton & M. D. Vernon. London: Academic Press.

_____ (1976b), Cognitive development in the neuroses and the szhizophrenias. In: *The Development of Cognitive Processes,* ed. V. Hamilton & M. D. Vernon. London: Academic Press.

_____ (1979a), The cognitive analysis of personality related to information processing deficits with stress and anxiety. *Bull. Brit. Psychol. Society,* 32:21. (Abstract of Invited Address.)

_____ (1979b), "Personality" and stress. In: *Human Stress and Cognition: An Information Processing Approach*, ed. V. Hamilton & D. M. Warburton. Chichester: Wiley.

_____ (1979c), Information processing aspects of neurotic anxiety and the schizophrenias. In: *Human Stress and Cognition: An Information Processing Approach*, ed. V. Hamilton & D. M. Warburton. Chichester: Wiley.

_____ (1981), A cognitive model of anxiety: Implications for theories of personality and motivation. In: *Stress and Anxiety*, Vol. 9, ed. C. D. Spielberger & I. G. Sarason. New York: McGraw-Hill.

Hebb, D. O. (1949), *The Organization of Behavior.* New York: Wiley.

Horowitz, M. J. (1976), *Stress Response Syndromes.* New York: Aronson.

_____ (1979), Psychological response to serious life events. In: *Human Stress and Cognition: An Information Processing Approach,* ed. V. Hamilton & D. M. Warburton. Chichester: Wiley.

Kahneman, D. (1973), *Attention and Effort.* Englewood Cliffs: Prentice-Hall.

Koriat, A., Melkman, R., Averill, J. R. & Lazarus, R. S. (1972), The self-control of emotional reactions to a stressful film. *J. Pers.,* 40:601–619.

Lazarus, R. S. (1966), *Psychological Stress and the Coping Process.* New York: McGraw-Hill.

_____ (1974), Cognitive and coping processes in emotion. In: *Cognitive Views of Human Motivation*, ed. B. Weiner. New York: Academic Press.

Martindale, C. (1975), The grammar of altered states of consciousness: A semiotic reinterpretation of aspects of psychoanalytic theory. In: *Psychoanalysis and Contemporary Science,* Vol. 4, ed. D. P. Spence. New York: International Universities Press.

Mischel, W. (1973), Toward a cognitive social learning reconceptualization of personality. *Psychol. Rev.,* 80:252–283.

Neisser, U. (1976), *Cognition and Reality: Principles and Implications of Cognitive Psychology.* San Francisco: Freeman.

Norman, D. A. (1976), *Memory and Attention: An Introduction to Human Information Processing.* New York: Wiley.

Peterfreund, E. (1971), *Information Systems and Psychoanalysis: An Evolutionary Approach to Psychoanalytic Theory. Psychol. Issues,* Monogr. 25-26. New York: International Universities Press.

Pylyshyn, Z. W. (1973), What the mind's eye tells the mind's brain: A critique of mental imagery. *Psychol. Bull.,* 80:1-24.

Sarnoff, I. (1971), *Testing Freudian Concepts: An Experimental Social Approach.* New York: Springer.

Seymour, P. H. K. (1976), Contemporary models of the cognitive processes: II. Retrieval and comparison operations in permanent memory. In: *The Development of Cognitive Processes,* ed. V. Hamilton & M. D. Vernon. London: Academic Press.

Silverman, L. H. (1972), Drive stimulation and psychopathology: On the conditions under which drive-related external events evoke pathological reactions. In: *Psychoanalysis and Contemporary Science,* Vol. 1, ed. R. R. Holt & E. Peterfreund. New York: Macmillan..

Thom, R. (1975), *Structural Stability and Morphogenesis: An Outline of a General Theory of Models.* Reading, Mass.: Benjamin.

Ursin, H., Baade, E. & Levine, S., Eds. (1978), *Psychology of Stress: A Study of Coping Men.* New York: Academic Press.

Warburton, D. M. (1979), Physiological aspects of anxiety and schizophrenia. In: *Human Stress and Cognition: An Information Processing Approach,* ed. V. Hamilton & D. M. Warburton. Chichester: Wiley.

Zeeman, E. C. (1976), Catastrophe theory. *Sci. Amer.,* 234:65-83.

DISCUSSION

COGNITIVE VERSUS PSYCHODYNAMIC
APPROACHES TO DEFENSE

Dr. Koriat: A very important feature of Dr. Hamilton's model is the attempt to bridge the gap between the psychodynamic and cognitive approaches to defense. Let me try to contrast the two. The most important organizing concept in dynamic psychology in the last thirty years or so was the concept of energy. Recently, with the rise of cognitive psychology, another concept came up—the concept of information. These are, in my view, the focal competing concepts that any serious theory of personality must deal with.

There are some parallels between the two concepts. Psychodynamic theories have tried to deal with the flow of energy within the organism, with the energy originating from the id and then being contained by the structures of the ego and superego before obtaining some access to awareness and behavior. In a similar way, cognitive psychology has tried to deal with the flow of information within the organism and with the way in which it is selected, organized, contained, or assimilated by the cognitive structures of the person. Where psychodynamic theories view the ego and the superego as internal representatives of the outside world and mediators between the impulse and its expression in behavior, cognitive theories view the cognitive structures as the internal representation of the outside world, and the mediators of the expression of information in behavior.

We agree that the major motivation for defense is anxiety. Anxiety, in the dynamic framework, results from the clash or discrepancy between the impulses of the individual and the structures of the ego, in the same way as cognitive frameworks see anxiety as resulting from a discrepancy between information coming through the senses and one's structures, schemata, and so on. Thus, defenses can be viewed as vicissitudes of drive energy or as vicissitudes of information. These are the two alternative conceptions, and the major problem facing us is to formulate a theory which encompasses both the concepts of energy and information.

While I think that Dr. Hamilton tried to take care of both concepts within the same theory, he missed, in my view, some of the important contributions of psychodynamic theory. Specifically, I miss two questions. The first question is: *Who is doing the fooling?* Somebody has got to be threatened, and I don't know where he is. One must determine exactly who is doing the fooling and who is being fooled. The second question is: *What for?* Why do we try to fool ourselves, what is the function of denial? These are questions which Freud tried to answer in a certain way, but I don't think that he succeeded. Cognitive psychologists are not interested in these questions because there is no person in cognitive theory.

Dr. Hamilton: What is the function of denial? My view is that the fundamental thing is the hedonistic need of the individual, and one way to achieve that is to avoid anxiety. *I consider anxiety as a burst of information which has to be kept in check.*

Dr. Werblowsky: The fascination of the computer model has always interested me. This is best seen in the Lévi-Strauss type of structuralism. The idea of explaining the human mind, the cosmos, and virtually everything in terms of binary oppositions clearly stems from being enamored of the computer model.

Dr. Elkes: Dr. Hamilton has drawn our attention to the need for new conceptual models and new languages. By pointing out the need to examine the stages of the process of denial at as fine a grain as we can, he actually demonstrated the limitation of the computer model as we now see it.

7

DENIAL IN CONCENTRATION CAMPS: SOME PERSONAL OBSERVATIONS ON THE POSITIVE AND NEGATIVE FUNCTIONS OF DENIAL IN EXTREME LIFE SITUATIONS

LEO EITINGER

Denial as a concept has been used in the medical literature throughout the last century, as described by Weinstein and Kahn (1955). Since Anna Freud (1936), it has been understood as one of the much used, but not very "highly estimated," defense mechanisms. The young child uses denial both naturally and constructively. Being unable to cope with a powerful, threatening outer world in a realistic way, it denies the physical menaces, and thus mitigates the unbearable situation. In psychiatric literature, denial is usually considered a very primitive defense mechanism, illustrating severe psychopathology, usually of psychotic character or typical of persons with few resources and/or weak egos. We shall later see that the occasion for the use of denial is not always as simple. In the present context, denial will be considered and dealt with as one of the many more or less successful coping mechanisms used

by the concentration camp inmates in their desperate attempts to
survive.

To relate even sketchily the vast literature concerning the prisoners' behavior in the camps, or to discuss the place and function
of denial in their actions and reactions, is virtually impossible
within the given limits of this presentation. Only a few reports can
be mentioned here: While the war was in progress, when the killing
of millions in the so-called extermination camps reached its greatest momentum, Bettelheim (1943) felt "objective enough"—to
quote him—to describe his observations from the pre-war camps.
He found only regression and "identification with the aggressor."
Cohen (1954), at that time a young medical doctor from the
Netherlands, observed mostly the negative side of concentration
camp behavior—the regression, depersonalization, resignation,
and extreme egotism. However, he also describes prisoners who
were altruistic and had feelings of compassion toward their fellow
prisoners.

Similar observations are reported by Lucie Adelsberger (1947,
1956), a psychologist who had been imprisoned in Auschwitz-
Birkenau and had survived the evacuation to Ravensbrück, where
she was liberated. She describes, in a deeply human and moving
way, both the positive and negative aspects of human reactions
and interpersonal relations. According to Adelsberger, there was a
"relapse to the animal state, but also a sublimation of highest degree." One example might be quoted from her report: "Themselves
already on the verge of starvation, they would sell their own bread
ration, in order to buy potatoes for a dying comrade, and thus give
him a last happiness." Only somebody who has a *real* understanding of what the expression "bread ration" means can fathom the
depth of this observation.

V. E. Frankl, who has published extensively about his experiences and observations in Nazi concentration camps, has written
an overview of the psychology and psychiatry in the camps
(Frankl, 1961). He quotes the last sentence of Baruch Spinoza's
"Ethics": "Sed *omnia* praeclara tam difficila quam rara sunt." (But
everything great is just as difficult to realize as it is rare.) There
were, according to Frankl, only a few who were able to preserve
their humanity, but they were an example to the others, an example which started a chain-reaction. For these people the life in the

camp was no regression, but a test and a moral progression—in some cases even a religious revelation.

Observations by prisoners without medical or psychological background, like Kautsky (1946), Wyller (1948), Adler, Langbein, and Lingens (1962), Langbein (1972), or the very moving history of the Norwegian Jew, Herman Sachnowitz (1976), the only survivor of a family of five brothers and three sisters, often describe seemingly contradictory findings, i.e., relapse to the animal state, but also a sublimation of the highest degree. But one is tempted to ask: Could it be otherwise? One must consider the incredible number of prisoners in the Nazi camps. In his classical book on the German SS imperium, Eugon Kogon (1946) writes that the average population in the camps of Nazi Germany and the occupied territories was about one million at any given time. Any attempt to generalize psychological reactions in a population of such a size must therefore be considered with the greatest caution. Nevertheless, it is worthwhile mentioning that the problem of denial has not been dealt with in detail by any of the above-mentioned authors. A modest study on the topic may therefore be in place.

Concentration camps were an integral part of the Nazi regime. Much deliberation and planning, organization and classification were used in order to get them going. During the Nazi rise to power in Germany in 1932–1933, the concentration camps were unorganized places where the different groups in the SS party were allowed to give vent to their aggressivity and to wreak vengeance on their political enemies in the other parties, mainly socialists. Later the camps became well-organized institutions run by the highest SS authorities, the official aim described as the "re-education of the inmates." The internees were not only expected to survive, but to be "transformed" into new individuals, better suited to live and cooperate with the new regime.

A German SS officer (Schäfer, 1934) wrote about the concentration camp Oranienburg, later known as the infamous Sachsenhausen: "Any idiotic system can put people into prison. What has been proven to be of great importance and value in the concentration camps, is the courage to bring about reforms which at first may appear to be unpopular and to re-educate people to be obliged to work in a decent way again. . . One can hardly believe how beneficial this training is for such vile and brutal people" (p. 48). After the war, we have been given a totally different description of the concentration camps. Even in the pre-war concentration camp, however, inmates were never considered worthy of "re-education." In all the existing camps the prisoners were treated with the utmost brutality and sadism, resulting in a high rate of mortality and suicide. But the possibility existed, though in most cases only theoretically, that the inmates would sooner or later be freed. This also applied to a far lesser degree to Jewish concentration camp prisoners before the war. (For example, Jewish prisoners who were fortunate enough to have family or acquaintances able to provide entrance visas for them to a foreign country, especially one that was overseas, had a reasonable chance of being released from the camp.) The decisive point was that there existed a *possibility* to survive.

This situation was radically changed after the infamous Wannsee Conference at which the Nazis decided to kill the entire Jewish population wherever the German military power enabled them to do so. (I am deliberately using the term "kill" and not "exterminate," because one kills a person and exterminates vermin.) To accomplish this aim, the so-called annihilation camps in Poland and Russia were established (e.g., Treblinka, Majdanek, Sobibor).

Amongst these camps, Auschwitz had a unique character. It was both an annihilation camp with gas chambers and crematoriums, where between three and four million people were killed, and at the same time, a vast work camp and basis of manpower for many branches of the German industry (coal-mining, chemical industries, weaponry, and many, many others). This double function of Auschwitz—the organization of mass murder on the one hand, and a work force on the other—put the inmates of Auschwitz in an ambiguous psychological situation. (As my personal experiences and observations are mainly from this camp, I am referring only to Auschwitz in the following.)

The admittance procedures signaled to even the very naive prisoner-to-be that something exceptional was happening. Jews arrested in Germany had to sign a paper on which they declared that they were freely delivering all their property and possessions to the German State, and that the State "as compensation" would take care of them and all their needs until the end of their days. (This was surely an unsurpassed cynicism.) Jews arrested in occupied countries (as I was, in Norway) were simply deported to Auschwitz while the local governments confiscated their property. In the camp itself, the SS no longer cared to hide that they considered this stay the last stop in a prisoner's life. We had to deliver all of our personal belongings, not only luggage and valuables, but also personal clothing and wedding rings, in short, absolutely everything. Completely naked, one went into the bath with only one's spectacles; and completely naked, one entered the camp. The SS did not bother to give any receipt for one's belongings; thus it was not difficult to imagine what one's fate would be. But even those who did not understand what was going on, or did not want to, were very soon confronted with certain realities. Having arrived in the "block," one of the first things one heard was that there was only one way out of the camp, i.e., through the chimney of the crematorium. One could hear this either in the most brutal way from a capo, or in a more fatalistic way from a fellow prisoner, who would just say, "Here everybody is killed—sooner or later." In some cases one received detailed information about the total death machinery in the camps from better-informed fellow prisoners.

Even in retrospect, I must say that the only rational reaction to this situation, especially during the years before the complete debacle of the German armies was obvious, would have been to take one's life. I do not want to take up the question of resistance, or of "dying as a man," because this is not a part of the problem to be discussed here. I am only stating that in a situation where one is sentenced to death, and where one knows that one is allowed to stay alive only as long as one's last strength, health, and working capacity are not completely exploited, the most "rational" act would be to avoid this last abuse of one's reserves. And, of course, there are many such examples. I personally remember a young man from Germany who had arrived with the same transport as I had. He told me quite calmly that he had not known where our transport was going, but seeing that we were in Auschwitz, and knowing what was going to happen, he did not want to let the Nazis decide *when* he was to die; *this* decision he wanted to make himself. He just as calmly tried to kill himself.

It is my contention that this real and extremely life-threatening situation provoked a serious *denial* reaction, and not, as is usually described, a repression only. Such denial was necessary to prevent the acceptance of a fatalistic logic that would lead to "the only possible consequence" in the camp—suicide. Thus, in some cases it was of immediate life-saving value.

Weisman and Hackett (1966) wrote that repression acts to inhibit potentially disruptive internal forces, while denial acts to protect against potentially destructive external forces. By accepting this definition, the mechanisms used in the camp should correctly be termed "denial." The next question is whether denial could also have been of positive value for the inmates of the concentration camp under circumstances other than the initial life-saving. Based on my own experiences and observations in Auschwitz, I would answer this question in the affirmative.

Before describing my experiences, a few references from the literature are pertinent. Already in 1950, Lewin had shown that denial has a positive function; according to him, however, it occurred in a quite specific context only—to generate unrealistic confidence and optimism. Experimental investigations of the effectiveness of denial as a coping strategy have been reported by Lazarus and his colleagues (1964, 1965), and the clinical aspect of the problem has been explored mainly by Hackett and Cassem (1970, 1974). In the coronary care unit where they made their observations, denial not only served to allay anxiety and maintain hope, but was also of general aid in the patient's recovery. Based on a denial scale developed by their group, Froese, Hackett, Cassem, and associates (1974) demonstrated that in the earliest stages of hospitalization for myocardial infarction, patients who used denial tended to gain control over their anxieties sooner than non-denying patients. During the acute state of the illness, denial as a means of coping could thus *not* be considered a dangerous mental mechanism or hazardous distortion of reality with tragic results.

Kroll, Silk, Chamberlain, and Ging (1977) describe an "epidemic of unexplained hospital deaths," which mainly befell patients in the intensive care unit. A questionnaire survey after the cessation of the "epidemic" showed that the patients who were theoretically most vulnerable used denial to cope with the unprecedented and frightening situation. The threatening, murderous piece of reality was denied and repudiated with a more benign explanation. Their denial reaction helped them to ward off anxiety, and made normal and continuous functioning at the hospital possible. The authors remark that "denial mechanisms often protect individuals and social groups from being overwhelmed by anxiety or panic that would otherwise paralyze all functioning and prevent even the initiation of constructive responses" (p. 1380). Furthermore, the denial of the patients was accompanied by preventive measures; thus, a normal life with normal psychological reactions could be reestablished in the hospital.

It should be made clear from the very outset that there cannot be a realistic comparison between the psychological situation of prisoners in Auschwitz (or other annihilation camps) and normal psychological or psychopathological reactions in persons outside the camps. Nevertheless, some parallels may be drawn. I would thus submit that even in the camp the denial reaction under certain specific circumstances had a positive function, helping the inmates to behave as though the most dangerous situations and severe anxieties did not exist, therefore allowing some of them to survive. This applied especially to the very early beginning of the uphill struggle of the newcomers during the first weeks and months in the camp. As several other authors have described, these first weeks—and sometimes even months—were the most difficult, dangerous, and devastating for the inmates. Only after being put to work or gaining a position in the camp where the immediate danger of death was *relatively* small, could one say that it was rational to harbor the hope that "something unforeseen would happen," and that one would be able to survive in spite of all the negative odds. The very few who could occasionally get hold of bits of news and thus follow the steady withdrawal of the German military forces had a small additional argument in favor of this faint hope.

After the initial stage, the psychological situation was already somewhat changed. One could afford to be more aware of the life-threatening situation, to assess it more rationally, and to strain every nerve in order to stay alive, "to become a witness and to tell the story." The impact of modifying one's awareness control from complete denial, to a more differentiated degree of understanding and emotional assessment of the real possibilities to survive, was not always easy to bear. It demonstrated to the experienced self-observer the difference between a rigid defense mechanism of total denial and the growing pains and pleasures of living emotions and reality orientation. Again, with all necessary reservations, this psychological situation can be compared to that of a coronary patient, who during the most acute and nearly fatal period copes with his life-threatening situation by complete denial, and only then starts to realize how severely ill he has been.

There was one category of prisoners about whom I am especially concerned—the doctors. Their psychological reactions would have been of extraordinary importance to their own possible survival and to that of their fellow prisoners. Even they had to cope with the actual situation by denial. Without using this defense mechanism, it would have been impossible for them to do their work and offer their medical help, insufficient as it was. In spite of everything that has been said against becoming "accomplices of the SS," the prisoner doctors alleviated countless sufferings and helped thousands and thousands of fellow prisoners to endure their fate. The fact that there remained a few hundred thousand survivors at the end of the war, the fact that not absolutely all prisoners succumbed to the ill treatment, is partly due to the prisoner doctors' efforts. This is nothing to boast of; those doctors who were fortunate enough to be able to help were grateful for the opportunity to do so. However, from a psychological point of view, it was only their denial of the realities which made it possible for them to act and work as if their human and/or medical activity was a normal one of real help to the fellow prisoners. For example, a colleague and I worked as prisoner doctors in the "infirmary" of a relatively small "side camp" of Auschwitz where most of the prisoners did forced labor in a plant producing anti-aircraft guns. One day a boy with terrible pains was brought to us from the factory. It turned out that he had a ruptured ulcer of the stomach. Under the most primitive conditions (on a kitchen table, with shoehorns as surgical hooks) we managed to close the rupture; improbable as it was, our patient survived. (Yet, as with other patients on whom we had to operate under similar conditions, or whom we could treat with drugs in the "infirmary," he had to go back to his work and his sufferings in the camp. Unfortunately, I am unable to say if the operation was a real success, i.e., whether the patient survived not only the operation, but also the war.)

There are also examples of prisoner patients whom we treated "against all possible odds," and who survived not only their disease, but also the camp. I have met them subsequently in different situations after the war, and have found these meetings among the most important and positive experiences in my medical life. The fact that one can be of help in the most hopeless of situations, and that this help can have long-lasting positive consequences for others, cannot be overestimated. One can hypothesize that such consequences were ultimately possible only with the help of denial at the time.

Another example occurred during the evacuation of Auschwitz for an unknown destination. The staff of the camp hospital marched as a closed group together with the other prisoners on one of the seemingly endless and hopeless "death marches." Late one evening, exhausted, we reached a barn in which we could stay overnight. A prisoner came to the camp hospital because he had severe pains in his legs and back, and asked for help. Hopeless as the situation was for everybody, he received some consolation and a pill "against the pains." Without complete denial of the actual facts of utter hopelessness and of the knowledge that everybody unfit to march along with the others was bound to be shot, even this very modest help would have been impossible. (I do not know if this fellow prisoner survived the march or not, but I know that the medical profession would have betrayed itself if the poor fellow had not received this small, perhaps pain-relieving, tablet.)

I furthermore submit, even though it may be somewhat debatable, that the "emotional blunting" that has been described as a practically universal defense mechanism amongst concentration camp inmates should be considered as a denial mechanism with a positive function. One's deep and unchanging grief, the trouble and concern about the fate of one's nearest, who had either been arrested at the same time with oneself or whose whereabouts were unknown, the murderous behavior of the guards, the killing of one's comrades, the flogging and the executions, in brief, the unbearable and incredible realities of daily life were to a certain degree dealt with as if they did not exist. One tried to avoid the awareness of the difficulty of the situation by a type of psychic withdrawal from the realities. It is true that basic psychology tells us that such primitive mechanisms are not very efficient, and that even this moderate effectiveness is achieved only at great costs. We furthermore know that in normal life a problem cannot be solved when there is no awareness of it, and that precluding or excluding awareness prevents a realistic solution. But in extreme situations, as in the concentration camps, there is no realistic possibility of *solving* the problems; therefore, denial in these situations must be considered as having a positive function.

Without being able to prove this statistically by any "hard documentation," other than personal impressions during the war and several hundred interviews with survivors after the war (Eitinger, 1964), I am of the opinion that the positive function of denial was not only time-limited. It was also very closely connected with the problem of interpersonal relations. Therefore, a few words on general coping in the camps are appropriate here: The people who were able to mobilize the most adequate coping mechanisms were those who, for one reason or another, could retain their personality and system of values more or less intact even under conditions of nearly complete social anomie. Those who were most fortunate in this respect were the persons who, thanks to their profession, could both show and practice interest in others, and who could retain their values inside the camp at the same level as outside the camp. The few fortunate ones were some doctors, nurses, even social workers and priests, as described by Kral (1951) in Theresienstadt (Terezin). They were more preoccupied with the problems of their fellow prisoners than with their own, and came through their trials in better mental condition than the average inmate of the camp. Only a tiny minority, however, had this good fortune. The large majority had to find other ways of surviving.

Prisoners who had been able to stay together with some members of their family, who could remain in contact with some of their pre-war peers, who were able to help others and/or to receive help (as described by Luchterhand [1967], among others) were those who resisted best. They were not completely deprived of all feelings of personal and human dignity and values either in their own eyes or in the eyes of their fellow inmates. These findings are to a certain degree the same for ex-prisoners interviewed both in Norway and in Israel. When asking the Norwegian ones what most helped them to survive, the answers were nearly stereotyped: "Being together with other Norwegians." The answers of the Israelis were much more varied because of the complex family and group relations they had during imprisonment.

The conservation of one's ability to make some of one's own

decisions was most important. In some cases it was only the decision about how to deal with the daily portion of bread, in other cases the question of keeping up personal hygiene. The decisive factor was always that the prisoners did not consider themselves completely passive. They did not lose their reasoning power, their ability to plan and to put their plans into action. They proved this by being capable of administering the diminutive remains of their right to decide for themselves, by showing that they were not willing to be completely overwhelmed by circumstances. They continued to be individuals and individualists.

The combination of being able to preserve some individuality, and some "old" real norms and values of life on the one hand, and to deny the outer danger on the other, seems to me to have been the most successful way of coping.

However, it must be stressed that not any kind of denial had a positive function. The most tragic one was a prisoner's inability to assess how far he could go in using the "medical way" in order to avoid excessive hard work, etc. While denial of the "general death sentence" could give positive results, denial of the camp's *tendency* was tantamount to being killed immediately. The first selections immediately after the Jewish prisoners had left the cattle cars at Auschwitz are rather well known by now. The SS doctor in charge sorted the arrivals just by a slight motion of a finger to left or to right, either glancing only at the new prisoners or asking them a question. The result of this selection was that the number of prisoners taken into the camp from Jewish transports amounted to an average of about 10% of all the people who were brought to Auschwitz. After arrival in the camp, the prisoners were asked if they had some serious disease. Those who really were chronically ill, or who hoped to get an easier life by saying that they were seriously ill, were selected at a roll call and sent to the gas chambers.

In other words, a prisoner who thought that he could gain some advantage by stressing his chronic ischiadic pains, or by aggravating a coughing period, was in a very serious and life-threatening situation. Inability to work was the main reason for being "selected" on a later occasion, i.e., for being sent to the gas chambers. This is perhaps one of the main reasons why so few conversion reactions were observed in the camps. Most of the prisoners knew that any secondary gain was impossible, and those who did not know were killed off very quickly. The extreme and chronically life-threatening situation "solved" all other problems and conflicts, making the neuroses' primary gain superfluous.

Prisoners who denied their being in a life-threatening situation by escaping into daydreams, who did not accept the grim reality of camp life and its immediate ghastly demands, who did not try to find an operative adaptational mechanism, were also "selected" very quickly. This general denial also occurred in the pre-war camps and resulted after a few weeks or even days in the death of the inmate. In Auschwitz a prisoner not able to grasp the total tendency from the outset, or who tried to escape reality by denial in fantasy, would hardly survive the first working day. It would be pointless to enumerate all the situations that could result in fatality for a prisoner who was not sufficiently reality-oriented. From the time alarm sounded in the morning, jumping out of "bed," precise and correct "building" of the covers, the role calls, standing in the right row, marching, until the last distribution of a lukewarm watery fluid which was sometimes called soup, sometimes tea or coffee, the whole day was controlled, and every moment full of danger. A fatal blow on the head was the most probable result of not assessing the bitter and grim realities of the moment, or trying to escape them by any sort of denial.

These were often prisoners who were completely isolated from their families, deprived of all contact with groups to whom they were related before the war, or people who quickly abandoned themselves and their inner-most values. People who were completely overwhelmed by the notion that they had nobody and nothing to struggle or to live for, who felt completely passive and had lost their ability to retain some sort of self-activity, were those who most easily succumbed. The symptoms of these feelings of hopelessness and submission could be seen quite early by experienced observers. Prisoners with such symptoms started to neglect their physical appearance, showing that their reality assessment was impaired insofar as basic needs of personal hygiene were concerned. When a prisoner could no longer "understand" how important it was for him to wash properly and to keep himself free from vermin, he was lost. Nobody in the camp could escape knowing the deadly danger of typhus (spotted fever) and the way it is spread by lice. Denial of this danger, neglecting the not very delicate but absolutely life-saving daily lice-inspection, was a nearly pathognomonic symptom of the approaching "giving-up syndrome," and of the very near and unavoidable tragic end of a prisoner's life.

Even though recent literature has shown the positive value of denial for the survival of patients suffering from serious illness, this positive side has never been discussed in detail in connection with survival problems in Nazi concentration camps. I have tried to show that the use of denial was rather complex, necessarily connected with other coping mechanisms, seemingly more contradictory than many other ways to deal with the meaningless conditions in the extermination camps. Denying death could be life-saving under certain circumstances, while denying the small seemingly unimportant facts of daily life and struggle would result in certain and premature death.

A more detailed analysis of the circumstances involved is able to explain the contradictions, showing that basic human values and positive interpersonal relationships were of salient importance even under these most extreme situations. This understanding will leave us with certain positive conclusions about the role of denial and its ultimate impact. In conclusion, I would therefore like to quote a paper by Sledge, Boydstun, and Rabe (1980) on the changes of self-concept related to war captivity. They write: "The subjective sense of having benefited from war-imprisonment experience is positively correlated with the harshness of the experience. We emphasize that this is a subject phenomenon and in no way implies absence of actual disability (which may or may not be present in individuals who report that they have benefited by their experience). This study did not deal with the issue of mental health or disability of POWs" (p. 443).

By comparing the incomparable, something similar may be said about the concentration camp survivors and the nature of this study.

REFERENCES

Adelsberger, L. (1947), Psychologische Beobachtungen im Konzentrationslager Auschwitz. *Schweiz. Z. Psychol.*, 6:124–131.
_____ (1956), *Auschwitz, ein Tatsachenbericht.* Berlin: Letner.
Adler, H. G., Langbein, H. & Lingens, E. (1962), *Auschwitz, Zeugnisse und Berichte.* Frankfurt: Europäishe Verlagsanstalt.
Bettelheim, B. (1943), Individual and mass behavior in extreme situations. *J. Abnorm. Soc. Psychol.*, 38:417–452.

212   LEO EITINGER

Cohen, E. A. (1954), *Human Behavior in the Concentration Camp.* London: Cape.

Eitinger, L. (1964), *Concentration Camp Survivors in Norway and Israel.* Oslo: Oslo University Press.

Frankl, V. E. (1961), *Psychologie und Psychiatrie des Konzentrationslagers,* Psychiatrie der Gegenwart III. Berlin: Springer.

Freud, A. (1936), *The Ego and the Mechanisms of Defense.* New York: International Universities Press, 1946.

Froese, A., Hackett, T., Cassem, N., et al. (1974), Trajectories of anxiety and depression on denying and non-denying acut myocardial infarction patients during hospitalization. *J. Psychosom. Res.,* 18:413-420.

Hackett, T. & Cassem, N. (1970), Psychological reactions of life threatening stress: A study of acute myocardial infarction. In: *Psychological Aspects of Stress,* ed. H. Abram. Springfield, Ill.: Thomas.

_____ _____ (1974), Development of a quantitative rating scale to assess denial. *J. Psychosom. Res.,* 18:93-100.

Kautsky, K. (1946), *Teufel und Verdammte.* Zürich: Gutenberg.

Kogon, E. (1946), *Der SS-Staat: Das System der deutschen Konzentrationslager.* Frankfurt: Europäische Verlagsanstalt.

Kral, V. A. (1951), Psychiatric observations under severe chronic stress. *Amer. J. Psychiat.,* 108:185-192.

Kroll, P., Silk, K., Chamberlain, K. & Ging, R. (1977), Denying the incredible: Unexplained deaths in a Veterans Administration hospital. *Amer. J. Psychiat.,* 134:1376-1380.

Langbein, H. (1972), *Menschen in Auschwitz.* Frankfurt: Europaverlag.

Lazarus, R. S. & Alfert, E. (1964), The short-circuiting of threat by experimentally altering cognitive appraisal. *J. Abnorm. Soc. Psychol.,* 69:195-205.

_____ et al. (1965), The principle of short-circuiting of threat. *J. Pers.,* 33:622-635.

Lewin, B. (1950), *The Psychoanalysis of Elation.* New York: Norton.

Luchterhand, E. (1967), Prisoner behavior and social system in the Nazi concentration camp. *Int. J. Soc. Psychiat.,* 13:245-264.

Sachnowitz, H. (1976), *Det Angar Ogsa Deg.* (It concerns you too also you.) Oslo: Cappelen.

Schäfer, W. (1934), *Konzentrationslager Oranienburg.* Berlin: Buch- und Tiefdruckgesellschaft.

Sledge, H., Boydstun, J. A. & Rabe, A. J. (1980), Self-concept changes related to war captivity. *Arch. Gen. Psychiat.,* 37:430-443.

Weinstein, E. A. & Kahn, R. I. (1955), *Denial of Illness.* Springfield, Ill.: Thomas.

Weisman, A. & Hackett, T. (1966), Denial as a social act. In: *Psychodynamic Studies on Aging,* ed. S. Levin & R. Kahana. New York: International Universities Press.

Wyller, T. (1948), *Fangeliv Og Fri Tanke.* (A Prisoner's Life and Free Thoughts.) Oslo: Cappelen.

8

DENIAL AND RELIGION

R. S. ZWI WERBLOWSKY

I would like to begin my contribution with a brief general consideration of the term "denial" and some of its implications. In current English professional usage the word "denial" serves more or less as a translation of Freud's *Verleugnung,* a word which etymologically includes the notion of lying: the attempt by a "lying" type of denial to refuse accepting a certain reality.

Of course, the English word "denial" could also be taken to refer not to Freud's favorite term, but to the notion of *Verneinung,* in the sense of rejecting on grounds of principle something the presence of which you admit. There is, I think, a huge difference between these two, and I will say more about this distinction shortly. My purpose is to sketch some aspects of the wide spectrum of culturally created, developed and constructed patterns of dealing with the problem of denial under its double aspect of *Verleugung* and *Verneinung.*

Normally we think of denial, in the sense of *Verleugnung,* either as a failure or a refusal. Clearly the two are not necessarily the same. Sometimes a failure to do something may, on closer psycho-

213

logical inspection, reveal itself to be a mechanism of refusal; but such is not always or necessarily the case. We must guard against dogmatic preconceptions, and each case requires a careful investigation of the mechanisms involved. There may be failure and/or refusal to *perceive*. Here the cognitive problem comes in, the problem of the perception of reality; or, if reality is perceived, failure and/or refusal to relate to it in a specific, relevant or meaningful manner.

This, of course, brings us up against another philosophical problem. My above description of the alleged failure and/or refusal to perceive and/or relate to reality is really uncritical and simplistic. I should rather qualify and say: to perceive, or relate to, what *others* consider to be reality. Then, of course, we must go on to ask: On the basis of what criteria? Are they social, cultural, or other kinds of criteria? Certain things are called "reality" simply because they are part of what sociological jargon calls the "social construction of reality." If one takes reality not as a metaphysical entity but as a social construct, then one also takes it for granted that the "reality" of the Hindu is very different from that of the Israeli. In other words: the reality you deny, refuse or fail to relate to, is very often what *others* consider to be reality.

The question is to what extent the definition of others imposes itself so much, or is so internalized, that you feel morally, socially or otherwise committed to it, and hence refusal is tantamount to denial. Prior to denial, and in order to make it "denial," there must be a basic assumption to the effect that one really ought to accept that particular social construct of reality.

All this is, perhaps, not very decisive for psychologists, but it may give you an idea of the way non-psychologists, and in particular social scientists (and I consider the student of comparative religion to be basically a social scientist) look at this problem. My remarks were designed to suggest that what in psychological discourse is normally referred to as a defense mechanism, in reality hides a great many philosophical problems. This does not detract from the reality that denial may, in fact, be just a defense mechanism. One may have to talk about defense and to analyze the mechanisms, but this must not blind us to the issue that lurking under the reality of defense mechanisms are a great many conceptual problems.

The concept of the social construction of reality, needless to say, involves the problem of the social and cultural conditioning of perception as a whole, and of the filtering of perception. A great deal has been said on this subject in this volume and it has been a major theme, whether explicit or implicit, whether elaborated or tacitly assumed in our discussions of "denial." Facets of the problem include the structuring of perception, the mechanisms of filtering perception, the "filtering out" as well as "filtering in," and in conjunction with these, the problem of "leaks" which, far from being accidents, may be part of the general configuration. They are not simply mishaps but part of the (unconscious) design of the whole perceptive process. We are dealing with a very sophisticated system of filtering, and within this feedback system, built-in provisions are made for certain leakages. But what is the locus of these leakages, and how many are there? At what point would excessive leakages make the whole mechanism self-defeating? And, in which cases do they have a reinforcing function?

The nature of the construction, as well as the filtering of perception, and the leaks (or the diverse choices of mechanisms of leaks) are more often than not cultural problems. They are not simply problems of the individual patient with whom the psychologist or the psychiatrist has to deal, but expressions of social constructs requiring the analysis of cultures and religions. If you happen to be, say, in Southeast Asia, you will want to understand how Hindus perceive the world as distinct from Buddhists; how a Madras Hindu filters in contrast to a Thai Buddhist; what "leakages" a Hindu system builds into its perceptive apparatus as compared to those of a Buddhist system. Sometimes these phenomena may be personal, whereas others may be physiologically general. All this requires large-scale comparative research. We all remember the exercises we did in our first term as psychology students – drawing something (e.g., a staircase) which can be seen in two different ways, as going up or as going down. (Incidentally, that's why Escher's drawings are such a major contribution to the psychology of perception.)

With these cultural distinctions in mind, perhaps we have not paid sufficient attention to a type of "denial" which is a reaction or alternative to overemphasis. I believe there is denial not only of reality, but also of overemphasis, and that we ought to take seriously into account the occurrence of denial as a defense mechanism against what is perceived as the lurking danger of overemphasis. Some people prefer to deny death because our life-and-health ob-sessed culture has not taught them how to relate to death but has inflated the latter to unmanageable proportions. Nihilism is fre-quently an insurance policy against disappointments resulting from naive or overidealistic optimisms. Similar observations could be made with regard to certain types of religious faith as well as atheism.

It may also be useful—and this would link up with the distinc-tion I made earlier between *Verleugnung* and *Verneinung*—to re-mind ourselves of the form of denial which is connected with re-nunciation. For example, when giving an account of Buddhism, I would always pair the concept of denial with that of renouncing, because there is an element of learned, culturally acquired denial in Buddhist metaphysics as well as in Buddhist psychology: the concept of *anatta*. This is the doctrine of "non-self," which says that there is no ultimate self or ultimate subject, and that the indi-vidual subject is what we might call an optical illusion; this is really a "denial" of one of our most basic and intimate experiences—that of being a "person." Putting the Buddhist view in different, non-Buddhist terminology, it is as if you were drawing two parallel lines on a blackboard—let us say, a railway track—which for rea-sons of perspective, you would not draw as parallel lines; but the point where these lines meet is *outside* the blackboard—they do not meet in an actual, drawn reality, but only in the beholder's im-agination.

That is exactly what Buddhism thinks about the human sub-ject: it is a construct of illusion. You believe that there is an ulti-mate point, but in reality, of course, there is no blackboard where the lines could meet, and the proof-of-the-pudding is that every subject, especially in the act of introspection, is or becomes an ob-ject. Psychology exists philosophically by virtue of the fact that the human being is its subject and object at the same time. The moment one turns one's own subjectivity into an object of psycho-logical analysis, the question becomes: Who or what is the subject that is contemplating this object? And then, of course, one is auto-matically stuck with an infinite regression because this can go on indefinitely. The further one pushes the analysis, the more the sub-ject in its turn becomes the object, and saying "object" already poses the assumption that behind it there is yet another subject.

There are two ways out: One says that there is some kind of hidden, mysterious, absolute Subject, which may be the soul or that divine spark in man of which some mystics talk and which cannot be grasped. In the terminology of Kant's philosophical psychology it would be called the "transcendental personality." It is "transcendental" because it is not to be physically or empirically grasped, but it must be there as a theoretical construct; otherwise there could be no objects or anything objectifiable as part of your subjectivity. The other adopts the Buddhist solution and denies the existence of a "self": it is an optical illusion. Once the "I" or "self-hood" disappears, there is *nirvana,* for once the illusion of a subject which could have objects disappears, the objects disappear as well.

Here we have a case of denial that denies what others consider to be reality: the reality of self, the ego, the transcendental personality, or the *atman* (which is the Hindu equivalent for the concept of the soul). But this can only be realized by the practical application of a form of denial, which is renunciation. It is not just cognitive denial, but a certain discipline and method that gradually detaches the person from his subjectivity and ego; such denial then becomes renunciation, and ultimately, a new type of reality.

So far I have mentioned denial as defense against overemphasis, and denial as renunciation. There is also denial as a defense mechanism, not against fears in general, but against a very specific type of fear—the fear of disillusionment. Here denial serves as a defense mechanism against false hopes.

Very often people are more afraid of the danger of disillusionment, i.e., of hopes that might prove vain and false, than of actual threats. Hence they take precautionary safeguards against hope. Part of religious—and, I think, psychological—therapy is to point to the realistic character of certain hopes, and to take away the fear of losing hope, by which some people are positively obsessed or paralyzed.

At this point the comparative religionist is tempted to take the bit between his teeth and gallop away, for hope, he may recall, is one of the three major "supernatural" or "theological" virtues of Christianity. According to St. Paul, Faith, Hope and Charity are the characteristic Christian virtues, and in later theology they have been contrasted as "supernatural" religious virtues over and against the so-called four natural "cardinal virtues" which Western ethics inherited from Aristotle. Medieval Christian theology thus knows seven virtues, namely, the four standard "natural" ones plus the three "supernatural" virtues of Faith, Hope and Charity. Here we have a religious tradition which inculcates a certain type of hope, and which even teaches that resistance to or denial of hope is, from the strictly theological point of view, as heretical as the denial of Faith.

It is a historical fact that people have not always "denied" the same things or in the same way. There have been cultures or cultural periods insisting that you have to see "reality" and never forget it. For example, if I were a historian of art, I would be able to tell you in greater detail at what periods it was almost *de rigueur* that on every painting of a table there should be a skull to remind you that there is an end to life: *memento mori*. This became a stylized motif, but it is enough to remind us that the details and modalities of the denial of things to be feared are neither universal nor necessary. One can, in fact, get cultural or individual styles in which the opposite takes place. As Shakespeare said of the madman: "He sees more devils than vast hell can hold," whereas we probably tend to deny devils.

Most of the discussions have been concerned with the mechanisms for the denial of actual or potential anxieties. I tried to draw attention to the phenomenon of the denial of hope and raised the question whether it was, perhaps, also an anxiety phenomenon, i.e., a mechanism against the fear of being disappointed.

Perhaps a word is in order here concerning a distinction that suggests itself in light of a point that came up repeatedly and insistently in discussions of hope. I already mentioned that in the Christian tradition hope is considered a supernatural virtue. I think we may interpret this psychologically to mean that even Christian philosophical and theological thinking is afflicted by the uneasy awareness that there is something problematic about the nature of hope, hovering—as it were—rather uneasily between reality and non-reality. Otherwise there would be no reason at all for not including hope, together with courage, prudence, patience and fortitude, among the other straightforward "natural" virtues. The very fact that this particular classificatory system puts hope in a different category seems to suggest that hope is perceived as somehow problematic, and at any rate different from the ordinary virtues.

I would suggest that, in order to make the difference clearer, we should try to distinguish between hope and optimism. Optimism is usually an attempt to imagine easy ways out, in fact not seeing reality; hope is in a different category altogether. If I were to stick to the medieval Christian definition of hope as a supernatural virtue, then I would probably say that optimism is a natural vice.

Before terminating my reflections, I would like to take up one of the standard anthropological definitions of man as the being that can say "no." In other words, there is a kind of denial (which is perhaps close to the type I discussed earlier under the heading of renunciation), the essence of which is the human capacity to say "no" to selected aspects of reality as part of his "realistic" view of reality. The whole area of ethics, for instance, is based on the perception of realities (e.g., evil) to which one says "no" — although not in the sense of denial by not perceiving them. There are many ways of saying "no." In fact, there is a very wide spectrum of types of denial, and the kind of denial that has been focused on thus far is only a segment of a much larger spectrum. Of course, one of the great problems to which I cannot address myself at present is precisely this subject of the different kinds of "no," and the implications of the difference between *Verneinung* and *Verleugnung*.

This could, perhaps, be linked up with Jung's conception of integrating the Shadow, the latter being exactly that part of the reality of the self which is repressed and denied. To say that the "shadow" should be "affirmed" is ambiguous. But, according to Jung, it has to be seen, accepted and integrated to enable us to say "no" to it and cope with it in the appropriate way.

Let me end by taking one or two very haphazard illustrations from the field of comparative religion, and pointing out different types of hope. There is, for instance, the denial of fatalism. There was a period, around the turn of the era, in the 1st Century B.C. and the 1st Century A.D., when the Mediterranean world was full of ideas about blind necessity, fate, *anangke*, etc., ruling the world. In that situation the belief in the presence and activity of individual gods or a Saviour-God helped people to free themselves from fatalism. The world is not ruled by a blind *fatum*, but there are individual gods with their whims, and you can propitiate them, pray to them, sacrifice to them. This is the stage in the development of classical religion which we could describe as the "denial of fatalism."

On the other hand, there must have been a situation when belief in the inescapable rule of causality and fate (as we find in late antiquity) was a liberating factor. The iron laws of the cosmos were a denial of the unbearable arbitrariness of unpredictable divine beings. The gods were so arbitrary, and their whims so unpredictable, that the result was, culturally, an unbearable pressure; the only way to deny this was the social construction of a reality based on the notion of a blind necessity, a rule, a *fatum,* which plays itself out and to which, as some of the great Greek tragedians put it, "even Zeus himself" was subject.

So, depending on the socio-psychological situation of a culture, what is perceived as oppressive in one particular context can appear as liberating in another. That is why you can in one instance feel impelled to deny one thing and affirm another, and vice versa.

I just said that fatalism might be considered a kind of anxiety release when it functions as a denial of ultimate despair. This denial is, I think, the guiding principle of most "religions of salvation," such as Christianity, Buddhism *(nirvana)*, and Hinduism *(moksha).* Human beings (and societies) can entertain perceptions of reality that lead to ultimate despair, which is something far worse than the idea of death. In fact, some people have sought death as a release. The whole debate about suicide, which began with the ancient Stoics, and went on throughout the Middle Ages and into the modern period is an example of this. For the ancient Stoics suicide was the highest affirmation of man's dignity. In a reality which man cannot deny, but which is no longer compatible with his dignity as a human being, the only dignified way out is suicide. The religious and philosophical debate about suicide as an unforgivable sin, or alternatively as an expression of man's dignity, is connected with this problem. By the way, it is rather interesting to note how a great poet instinctively adjusts to a sense of, and intuitive feeling for, these cultural realities. In Shakespeare's dramas, the action of which takes place in a pagan, non-Christian, classical setting, suicide receives a positive rating; in the plays that take place in a Christian setting, suicide is a far more dubious affair.

I mentioned earlier the notion of hope as a "supernatural" virtue, citing it as evidence of a Christian awareness of the problematic character of this quality. Continuing this line of thought, still in a traditional Christian theological idiom, one might say that the idea of hope, which takes you beyond ultimate despair, and which in fact enables you to deny despair, is precisely the belief in the Resurrection—but a resurrection which, by definition, is conceivable only through and beyond the Cross. There is no room for hope within a Christian framework if you deny the Cross. You can affirm Resurrection only if you have affirmed the Cross. Here the whole problem of denial and hope is expressed in a highly dialectical way. The comparative religionist, analyzing the symbolic "dressing-up" of realities in the various religious traditions, cannot help feeling that they really have something to say. There is, among other things, a belief in the *risk* of the various possibilities. Evidently most religions somehow try, on the popular level, to provide a system of defense mechanism denials. But these very same religions, on other levels, can also insist on certain realities being perceived and on nothing being filtered out. On the contrary, they really fill Hell with more devils than it can hold, precisely as a different kind of feedback loop, namely, to prevent people from denying the dangers—hence, often exaggerating the dangers rather than playing them down. Better to fill Hell with more devils than it can hold than allow someone to say there was no Devil!

Sometimes religions seem to promise easy comfort. Sometimes they demand an excessively sober look. If a classical Hindu text tells you that you may have to reckon with a minimum of ten thousand rebirths in this Vale of Tears, until you can finally exhaust your karma and approach liberation, I'm not sure it is all that comforting an idea.

DISCUSSION

WHICH "REALITY" IS DENIED?

Dr. Spence: If we think of reality as being of many kinds, then it is really hard to talk about denial in the way we have been used to talking about it. Denial in the Freudian sense implies that we see reality as it truly is, whereas the patient does not, and therefore he is denying. Dr. Werblowsky's point, with which I agree, is that many realities mean many views of the world and therefore the term "denial" implies making a value judgment concerning the various views of the world.

Dr. Lazarus: I would like to bring you back to a dilemma that psychology has had for a long time, that expresses this whole question of identifying reality and its role in psychology. Classical perception in psychology has always concentrated on the problem of *veridicality*, that is to say, describing what is real or true in the environment in which we live, and it dealt with "cool," nonemotional aspects of perception. On the other hand, "the new look" in perception focused on *individual differences* and on "hot" *emotional* aspects. A great deal of its attention was directed at how we pro-

223

tect ourselves against threatening aspects of our lives, which is directly related to the issue of denial and defense. The dilemma is that these two ways of asking questions about our relationship to the world have never been resolved. No one has ever integrated the two questions. They are both difficult, and they are both essential parts of the adaptational problem. On the surface they appear to be antithetical; yet they cannot be antithetical because both are part of the process of human adaptation.

Dr. Goldberger: There is an in-between position between "pure perception" and the "new look perception," which is often overlooked. It says that perception may be influenced to some extent by needs, wishes and personality predispositions, but only within certain, rather narrow confines.

Dr. Lazarus: If needs and personal characteristics determine perception only in highly ambiguous situations, ambiguity becomes very important. It is also very frequent, particularly when considering social events. The perceptionists have dealt with physical objects because they are unambiguous, unless presented in suboptimal conditions. *Most of what we deal with in the social context is highly ambiguous, and leaves an enormous latitude for varieties of viewpoints.*

Dr. Werblowsky: This reminds me of an experience I had in a Zen monastery in Japan, where I spent some time as a novice trained in Zen. One day we had to scrub floors particularly hard since the next day was the annual celebration of Buddha's birthday. The great Zen master came along and saw me scrubbing heavily. He looked at me quizzically and said: "Aren't the two of us big idiots? After all, the Buddha is either born inside us every minute or he is never born at all! But nevertheless, you go on scrubbing the floor and decorating the temple." I suddenly felt that here was a man who could take the two horns of a dilemma in one grasp. There was a denial and affirmation of symbolism on different but complementary levels at the same time.

9

ANTICIPATORY STRESS AND DENIAL

SHLOMO BREZNITZ

In contrast to physiological stress, psychological stress never acts purely in the present. The psychological processes relate either to a distressing event in the past, or one anticipated in the future. Issues of psychological coping and adaptation are thus concerned primarily with the notion of *threat*, which deals with the anticipation of future stressors, or the notion of *trauma*, which deals with the recovery phase following past stressors. A full account of a person's psychological reaction to a particular stressor should describe the entire sequence — both the anticipation and the recovery.

There is a growing literature on systematic experimental analysis of reactions of human subjects to anticipatory stress in the laboratory (Lazarus, 1964, 1966; Breznitz, 1967; Niemela, 1969; Elliot, Bankart, and Light, 1970; Epstein and Clarke, 1970; Epstein and Roupenian, 1970; Folkins, 1970; Breznitz, 1971, 1972; Monat,

Thanks are due to the Hadassah Hospital, Jerusalem, and to the Medical School of the Hebrew University for providing the subjects for this research.

Averill, and Lazarus, 1972; Breznitz, 1976; Averill, O'Brien, and DeWitt, 1977). The main focus of this research effort is to investigate the psychological importance of the various parameters of threat. It is of some interest to note that post-stress recovery remains an almost entirely neglected area of study in the laboratory.

When leaving the controlled laboratory situation and venturing to investigate real-life stressors, the emphasis changes dramatically. While there are countless records of reactions to psychic trauma, particularly in the context of the psychodynamic clinical tradition (Horowitz, 1976), research on coping with well-defined external impacts is quite scarce (Baker and Chapman, 1962). Considering its importance, the study of the anticipation of serious real-life dangers has unfortunately received even less systematic attention (Janis, 1958; Mechanic, 1962; Shannon and Isbell, 1963; Fenz, 1964).

The study of denial-like processes and phenomena make the anticipation of meaningful real-life dangers particularly interesting. It is when the signified loss and harm are still only cognitively present, and have not yet materialized, that defenses such as denial may come to play an important role in the coping process. In the recovery phase after the event has already taken place, denial of the facts and some of their obvious implications, while sometimes present, indicates an objectively serious distortion of reality on the border of pathology. During the anticipatory phase, however, it is much easier and common to deny certain painful facets of the impending future.

Stress and Coping under Conditions of "Temporal Certainty"

"Temporal certainty" denotes exact information concerning the time when the anticipated danger will materialize. Situations which have this property provide a particularly good opportunity for studying the evolution of coping strategies in time. The main methodological advantage of employing the temporal certainty paradigm lies in the fact that it allows the researcher to make a relatively "safe" assumption, that *the intensity of the stress grows with the imminence of the danger.* Provided that the first test of a person does not coincide with the initial announcement of the threat (which causes a dramatic elevation in stress), and that the particular danger cannot be sufficiently defused by protective action during its anticipation, a second test, one closer to the critical timing of the danger, will be indicative of higher stress levels. The justification and further elaboration of this important assumption appears elsewhere in this volume (see Chapter 11 by Breznitz). At this point, suffice it to say that if a particular threat produces a fear reaction, for example, the intensity of fear will grow with the imminence of its execution. Temporal certainty is thus operating on the subjective level of the threatened individual, who must have sufficient cues to judge the imminence of the danger.

The above assumption makes it possible to take a closer look at the coping process during the various stages of anticipation. What happens as the danger comes closer and closer? Which defenses will have to go and which will replace them? As the frightening event becomes imminent, is there a way to deny its threatening psychological implications? These are some of the questions the research reported here attempts to explore in the context of meaningful and intense real-life stressors.

THE STRESSORS

Two controlled field experiments were carried out in order to test the generality of the results. One dealt with *anticipation of surgery*, the other with *anticipation of a major oral examination*. While both situations produced stress of high intensity, they varied in many respects. The kind of objective danger involved, the implications to the future, previous experience with similar threats, amount of control over the outcome, ability to utilize the anticipation phase for preparation, and differences between the subject populations are among the most obvious dimensions on which the two field experiments differed.

In both instances, however, subjects had clear information as to exactly when the event would take place. This, in conjunction with essential similarities in experimental design and measures of stress reaction, allowed us to view the two studies *as independent replications of some basic features of anticipatory stress*. Needless to say, any similarities discussed will be of particular conceptual value precisely because of the obvious differences between the two situations. Since the main aim of this research was to explore the central issue of defensive, denial-like behavior during anticipatory stress, the rationale for such simultaneous attack on the problem is clear — we are essentially looking for the context-free and content-free elements of coping which transcend stressors.

Following Janis' now classical study of surgical patients (Janis, 1958), both preoperative and postoperative stressors became quite popular research themes (Andrew, 1970; Johnson, Leventhal, and Dabbs, 1971; Auerbach, 1973; Cohen and Lazarus, 1973; Spielberger, Auerbach, Wadsworth, Dunn, and Taulbee, 1973; Martinez-Urrutia, 1975; Chapman and Cox, 1977). Most of these studies focused on the presumed relationships between preoperative fear and postoperative adjustment. Our focus of interest, however, is tracing the course of the fear reaction during the various stages of the anticipation phase proper.

A similar point can be made concerning the stress of anticipating important examinations (Mechanic, 1962; Morris and Liebert, 1970; Sarason, 1973). In order to ensure that the examination will indeed be a meaningful and intense stressor, third-year medical students awaiting their oral examinations in anatomy were chosen as subjects.[1]

EXPERIMENTAL DESIGN

Since our main interest lay in exploring the changes in coping and defense during the anticipation of the surgery/examination, it followed that subjects must be tested at least twice before the event. A yet better tracking of changes in time would have required at least three or four different tests, but unfortunately technical difficulties related to hospital arrangements made it impossible to conduct more than two tests. The initial design problem was thus the optimal timing of these two tests. The final choice was different for the two stressors.

In the anticipation-of-surgery study, a thorough analysis of the hospital situation indicated that irrespective of the length of time a patient spent in the hospital, the actual scheduling of non-acute surgery took place around noon of the preceding day. It was

[1] The faculty and students of the Medical School of the Hebrew University, Jerusalem, regarded this particular examination as the most frightening experience of the entire medical training. The local folklore richly elaborated the various threats implied by this test.

then that the patients were told that their operation "will definitely take place tomorrow," thus providing the temporal certainty which is a basic feature of our research paradigm. The first test (Test 1) was thus conducted shortly after the above information was given to the patient, i.e., during early afternoon on the day before the operation.

In order to maximize the impact of imminent danger, the second test (Test 2) was given about fifteen minutes prior to the subject being taken to the operating hall, or, whenever applicable, about fifteen minutes before receiving premedication. While in the second case the operation itself was still one hour away, the relevant psychological processes were assumed to be affected by the premedication, and any later testing would have been misleading.

In the anticipation-of-examination study, considerations of maximizing the students' cooperation made it imperative that if the second test (Test 2) was to be given about fifteen minutes before the scheduled exam, Test 1 should be given at least a few days before. Consequently, it was given between three to five days prior to the examination, when the students were still willing to spend the time on something other than studying. It was during Test 1 that the cooperation for the crucial last-moment Test 2 was secured.

DEPENDENT VARIABLES

Any probe attempting to reveal the ongoing cognitive processes during anticipatory stress interferes with these very processes. Not unlike Heisenberg's principle of indeterminacy, cognitive functioning in order to be observed must be elicited by some indirect probes which change it. This is particularly relevant in the case of denial and other kinds of psychological defenses, since the probe can well have a cue function, and thus actually instigate the defensive process.

There is, of course, no simple solution to this problem, but it emphasizes the need for a multilevel approach. The unveiling of some of the defensive processes occurring during anticipation of a stressful event must be attempted by different probes simultaneously. Some processes are fully conscious, and the surgical patient or the medical student while in control of the verbal channel may decide whether to communicate them to the researcher. At the same time, other processes can be effectively approached only by the indirect methods of projective and semi-projective techniques.

This research utilized two different methods:

(a) *Direct questions* on a variety of aspects related to the surgery or examination (e.g., Are you afraid of the surgery/exam? What specifically scares you? Do you want to learn more about your surgery? Do you prefer total/local anesthesia? What grade do you expect to get in the exam? Do you need a lot of luck to succeed? Do you try not to think about it? How long is it since you learned about the surgery? How long is it since you decided to take the exam now? etc.).

(b) *A specially devised word association test (WAT)* to study the "deeper" aspects of the underlying cognitive mechanisms. As in Epstein (1962) and Epstein and Fenz (1962), the additional advantage of the WAT consisted of sampling stimuli with varying degrees of relevance to the particular area of stress. Thus, some stimulus words were "neutral" while others were "relevant" to the threat. Out of all initial possible words, only those for which five judges independently agreed to their relevance were accepted into the final list. The two lists of stimulus words appear in Table 1.

The WAT was given orally and the reaction times were measured.

SUBJECTS AND CONTROLS

In the anticipation-of-surgery study, the sample was deliberately a highly heterogeneous one. The first 70 surgical patients who could be tested served as the experimental group. The following reasons led to exclusion of subjects:

(a) Patients who for some medical reason could not fully cooperate were not tested. Among them were patients who were in great pain, patients who were heavily drugged, and patients who were attached to some medical instrument that hampered their freedom of speech or movement.

(b) Patients who were too young to understand the various testing procedures were excluded.

(c) Patients whose knowledge of the language (Hebrew) was insufficient for the various verbal tasks were excluded.

(d) Patients who were hospitalized in a critical condition or with an acute problem were excluded because they did not antici-

TABLE 1
STIMULUS WORDS FOR WAT (TRANSLATED FROM HEBREW)

Anticipation of Surgery
picture, prescriptions, fate, chair, surgery, nurse, act, fear, anticipation of surgery, flower, crime, pain, dream, health, punishment,
tree, knife, gaiety, bed, darkness, conscience, anesthesia, apprehensions, loneliness, soon.

Anticipation of Examination
picture, success, fear of failure, wrong, excuse, justice, least of all,
sorry, let it be, to copy, waste of time, lamp, fear of the exam, luck,
excitement, grade, crime, fed up, tree, what will they say about me,
disappointment, to postpone, flower, let it be over, punishment,
conscience, music, they are still waiting for the answer, will fail me,
indifference.

pate the need for surgery before hospitalization.

(e) Finally, any patient whom the physicians or the nurses in
the surgical ward advised to be left alone was excluded as well.

Consequently, our sample does not represent the entire population of surgical patients. Medical diagnosis and type of surgery
did not, however, constitute a selection factor. Major and minor
surgery, as well as total and local anesthesia, were all represented.
This is in sharp contrast with those studies attempting to investigate postoperation adjustment, which must control for diagnosis,
prognosis, and type of surgery. No such need is implied, however,
if the defensive processes during the preoperative stage are the focus of the research.

All subjects were tested twice and served as their own controls. It is difficult to conceive of any control group that can meaningfully respond to direct questions concerning impending surgery.
The answers of nonsurgical subjects would be totally irrelevant
and misleading. Thus, only the WAT could be meaningfully administered to control subjects, and consequently, 70 healthy individuals comparable to the experimental group in age, sex, and education, were tested twice with the WAT. The inter-test interval was
also equated to that of the experimental group.

In the anticipation-of-examination study, the sample was
highly homogeneous. All the third-year medical students who registered to take the oral in anatomy in that particular term partici-

pated in the research. Thirty-six of them were randomly chosen to participate in the experimental group, and they were tested twice. The remaining 18 students were tested only on Test 2, i.e., just prior to entering the examination room. They were labeled as Control (a) and enabled us to explore the impact of Test 1 on Test 2.

A second control group, Control (b), consisted of 23 third-year students (not from the medical school), who during the period of study did not anticipate any major examinations. They were tested twice, with the inter-test interval equated to that of the experimental group.

The pulse rate of subjects in the experimental group was counted manually at the wrist for one minute at the beginning and end of each word association test.

RESULTS

CATEGORIZATION OF WAT RESPONSES

Since analysis of denial-like responses cannot rest entirely on answers to the direct questions, our first task is some meaningful categorization of the WAT responses. The emphasis on coping and defense determined to a large extent the content of the various categories, and they all attempt to describe the way the individual deals with the threatening situation.

The dimension of relevance built into the stimulus list provides the opportunity to test the person's reaction in various contexts. The distribution of certain appropriate responses is to a great extent influenced by the particular stimulus word, both in terms of its content and grammatical features (Cramer, 1968).

At the onset of the categorization process, there was a list of possible categories. In order not to force our preconception upon the data, the final list could be determined only after working with the actual data. To ensure maximal reliability, a system of precedents was used. Three clinicians independently judged each stimulus-response combination. Following the analysis of a particular subject, they compared notes and argued about any differences of opinion. If unable to agree, they took a vote which was then put down in the "Book of Laws," together with the specific example and the rationale for their decision. The "Book of Laws" was binding, and any new stimulus-response combination was first checked against already available precedents. If an exact precedent was found, it was blindly followed. In this way perfect inter-judge reliability could be obtained.

The categories are not mutually exclusive because some are semantic and others formal. The same categories were found appropriate, however, in both field experiments despite the different nature of the threats. The specific stimulus-response combinations as well as the examples in the "Book of Laws," of course, differ. Table 2 presents the main categories used in both studies.

Table 2 indicates that an affinity exists between the response categories and the psychoanalytic formulations of intrapsychic defense mechanisms. While the usage of such an approach to external stressors has always been quite popular (Grinker and Spiegel, 1945; Cohen, 1953; Janis, 1958), it should not be interpreted in our case as necessarily reflecting a theoretical position. At the same time, however, a serious external threat cannot ever be seen as unrelated to some intrapsychic anxieties which it typically evokes. This has been convincingly described by Janis (1958) in the first half of his book on presurgical stress, dealing with an in-depth analysis of a single subject. A similar point was made by Mechanic (1962) in relation to anticipation of important examinations. "Thus, the examinations represent not only an academic challenge but also a challenge to self-esteem, to the role as husband and father, and to the future role as a professional" (p. 25). "Furthermore, there are no pure fears inasmuch as all external dangers also have symbolic significance" (pp. 65–66).

Therefore, it is not surprising that the data meaningfully lend themselves to a taxonomy which is reminiscent of the psychoanalytic defenses of the ego against anxiety. The subjects in both of our studies undoubtedly experienced a mixture of fear and anxiety at the same time.

Not all of the responses were categorized; some did not fit any existing category, nor any possible new one. Such responses (about 30% of total responses) were not indicative in any sense of the way a person reacts to the threat. Most of such responses were simply statements of fact.

OPERATIONAL DEFINITIONS OF "DENIAL"

Using a narrow definition, "denial" can be operationalized on three different levels:

TABLE 2
CATEGORIZATION OF RESPONSES TO THE WAT

Code	Description	Illustration	
		Stimulus	Response
A	*Apprehension,* anxiety, fear, concern with implications of the threat.	success excitement apprehensions fear	failure from the exam surgery my own, of suffering
Ag	*Aggression*	let it be will fail me tree	that you die satan (name of the professor) to hang
Bl	*Blocking,* lack of response for at least 15 seconds, or if subject claims that: "Nothing comes to mind."		
C	*Compartmentalization,* avoiding the frightening context of surgery/exam, relevant to stimulus but not to its context.	failure knife excitement	in sports, business bread girls, happiness
D	*Dissociation.* No obvious relevance to the stimulus.	surgery apprehensions sorry justice	flower pillow pickled cucumber imagery
Den	*Denial* of fear	fear of future will fail me fear apprehensions	never, none no, not afraid, nothing none none, nonexistent
P	*Projection*	least of all fear of failure fear	him (name of peer) yourself he is scared his problem (name)
In	*Intellectualization*	fear of exam crime tree conscience	a chapter in Freud's book and punishment of knowledge censor, superego

TABLE 2—*Continued*

Code	Description	Stimulus	Response
		Illustration	
R	*Reversal* of the stimulus, antonym	success wrong loneliness darkness	failure right society light
Ra	*Rationalization*	fear of exam will fail me surgery anesthesia	helps to study the weather, bad luck scratch just sleep
Sy	*Synonym*	picture indifference fate apprehensions	printing, photo apathy luck worries
X	*Explanation* of the stimulus	crime pain wrong indifference	immoral behavior physical suffering mistake not caring
E	*Echo.* The stimulus or part of it is returned as a response.	fear of failure grade fear soon	failure grade fear soon
St	*Stereotypy.* Perseveration, the same response to at least 4 different stimuli.	picture success fear luck	big big big big
W	*Wishful thinking*	success grade surgery dream	great excellent, A will succeed pleasant
Z	*Avoidance* of the threat, by resorting to common neutral utterances. Usually a phrase containing more than a single word.	justice waste of time loneliness punishment	should exist waste of money sometimes good, sometimes bad if deserved

(a) Assuming that on Test 2 all subjects are highly stressed, responses "denying" the intensity of fear reaction to the imminent stressor indicate denial.

(b) Assuming that WAT responses are to a great extent "unconsciously" determined and the subjects cannot control them, the category of "denial" indicates denial.

(c) Assuming that WAT responses are under less cognitive control than those to the direct questions, if a subject claims on the latter that he is unafraid and yet his WAT indicates fear, this would imply denial.

As our analysis unfolds we shall resort to a broader definition of denial and denial-like responses.

PREVALENCE OF "DENIAL"

Considering the kinds of stressors used in this study, there was little doubt that the fear reaction to them would be intense, particularly on Test 2, when the threatening event was imminent. At the same time, the fact that in the anticipation-of-examination study we could take the pulse rate of subjects, allows us to check this assumption against the psychophysiological index of heart rate. The results show that the mean heart rates on Test 1 before and after the WAT were 85.1 and 83.0, respectively. On Test 2, however, the means were 108.6 and 104.4, indicating high arousal. (The differences between the tests both before and after the WAT, were found to be significant at the $p > .001$ level.)

The assumption that on Test 2 subjects were highly stressed thus appears to be a plausible one. And yet, 20 out of 36 subjects responded to the direct questions concerning their fear by claiming either "low fear" or "no fear." Such responses can be viewed as denial using our first operational definition.

The category of "denial" on the WAT was given by 26 subjects in the anticipation-of-examination study on Test 1, and by 30 out of 36 subjects on Test 2. In the anticipation-of-surgery study, out of 70 subjects, "denial" was used by 28 on Test 1 and 37 on Test 2. Thus, according to our second operational definition, some degree of denial was found in many of our subjects.

All but one subject in the anticipation-of-examination study gave fear responses on the WAT, even those who denied fear on the direct questions. Very much the same pattern was found in the anticipation-of-surgery study, indicating that by the third criterion denial was once more found to be a highly frequent response.

The above three kinds of denial do not necessarily reflect the same underlying psychological process, and indeed, there are additional possible ways to measure this complex defensive process.

Our main research interest was not to just demonstrate denial, but rather to study the changes in coping and defense during the anticipation period proper. Thus, the main source of information lies in whatever systematic changes took place on the WAT between Test 1 and Test 2. It is precisely this issue that we now proceed to investigate.

RESPONSE REPRODUCTION

The subjects in this study were not specifically requested to reproduce on Test 2 the responses they gave on Test 1. Therefore, reproduction failure does not necessarily indicate emotional problems, particularly in view of the significant test-retest interval (Rapaport, Gill, and Schafer, 1968).

Broen and Storms (1961, 1966) view anxiety and arousal as responsible for reproduction failure under stress. According to their analysis, anxiety, following the Hullian model, multiplies the habit strength of the various responses. Postulating a reaction potential ceiling effect, additional anxiety beyond a certain level will lead to temporary breakdown of the differences between various response tendencies, thus causing reproduction failure. Consequently, they would predict a main effect of reproduction failure in the experimental groups compared to the controls.

We submit that successful reproduction actually indicates stability of the hierarchy of responses to a particular stimulus (Breznitz, 1968). *Cognitive preoccupation with thoughts in a certain area should lead to changes in one's hierarchy of responses in that area, and consequently to reproduction failure.* In other context areas with which they are not thus preoccupied, subjects should demonstrate greater stability of responses. We can safely assume that *subjects in the anticipation-of-examination study spend more time between Test 1 and Test 2 thinking about the impending examination than about some of the neutral nonrelevant topics.* By the same token, subjects in anticipation of surgery are assumed to be more cognitively preoccupied with thoughts concerning their operation than with less relevant themes.

The above analysis leads to the prediction that *responses to "relevant" stimuli will change more between the two tests. In other words, changes in the WAT may serve as a measure of cognitive preoccupation.*

Table 3 presents the data on reproduction.

TABLE 3
RESPONSE REPRODUCTION ACCORDING TO STIMULUS RELEVANCE

	Anticipation of Surgery (N = 70)		Anticipation of Examination (N = 36)	
	Experimental	Control	Experimental	Control
All stimuli	28.7%	57.3%	36.1%	64.0%
5 most neutral stimuli	39.0%	49.0%	54.1%	65.3%
5 most relevant stimuli	18.6%	62.3%	27.3%	70.6%
Stimuli with greatest difference in reproduction	apprehension, anticipation of surgery, soon		fear of failure, excitement, grade, disappointment	
Stimuli with smallest difference in reproduction	act, fate, chair, flower, tree		picture, lamp, tree, flower	

Table 3 indicates that there is indeed a small general effect of reproduction failure in the experimental groups, but most of the change takes place in the responses to relevant stimuli. Thus, while there is in principle no contradiction between the reaction potential ceiling effect hypothesis and our cognitive preoccupation hypothesis, the latter appears to better account for the results. This is probably particularly true in stresses with temporal certainty. As the person comes closer to confrontation with the danger, he tends to spend more time thinking about what lies ahead. These thoughts about the relevant content area interfere with previous thoughts, and, in fact, change the response hierarchies to the relevant stimuli. It is a case of *self-produced interference via cognitive preoccupation.*

This phenomenon illustrates the limits to successful denial. A threatened individual may prefer *not to think* about the impending danger, but as the critical time approaches his ability to actually distract his mind is gradually weakened. This "process of involvement" is not just a function of the proximity of the danger, but also reflects its total duration.

CHANGES IN MODES OF REACTING TO ANTICIPATORY STRESS

The categorization of WAT responses makes it possible to analyze the cognitive changes that take place between Test 1 and

Test 2. Table 4 presents the percentage of occurrence of each response category based on the total number of responses, i.e., subjects × responses in each study.

Even a superficial glance at Table 4 clearly indicates that the number of categories used in this study is far too large. It seems that only a few of the categories receive a significant number of responses, whereas many others are very rarely used. Thus, it appears that the following categories can be discarded without much loss in terms of our data: aggression (Ag), projection (P), and rationalization (Ra). (They received less than one percent of responses on each test.)

On the other hand, the following categories seem to be particularly important: apprehension and anxiety (A), denial (Den), reversals or antonyms (R), stereotypic responses or perseveration (St), and wishful thinking (W).

Before trying to analyze the results in greater detail, a few additional comparisons have to be made first. Thus, the question has to be posed: To what extent is there an influence of the first test on the second test? As was already stated in the design section of this study, in the case of anticipation of examinations, there was a special control group specifically designed to answer this problem. In this group subjects were used who received only the second test, prior to their entering the examination hall. Table 5 presents the second test results of these subjects compared with experimental subjects who received both tests.

Table 5 clearly indicates that there is no effect of the first test on the second test. This is probably at least partially due to the limited amount of control that our subjects have over their own responses to the word association test. This finding allows us to examine the results of the two tests with confidence that they are *not* due to test-retest effects, and are due, rather, to the fact that the danger is coming closer.

Before looking at these changes, the status of the frequencies themselves would be better understood if compared with those of the appropriate control groups. Table 6 presents the percentages of responses to the main categories in the control groups for both studies.

Comparison of the frequencies of the various response categories of Table 6 with those of Table 4 shows that, with the single

TABLE 4
PERCENTAGES OF RESPONSE CATEGORIES BY TESTS AND BY STUDIES

Category	Anticipation of Surgery		Anticipation of Examination	
	Test 1	Test 2	Test 1	Test 2
A	12.6	10.8	17.3	18.4
Ag	0.2	—	0.9	0.4
Bl	2.9	1.6	2.7	1.2
C	10.4	7.0	5.5	2.4
D	0.9	1.7	1.5	0.1
Den	4.0	7.2	5.8	8.3
P	0.4	0.2	0.6	0.5
In	1.6	0.7	2.0	1.1
R	3.6	3.4	8.1	6.8
Ra	0.2	—	0.9	0.9
Sy	5.6	4.6	3.6	1.7
X	1.8	1.8	0.3	0.5
E	1.4	0.4	1.0	0.8
St	4.2	9.1	6.0	11.2
W	18.4	18.9	20.5	17.6
Z	5.6	3.9	3.6	2.4
Uncategorized	26.2	28.7	19.7	25.7
Total	100.0	100.0	100.0	100.0

TABLE 5
THE EFFECT OF TEST 1 ON TEST 2

Category	% in Experimental Group (Test 2 following Test 1)	% in Control Group (Test 2 only)
A	18.4	16.8
Den	8.3	8.6
R	6.8	7.0
St	11.2	12.3
W	17.6	16.4

TABLE 6
PERCENTAGE OF MAIN RESPONSE CATEGORIES IN CONTROL GROUPS

Category	Anticipation of Surgery		Anticipation of Examination	
	Test 1	Test 2	Test 1	Test 2
A	11.9	13.3	10.7	9.0
Den	0.8	0.9	2.6	3.4
R	3.9	3.7	7.1	6.9
W	3.2	3.6	12.4	11.1
St	1.4	3.9	3.4	2.7

exception of the category of reversal, the frequency of the main categories is higher in the experimental groups than in the control groups. The results are significant in both studies for denial, wishful thinking, and stereotypy, and for apprehension in the anticipation-of-examination study only. It should be recalled at this point that the latter category actually indicates the absence of defense. It will be discussed at some length later in this chapter.

At this point we are ready to look more closely at Table 4 to see which of the categories show distinct changes between Test 1 and Test 2. The frequency of the following responses decreased between the two tests: aggression, blocking, compartmentalization, projection, intellectualization, and category Z, namely, general statements or phrases. These changes generally occurred in both studies reported here. This is of particular interest due to the marked difference in time periods between the two—in the anticipation-of-surgery study, the test-retest interval was less than 24 hours; in the anticipation of exams, a few days.

Two categories noticeably increased over time in both studies (and not in the control groups): denial and stereotypic perseveration.

Categories A (lack of defense), R (reversal), and W (wishful thinking) were among the most stable in the entire list. This may be indicative of certain psychological advantages in the usage of these categories.

THE TAXONOMIC VALUE OF THE CATEGORIES

In order to ascertain the taxonomic value of the categories, rank-order correlations of the category frequencies in both studies were computed. For Test 1, Rho = .66, and for Test 2, Rho = .88.

This suggests that the categories indeed had a taxonomic value which transcended the specific context of each study.

There is another way to test this, namely, by utilizing evidence related to reaction times. (The mean reaction time for each response category was computed for all groups.) If the response categories indicate distinct kinds of information-processing, this should have some implications for reaction time, i.e., reaction times should be different for different categories. Whereas this can in principle be computed by looking at the test-retest reliability of reaction times within each study, even if found, such reliability might be explained away in terms of response reproduction. After all, the same category, if used twice, might actually indicate exactly the same response. How much more convincing if it could be shown that the response categories reliably showed differential reaction times between different studies.

The rank-order correlation between the mean reaction times of all response categories was computed for both tests. Whereas for Test 1 the rank-order correlation is minimal, namely, Rho = .14, the situation changed entirely in Test 2. Here *the correlation between the reaction times of the categories in the two different studies is Rho = .86 (p > .01)*. This finding dramatically supports the status of the response categories used in these studies.

Furthermore, in terms of the information-processing analysis of the various coping mechanisms used by our subjects, it seems that different coping strategies require different processing times.

Computing the rank-order correlation between the experimental and control groups in the anticipation-of-exam study, the correlation was Rho = .11 for Test 1 and Rho = .09 for Test 2. Thus, the categories require reliably different times only when there an actual threat is imminent. Phrased differently, *these response categories probably have an entirely different meaning in the control group and in the experimental groups.* The fact that the same responses are categorized in exactly the same way does not imply that their psychological status is the same.

The fact that the correlation between the two experimental groups for Test 1 is a small one has a clear explanation. After all, the two studies differ in terms of the imminence of danger during the first test. On the second test, however, the subjects in both studies are only a few minutes removed from the materialization of the danger. In this sense, therefore, they are more comparable on the second test than on the first.

In view of the fact that the different response categories do indeed seem to imply that differential processing time is required, it might be of some interest to look at the times themselves. Table 7 presents the mean response times for the main categories.

Since the data on which this table is based relate to responses and not necessarily to different individuals, no statistical tests were computed. At the same time, however, Table 7 indicates some interesting patterns. Thus, responses which are stereotypic or reversals seem to be quickest of all, followed by denial, then apprehensions and wishful thinking, and finally compartmentalization, which seemed to take a particularly long time. It might be postulated that the easier a particular response is, the less time it takes. This does not mean that the response is necessarily a more appropriate one, but that there is perhaps a smaller amount of conflict involved.

Therefore it makes sense that responses of perseveration are very short indeed, since they imply that a person is actually not paying much attention to the stimulus itself, responding with a ready-made answer. Reversals or antonyms are also very efficient in the sense that they are paradigmatic responses which do not directly deal with the content of the stimulus. The fact that denial takes less time than lack of defense is also of some interest in view of the fact that it presumably serves a hedonistic principle of some sort. The relatively longer durations of responses belonging to the categories of wishful thinking, and particularly compartmentalization, seem to indicate that these modes of coping become relatively inefficient, particularly on the second test, when the danger is imminent. Needless to say, these results open fascinating possibilities for a more sophisticated analysis of coping. However, much additional research must be conducted before such refined interpretations can be made.

STAGES IN COPING WITH ANTICIPATORY STRESS

The particular within-subject design employed in this study allows us to go beyond the simple counting of response categories on both tests. More specifically, we can try to analyze the history of each response in terms of its source, or alternatively, the prog-

TABLE 7
MEAN REACTION TIMES ACCORDING TO CATEGORIES (TEST 2)

Category	Mean RT (in seconds)	
	Surgery	Examination
A	3.46	2.08
C	3.54	3.09
Den	2.98	1.67
R	2.45	1.47
St	2.19	1.57
W	3.05	2.89

nosis of each response in terms of its target. Any attempt to look for directionality in the evolution of the cognitive patterns of coping must necessarily look for asymmetric relations between categories. More specifically, only if we discover that certain response categories typically change into other specific categories will we be able to postulate a certain pattern of coping over time.

An example may illustrate this argument. Consider the case of two response categories, let us say A and C, which change one into another in addition to other responses. Let us also assume that the chances of category A on the first test turning into category C on the second test are not drastically different from a change in the opposite direction. In such a case, it would be impossible to postulate whether category A is more advanced in terms of coping than category C, or vice versa. However, if we discover a totally asymmetrical relationship, namely, that whereas there are many changes from C to A, A does not change to C, this may indicate that A on some dimension follows C. With growing proximity of the threat, A in our example can be viewed as more fitting than C, or alternatively, a more advanced stage in the process. It follows, therefore, that the key to our thesis lies in looking at asymmetric relations.

In order to facilitate such an analysis it was necessary to further reduce the number of categories used. Thus, it was thought worthwhile to define a broader category which would be called "avoidance," which combines the following previous categories: blocking (Bl), compartmentalization (C), projection (P), intellectualization (In), rationalization (Ra), and general phrases and statements (Z). The single avoidance category indicated attempts by the person to avoid the threatening information or its implications by refraining from responding (blocking), by trying to see the stimulus out of the context of the threat (compartmentalization), or resorting to a variety of other cognitive tricks and devices to defuse the threatening nature of the stimulus. On the basis of Table 4 and the subsequent analysis of our data, it was thought worthwhile to test for asymmetric relationships between this new category of avoidance and the remaining categories, particularly the most frequent ones.

All the evidence so far indicates that in spite of the important differences between the studies, the response categories used seem to apply adequately to both. It is, therefore, possible to look at the changes between Test 1 and Test 2 in data combined from both studies. This was thought particularly useful in view of the larger number of responses that could be utilized this way. Table 8 presents the combined data for all the major categories used. It also deliberately includes the category of "uncategorized" in order to test its diagnosticity.

Table 8 indicates that although most of the responses tend to remain within the same category on both tests, there are sufficient changes to be able to test the asymmetric relations described above. Avoidance responses on the first test tended to change more often to other categories than vice versa. More specifically, the chances of transition from avoidance to wishful thinking or denial are much higher than from wishful thinking or denial to avoidance.

Asymmetric relations can also clearly be seen in relationship to perseveration. This particular response category either remains stable on both tests, or receives input from other categories. Following the logic described above, we would thus argue that perseverations indicate a more advanced stage in the process of reacting to imminent threat.

Rather than trying to explicate all the intricacies of Table 8, it is possible to extract from it a preliminary model which describes the postulated sequence of steps involved during the entire process of anticipation as discussed in these studies. A word of caution is now proper: It should be stated that even though we are using process methodology and each subject is studied more than once, *the number of discrete stages that can be discovered by this method cannot be greater than the number of discrete tests used.* Thus, since we have tested our subjects in both of the studies only twice,

TABLE 8
RESPONSE CHANGES FROM TEST 1 TO TEST 2

Test 1 \ Test 2	Avoid	W	A	Den	St	Uncategorized	Total
Avoid	160	28	38	17	10	182	435
W	13	201	23	7	13	99	356
A	11	29	176	29	16	67	328
Den	3	6	13	61	3	25	111
St	3	2	2	2	55	99	163
Uncategorized	47	45	29	11	102		
Total	237	311	281	127	199		

any attempt to postulate a sequence of steps which consists of more than two such steps is clearly highly speculative. While the asymmetric relationships do indicate a certain amount of directionality, there is not a single subject who was followed through the various stages postulated. Moreover, different sections of the model are based on data from different subjects and from different stimuli. The present model, which appears in Figure 1, must therefore be viewed with extreme caution and at best poses some of the questions which need to be elucidated by further investigation.

Our initial assumption is that there are two kinds of responses belonging to category A. On the one hand, there are responses which indicate that a particular individual did not yet resort to defensive mechanisms in dealing with the threatening information. Such responses are indicated by the label "anxiety 1." Anxiety 1, then, is the beginning of the entire defensive process. Anxiety 2, on the other hand, indicates that the person is no longer able to sustain a defensive construct in the face of imminent danger. On the face of it, both look the same, and a superficial analysis will clearly pool them together. The sequential analysis makes it possible, however, to look at the history of a response as well as its future. It is on the basis of such an analysis that we suggest that there must be two distinct kinds of anxiety, which from the point of view of the person involved are totally different. In the case of anxiety 1, everything is still possible, and a person may engage in a variety of defensive behaviors, all of which may alleviate the anxiety. In the case of anxiety 2, however, it is almost too late, since the person already tried the various defensive devices and found them lacking.

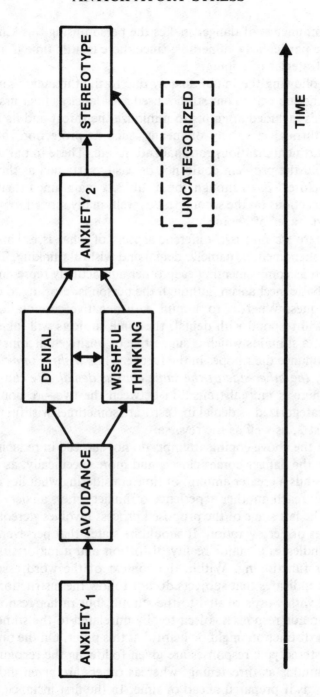

FIGURE 1
Reactions to Anticipatory Stress (the Process of Involvement)

The imminence of danger makes the person using this kind of response particularly vulnerable since there is little time to resort to new strategies of coping.

Following the initial anxiety due to the threatening information, the subjects in our studies used avoidance as their first strategy. This included attempts to minimize the threat and its implications through a variety of means, such as projection, blocking, compartmentalization, rationalization, etc. These initial attempts to avoid the problem could not be easily sustained as the danger came closer. Even though some subjects maintained their avoidance reactions on the second test as well, many moved to more advanced stages of coping.

Here we find two different aspects of what is essentially the same phenomenon, namely, denial and wishful thinking. They can be seen as complementing each other and actually representing the same basic mechanism, although the person is resorting to different techniques. Whereas to stimuli with negative connotations subjects will respond with denial, the same subjects will take advantage of a stimulus which is suggestive of positive outcomes to further enhance their hopes in the future. Thus *wishful thinking is, in a way, the other side of the same coin as denial.* We can also see that there is mutual transition between the two — responses that were categorized as denial in Test 1 are sometimes wishful thinking on Test 2, as well as the reverse.

If the above coping attempts do not succeed in reducing anxiety, as the danger comes closer, and more specifically, as the person spends a greater amount of time considering what lies in store, he may reach another experience of anxiety, i.e., anxiety 2.

The last stage of the proposed process involves stereotypic responses of perseveration. It should be stated that perseveration as such indicates a major reality distortion and a major shift from proper functioning. Within the context of the word association test, it indicates that subjects do not follow the instructions to respond with words related to the stimuli, but rather respond with ready-made responses, often totally unrelated to the stimuli.

A distinction might be helpful at this point. On the one hand, some stereotypic responses are given following the recognition of the stimulus as threatening, whereas others are given indiscriminately, as if prepared ahead of time. In the first instance, we can talk of filtering of the threatening information and attempts to block it at some level of the process. In the second case, there need not be any registration of the information at all, since the response is pre-planned and unrelated to the stimulus. The present model postulates that the first kind of stereotypy (in which there is still a certain amount of information-processing) is a direct continuation of the process as it was described so far. Experiencing anxiety 2, subjects defend against the threatening information by shifting at the last moment to perseveration. When this tendency is generalized to stimuli which are not threatening and not associated with anxiety in the past, it indicates that we are dealing with a second kind of stereotypy, namely, *intentional stereotypy*. As the model indicates, even responses which were uncategorized in the past and not associated with any of the response categories may change to stereotypic perseverations when the danger comes very close.

As was already indicated, there is no claim that any subject has to pass through all of these stages. The only claim is that these stages are indeed sequential in the sense that the movement is over time, whether suddenly or gradually. The data of these studies also indicate that there is very little movement backwards. A much more sophisticated process methodology would be needed in order to verify the actual transition of any particular subject through the various steps proposed here.

As the anticipated danger comes closer, it gradually starts to monopolize all attention. Whether it is anticipation of surgery or exams, or any other important experience, cues which signal the imminence of the danger lead to growing cognitive preoccupation with its nature. How will it be? Will I be able to bear myself properly? Is there anything I can do about it? (This increasing cognitive preoccupation with a particular problem was mentioned in an earlier section when discussing reproduction of responses to the WAT. Subjects have difficulty in reproducing their responses to relevant stimuli, probably due to the fact that they have been thinking about this particular content area quite often between the two tests.)

It is our view that it is this increasing cognitive preoccupation which leads a person through the various stages of coping represented in the model appearing in Figure 1. The more a person becomes involved with the impending danger, the greater the chances that he will find any self-produced reassurances unsatisfactory, and will have to sooner or later move to other kinds of defense.

The fact that a significant number of subjects showed stereo-typic responses deserves particular mention in this context. After all, as Rapaport, Gill, and Schafer (1968) and others have often claimed, perseverations on the WAT are indicative of schizo-phrenic patients. That normal people under the extreme stress of imminent surgery or important examination also exhibit perservera-tion suggests how far the coping process may have progressed.

There are two ways to consider these data: on the one hand, it can be claimed that it is the *proximity* of the danger that serves as the trigger for these symptomatic responses. In his book on stu-dents under stress, Mechanic (1962) describes the dramatic changes which took place as the examination came closer: "The weekend prior to examinations, severe psychosomatic symptoms seemed to appear. A few students actually became sick, probably attributa-ble in part to the increased vulnerability resulting from the physical and mental exhaustion that had accompanied study and from keeping late hours. Many students reported having stomach aches, anxiety attacks, increased problems with asthma, and some rashes and allergies. Appetite and eating patterns also seemed affected, and a number of students reported difficulty in sleeping. On the morning of the examinations most students reported stomach pains; a number reported diarrhea; and a few reported that they had been unable to hold their breakfast. As one student said: 'I was real scared. I never was so scared in my whole life' " (p. 162).

This list of all the classical symptoms of intense stress sup-ports the notion that proximity of the impact exerts tremendous influence over the students involved. Needless to say, anticipation of surgery leads essentially to the same apprehensions.

There is, however, yet another way to view this process. In-stead of concentrating on the proximity of the danger, it might be worthwhile to look at the *total duration of anticipation*. There are some studies which support the notion that duration of anticipa-tion of a threatening event indeed increases the total amount of difficulties experienced (Breznitz, 1967, 1968; Nomikos, Opton, Averill, and Lazarus, 1968; Mansueto and Desiderato, 1971; Brez-nitz, 1971). This notion of "incubation of threat" is clearly in line with the general position stated by Selye (1956) concerning the var-ious stages of the general adaptation syndrome. Selye is quite explicit about the fact that duration of impact is among the most important factors leading to eventual exhaustion of adaptation resources.

We claim that psychological exhaustion may set in if a person is preoccupied with a particular important threat for long periods of time. As Mechanic (1962) pointed out: "For those who had started studying intensively at an early date, exhaustion crept in and they lost their desire and motivation to study" (p. 142). A brief glance at Figure 1 indicates that we postulate that time accounts for the transitions from left to right; namely, from initial attempts at coping to more advanced and extreme attempts. Anxiety 2 and stereotypy can clearly be seen as symptoms of "psychological exhaustion."

In order to submit this notion to empirical test, the correlation between duration of anticipation and stereotypic responses was computed in both studies. It was found that in the anticipation-of-surgery study, the correlation between the amount of time the patients knew that they would have to have an operation and the frequency of stereotypic responses was $r = 0.56$ $(p < .01)$, and in the anticipation-of-examination study $r = 0.41$ $(p < .05)$. These results clearly support the notion that it is not only the proximity of the danger as such, but rather the amount of time spent living with that danger that accounts for the advanced stages of the process.

Psychological exhaustion comes about through what we label *"the process of involvement."* By getting more and more involved in the threat to the exclusion of other content areas, people waste their reassurances and their psychological resources. If this process is allowed to go on for a long period of time, exhaustion may set in.

FACETS OF DENIAL

Even when using the narrow definition of denial, this category is not without its interest. A few of the potentially important findings are as follows:

1. In the anticipation-of-surgery study it was found that frequency of denial on the first test correlated significantly with amount of time the patient had known about his or her surgery. This is of particular interest in view of the above analysis concerning the influence of duration of anticipation on the process of involvement.

2. In the same study, denial on the first test correlated significantly with the tendency of patients to answer in the negative the direct question concerning their fear. This finding illustrates some of the pitfalls of research which does not utilize a multilevel methodology. Thus, for instance, using only direct questions in attempts to reach conclusions about the amount of apprehension of the subjects may be quite misleading. Among those who claim that they are unafraid of impending surgery are surely at least some who are so advanced in their anxiety and fear that they resort to this rather primitive defense of denial. Unless one uses a multilevel methodology or a process methodology which allows studying the same person on more than one occasion, it is impossible to distinguish between the two. This difficulty might be partially responsible for Janis' (1958) finding that some subjects who were not "sufficiently scared" before surgery had greater difficulty in adapting to the postoperative phase. It is conceivable that subjects who exhibited these difficulties were in fact in the denial stage prior to surgery, indicating a substantial amount of fear and anxiety. The practical suggestion in such a situation would clearly stress the need to refrain from additional threatening information prior to the operation.

3. A significant correlation was found between denial and responses to the question: "Do you often think about the surgery?" As one would expect, subjects high on denial claimed that they didn't think about it as often as those low on denial.

4. Of particular interest is the significant correlation between denial and preference for total (rather than local) anesthesia. As total anesthesia implies lack of awareness, its preference is another indicator of denial. This relationship suggests that denial acts as a general orientation with implications beyond the cognitive manipulation of threatening information. It shows a clear preference for certain situations and behaviors as well.

Much more important, however, is the fact that *the entire sequence of transitions from one response category to another can be viewed as representing different aspects of denial.*

Thus, avoidance reactions indicate denial of certain immediate implications of the threatening information. A person attempts to deny the relevance, the urgency, or other aspects of the information by resorting to projection, rationalization, compartmentalization, blocking of the stimulus, etc.

In the next phase, namely, wishful thinking and denial proper, we have indications of another facet of the denial tendency. Whereas denial indicates an attempt to negate threatening information, wishful thinking can be seen as an attempt to actively seek out certain positive aspects of what is essentially a negative situation. These two, therefore, can be viewed as essentially denial-like behaviors.

Stereotypy is obviously indicative of denial; in this case denial of the stimulus itself. By putting a barrier between the information embedded in the stimulus and the understanding of its potentially anxiety-provoking implications, the subject protects himself from the stimulus. The barrier in the case of stereotypy consists of responding with unrelated, ready-made responses.

It is worth mentioning that our data indicate two kinds of stereotypy (as mentioned earlier). Whereas some stereotypic responses are given consistently to certain specific stimuli, others are given haphazardly to any stimulus, even if it is not particularly threatening. In the first case we have, therefore, what Spence (Chapter 4) would label "leakage." In order for a subject to know when to respond with a stereotypic response he must on some level register the undesired stimulus and its threatening information. The second kind of stereotypy indicates a generalized tendency to deny the stimulus without any discrimination whatsoever.

This notion that all of these coping strategies actually represent different kinds of denial is further developed in Chapter 10 (by Breznitz).

REFERENCES

Andrew, J. M. (1970), Recovery from surgery with and without preparatory instruction from three coping styles. *J. Pers. Soc. Psychol.*, 151:223–226.

Auerbach, S. M. (1973), Trait-state anxiety and adjustment to surgery. *J. Consult. Clin. Psychol.*, 40:264–271.

Averill, J. R., O'Brien, L. & DeWitt, G. (1977), The influence of response effectiveness on the preference for warning and on psychological stress reactions. *J. Pers.*, 45:395–418.

Baker, G. W. & Chapman, D. W. (1962), *Man and Society in Disaster.* New York: Basic Books.

Breznitz, S. (1967), Incubation of threat: Duration of anticipation and false alarm as determinants of fear reaction to an unavoidable frightening event. *J. Exp. Res. Pers.*, 2:173–180.

_____ (1968), "Incubation of threat" in a situation of conflicting expectations. *Psychol. Rep.*, 22:755–756.

_____ (1971), A study of worrying. *Brit. J. Soc. Clin. Psychol.*, 10:271–279.

_____ (1972), The effect of frequency and pacing of warning signals upon fear reaction to threat. *Sci. Rep.* (Ford Foundation).

_____ (1976), False alarms: Their effects on fear and adjustment. In: *Stress and Anxiety,* Vol. 3, ed. I. G. Sarason & C. D. Spielberger. New York: Wiley.

Broen, W. E., Jr. & Storms, L. H. (1961), A reaction potential ceiling and response decrements in complex situations. *Psychol. Rev.*, 68:405–415.

_____ _____ (1966), Lawful disorganization: The process underlying a schizophrenic syndrome. *Psychol. Rev.*, 73:265–279.

Chapman, R. C. & Cox, G. B. (1977), Determinants of anxiety in elective surgery patients. In: *Stress and Anxiety,* Vol. 4, ed. C. D. Spielberger & I. G. Sarason. Washington, D.C.: Hemisphere.

Cohen, E. A. (1953), *Human Behavior in the Concentration Camp.* New York: Norton.

Cohen, F. & Lazarus, R. S. (1973), Active coping processes, coping disposition and recovery from surgery. *Psychosom. Med.*, 35:375–389.

Cramer, P. (1968), *Word Association.* New York: Academic Press.

Elliot, R., Bankart, B. & Light, T. (1970), Differences of motivational significance of heart-rate and palmar conductance. *J. Pers. Soc. Psychol.*, 14:166–172.

Epstein, S. (1962), The measurement of drive and conflict in humans: Theory and experiment. In: *Nebraska Symposium on Motivation,* ed. M. K. Jones. Lincoln: University of Nebraska Press.

_____ & Clarke, S. (1970), Heart-rate and skin conductance during experimentally induced anxiety: The effects of anticipated intensity of noxious stimulation and experience. *J. Exp. Psychol.*, 84:105–112.

_____ & Fenz, W. D. (1962), Theory and experiment on the measurement of approach-avoidance conflict. *J. Abnorm. Soc. Psychol.*, 64:97–112.

_____ & Roupenian, A. (1970), Heart-rate and skin conductance during experimentally induced anxiety: The effects of uncertainty about receiving a noxious stimulus. *J. Pers. Soc. Psychol.*, 16:20–28.

Fenz, W. D. (1964), Conflict and stress as related to psychological activation and sensory, perceptual and cognitive functioning. *Psychol. Monogr.*, 78:1–33. (Whole No. 585.)

Folkins, C. H. (1970), Temporal factors and the cognitive mediators of stress reaction. *J. Pers. Soc. Psychol.*, 14:173–184.

Grinker, R. R. & Spiegel, J. P. (1945), *Men under Stress.* New York: McGraw-Hill.

Horowitz, M. J. (1976), *Stress Response Syndromes.* New York: Aronson.

Janis, I. L. (1958), *Psychological Stress.* New York: Wiley.

Johnson, J. E., Leventhal, H. & Dabbs, J. M. (1971), Contribution of emotional and instrumental response processes in adaptation to surgery. *J. Pers. Soc. Psychol.*, 20:55–64.

Lazarus, R. S. (1964), A laboratory approach to the dynamics of psychological stress. *Amer. Psychol.*, 19:400–411.

_____ (1966), *Psychological Stress and the Coping Process.* New York: McGraw-Hill.

Mansueto, C. S. & Desiderato, O. (1971), External vs. self-produced determinants of fear reaction after shock threat. *J. Exper. Res. Pers.*, 5:30–36.

Martinez-Urrutia, A. (1975), Anxiety and pain surgical patients. *J. Consult. Clin. Psychol.*, 43:437–442.

Mechanic, D. (1962), *Students under Stress.* New York: Free Press.

Monat, A., Averill, J. R. & Lazarus, R. S. (1972), Anticipatory stress and coping reactions under various conditions of uncertainty. *J. Pers. Soc. Psychol.*, 24:237–253.

Morris, L. & Liebert, R. (1970), Relationship of cognitive and emotional components of test anxiety to psychological arousal and academic performance. *J. Consult. Clin. Psychol.*, 35:332–337.

Niemela, P. (1969), Heart rate response during anticipation of an electric shock of variable probability. *Scand. J. Psychol.*, 10:232–242.

Nomikos, M. S., Opton, E. M., Averill, J. R. & Lazarus, R. S. (1968), Surprise versus suspense in the production of stress reaction. *J. Pers. Soc. Psychol.*, 2:204–208.

Rapaport, D., Gill, M. M. & Schafer, R. (1968), *Diagnostic Psychological Testing,* ed. R. Holt. New York: International Universities Press.

Sarason, I. (1973), Test anxiety and cognitive modeling. *J. Pers. Soc. Psychol.*, 28:58–61.

Selye, H. (1956), *The Stress of Life.* New York: McGraw-Hill.

Shannon, I. L. & Isbell, G. M. (1963), *Stress in Dental Patients: Effect of Local Anesthetic Procedures.* Technical Report No. SAM-TDR-63-29. Brooks Air Force Base, Tex.: USAF School of Aerospace Medicine, May.

Spielberger, C. D., Auerbach, S. M., Wadsworth, A. P., Dunn, T. M. & Taulbee, E. S. (1973), Emotional reactions to surgery. *J. Consult. Clin. Psychol.*, 40:33–38.

10

THE SEVEN KINDS OF DENIAL

SHLOMO BREZNITZ

Denial as a defense mechanism is viewed within the context of this chapter as a process through which a person attempts to protect himself from some painful or frightening information related to external reality. By contrast to repression and other intrapsychic mechanisms, denial deals with problems emanating from the outside. More specifically, I am interested here in pursuing the various kinds and processes of denial and the ways they evolve in relation to anticipatory stress, namely, a situation in which there is some threatening information concerning an impending real danger to a person. As seen in anticipatory stress situations (see Chapter 9 by Breznitz), when the danger comes closer, the person involved attempts to deal with it by a variety of changing mechanisms. It is of some interest that all of these mechanisms reflect various kinds of denial—whether they are attempts to avoid the information, minimize it by indulging in wishful thinking, deny its emotional implications, or even not attend anymore to surrounding stimuli, and try to protect oneself by ready-made stereotypic responses. In the case of avoidance, it might be denial of the urgency or immediacy of the situation and the need to take any action. In the case of wishful thinking, it is the denial of the implications for the person of the impending danger or harm and an attempt to concentrate on the positive aspects of the situation. In the case of denial of fear, it is the more obvious attempt to control the emotional impact. I would also like to posit, however, that stereotypic behavior reflects as well a kind of denial—denial of the information conveyed by the stimulus.

This chapter attempts to explicate a relatively simple model of denial-like behaviors. This model can serve as a framework toward a taxonomy of the various kinds of denial, as well as an analytic framework toward a better understanding of the various components of this potent and prevalent response to stress. More specifically, *I postulate seven kinds of denial, each related to a different stage in the processing of the threatening information.* These kinds of denial represent progressive attempts by the individual to protect himself from the impending danger by resorting to different strategies. They may be understood as different ways to bias his perception of the world in a manner more appropriate for him and more in line with the pleasure principle.

In order to facilitate the intuitive analysis that will be presented, the model resorts to some meta-questions which the threatened person presumably attempts to answer. These meta-questions, in spite of their verisimilitude to an actual ongoing process of appraisal, should not be seen as representing the way in which primary and secondary appraisals operate in fact (Lazarus, 1966). The status of the meta-questions in the model will be further discussed at a later point in this analysis; at this juncture their main contribution lies in facilitating the taxonomy of the various kinds of denial. In no way do I argue that these questions replicate the cognitive process, consciously or unconsciously, while a person is confronted with an objective threat. The model is presented in Figure 1.

Let me attempt a brief analysis of the model. I start by assuming that a person is confronted by a situation in which he is objectively helpless. This implies that there is no way in which he can engage in instrumental action that will reduce the probability or the intensity of the danger in front of him. Next I assume that the threatening information is sufficiently clear and strong to be above the necessary threshold for its perception and registration. By postulating such obviously threatening information, I make sure that

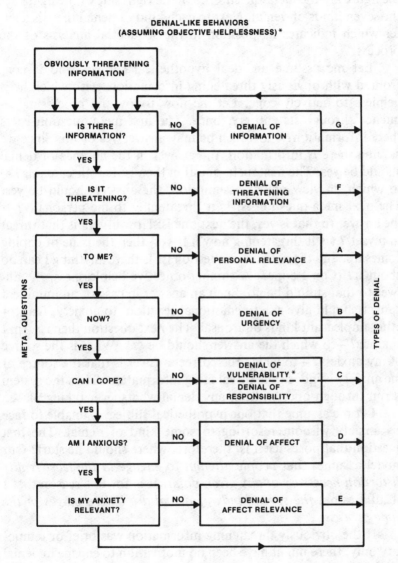

DENIAL-LIKE BEHAVIORS
(ASSUMING OBJECTIVE HELPLESSNESS) *

FIGURE I
The Seven Kinds of Denial

we are dealing with a stimulus definition of stress, irrespective of the particular response that a person will make. On the left side of the figure are the meta-questions. On the right side of the figure are the seven kinds of denial. Next to each kind of denial there is a letter which indicates its position in the sequential analysis of the process.

Let me assume an ideal hypothetical subject who is confronted with obviously threatening information, with which he is helpless to actively cope. Let me now follow the processing sequence through its entirety, once. The first meta-question is: Is there information? — to which he may answer yes or no. Since we assume there *is* information, the answer in the absence of denial should be yes. The next meta-question then is: Is it threatening? — to which, in view of our assumption, the answer should be yes. The next meta-question is: Is it threatening to me personally? If the answer to that is yes, the next one is: How urgent is that threat to myself? (Is it threatening now?) If yes, then the issue of coping comes up, and the next meta-question is: Is there anything I can do about it? (Can I cope?) Assuming objective helplessness, the answer to that should be no. Such an answer in case of an imminent danger should give rise to emotional reaction, to anxiety, fear, or other unpleasant kinds of arousal. The next question then is: Am I anxious? — to which the answer should be yes. What is the source of my anxiety? — to which the correct answer is that the source of the anxiety is indeed the threatening information. Thus the system is run through once without any denial whatsoever taking place.

Let me assume that our hypothetical subject is unable to face his anxiety without resorting to some kind of denial. The first question that poses itself is, therefore, where should he start? Our model assumes that *people attempt to engage in the least reality distortion necessary at any given point*. It is for this reason that I postulate that *the seven kinds of denial are indeed stages in the same process*.

If the obviously threatening information was brief or temporary only, there might have been no motivation to engage in denial at all. The problem, however, is that the threat is actually coming closer in time, and in addition, new incoming cues may signify its intensity, probability, and imminence. My model suggests that the first attempt to deny starts with the meta-question concerning personal relevance. Thus, a person will perceive the information as threatening, but may attempt to deny its personal relevance. By responding with a "no" to this specific meta-question, he engages in the first kind of denial, labeled *"denial of personal relevance."* It is denoted by the letter A, signifying its primacy in the entire sequence.

Denial of personal relevance is very well known and very frequent. Often a person will face a danger and yet perceive it as entirely devoid of any personal threat to himself. By maintaining this posture, he may indeed enjoy the advantages of denial, at least for a while. If the threatening information will not just disappear, and new signals indicate that it is actually coming closer, sustaining the belief that it does not concern him personally will become increasingly difficult. Once that belief starts to weaken, the next question concerning urgency becomes more salient. The person may now become concerned with time—how much time went by, how much time is left, what can be done to utilize time? If the denial tendency is still operative, and the person in our illustration is unable to face reality without the protective veil of distortion, he may now bias the information-processing at the next stage, namely, denying the urgency of the danger. Thus the answer to the first three meta-questions will now be yes—yes, there is information; yes, it is threatening; yes, it is threatening to me; but no, not yet, not now. Thus the second kind of denial is *"denial of urgency,"* and it is denoted by the letter B.

As the information continues to penetrate, even this solution may turn out to be impossible to maintain. While the urgency of the danger becomes more and more obvious, the next question dealing with protective behavior gains importance. It now poses a new option for denial, namely, *"denial of vulnerability."* Since my illustration assumes a situation of objective helplessness, a person who maintains that he can cope with the situation is in fact denying his vulnerability. In cases where there is a certain amount of objective control over the danger, there is a different kind of denial, which is diametrically opposed to denial of vulnerability. It is *"denial of responsibility."* By denying the ability to do something about the danger, a person may abdicate his responsibility for what lies in store, and for not taking any action. Thus, Type C denial is either "denial of vulnerability" (in the case of objective helplessness) or "denial of responsibility" (in the case of objective control). In both instances, however, the cognitive mechanism through which the pleasure principle is served is essentially the same. It consists of psychological manipulation of the perceived level of control either one way or the other way, contrary to its objective state.

If the threatening information does not terminate at this point, the psychological construction maintained by denial of vulnerability or responsibility will also be short-lived; sooner or later it will become impossible to maintain, and the answer to the meta-question will change from yes to no — no, I cannot cope. This automatically leads to anxiety.

The next stage during which the denial tendency can still intervene and reduce the anxiety is specifically tied to the perception of one's own emotions. By denying the affect itself, the person may, at least for a while, gain some psychological comfort. Thus, the fourth kind of denial is *"denial of affect,"* denoted by the letter D.

Once affect cannot be denied any longer, it may still be explained away. Trying to account for perceived emotionality by resorting to explanations and attributions unrelated to the objective facts can still result in some psychological advantage. There are many indications, those from analysis of intrapsychic processes as well as reactions to external stressors, that people may for some time maintain the illusion that their fears, worries, and anxieties relate to something other than the primary threat in front of them. This fifth kind of denial, *"denial of affect relevance,"* is denoted by the letter E.

Once this defense breaks down, there are no new meta-questions which may serve as the focus for the next stage of denial. There is no other possibility but to try to distort the answers to the preceding questions, those that were not tampered with yet.

The next possibility of denying threatening information and its implications to a person focuses on distorting the nature of the information itself. By using a filtering device, sifting information in a biased fashion, those aspects of the stimulus situation which are particularly threatening can be minimized, reduced, or even avoided altogether. In this case, we reach a stage of *"denial of threatening information,"* denoted by the letter F. This step in the denial sequence illustrates the need to invest greater amounts of energy in distorting objective reality. It is not just a function of the various evaluative processes taking place in the mind of the perceiver, but rather a brutal attempt to interfere with the kind of information that enters the processor in the first place. Much psychological literature and experimentation in relation to the influence of motivation on perception has dealt specifically with this kind of denial. The best example is the advent of the "new look" in perception, particularly the issue of perceptual defense (Lazarus and McCleary, 1951; Postman, 1953; Allport, 1955; Goldiamond, 1958; Bevan, 1964).

If the threatening aspects of the impending danger spread to gradually more and more content areas, the filter itself may become insufficient. Often, in this situation, there is no room for additional denial. It was attempted, it may have achieved its purpose for a while, and it ultimately failed. Only in very extreme cases is there yet another option available. By not taking chances with any information coming from the external world altogether, the need for a filter becomes superfluous. This implies denial of information in its totality. It is only in the rare extreme case of a psychotic withdrawal that such a pattern develops fully. In a more or less restricted form, however, it may become operative in extreme situational stresses as well. The stereotypic responses of perseveration by the subjects in the experiments previously discussed (see Chapter 9 by Breznitz) illustrate the point. By denying the informational value of the stimulus, they made sure that it would not be allowed passage through their already shaken and much weakened protective filters. Any such passage might induce additional anxiety; by resorting to perseveration there was no need to attend to the stimulus at all. This last stage of denial, *"denial of information,"* is denoted by the letter G.

ASSUMPTIONS AND CONSTRAINTS

The sequential analysis presented in this model is based entirely on the assumption of an ongoing continuous objective input of threatening information. It indicates that at any point *the need to switch to a more advanced category of denial is due to the fact that objective reality makes it impossible to maintain the previous level of adjustment.* This can be viewed in at least two ways: On the one hand, in the situation of anticipatory stress there are growing cues of imminence of the danger. Thus, even if there is no change in the actual content of the information, the very fact that the materialization of the threat is getting closer may suffice to facilitate the progression of denial-like tendencies. On the other hand, even if there are no new cues whatsoever, not even cues of imminence, the very fact that the information is still there and available, makes it more potent and reliable. It is therefore suggested that only when dealing with sufficiently prolonged threats can we witness the processes that have been postulated in our model. (See Chapter 11 by Breznitz.)

It follows that even in situations of objective helplessness, if for some reason the danger goes away or materializes very quickly, before there is sufficient time to move through the various stages of denial-like behavior or before there is sufficient time to exhaust one's options for coping and adaptation, denial can indeed serve an important psychological function. Threats which turn out to be false alarms illustrate this particularly well.

There is no claim in this model that each person has to go through the entire sequence. Indeed it might very well happen that the implications of threatening information are so overwhelming that a person will immediately move into very advanced stages of denial. Thus, for instance, fainting or entering the state of emotional shock, so frequently reported in situations of major personal disaster, is a case in point. Fainting and emotional shock are both states in which there is denial of information altogether. It is also possible for a person to deny at level B before ever experiencing level A, or start directly with level D before experiencing any of the preceding ones. However, it is proposed that *in no case will a person move backwards, i.e., to a less advanced stage of denial. The process may start at any level depending on one's predisposition and the intensity of the threat. Once it starts, however, it can only go in one direction, namely, forward.* It can only proceed toward more advanced stages of denial, never to the less advanced ones. Essentially, it is claimed that *the seven kinds of denial form a Guttman scale.* As such, *directionality* and *intensity* are implied (without actual experiential passage through the entire sequence).

It must also be explicitly stated that denial begins only after the program has been mentally run through in its entirety at least once. The reason for this is the postulate that anxiety and other unpleasant affects motivate the tendency to deny in the first place. Thus, at some initial stage, a certain amount of anxiety must be evoked by the threat in order to instigate the denial. Any other analysis, I am afraid, will inadvertently lead to the logical problems of the homunculus, which should be avoided at all costs. Denial, in my analysis, is therefore a mechanism that is evoked by appraisal of information, which leads to certain psychological discomfort that a person wants to reduce. It is therefore essentially an escape from psychological pain rather than its total avoidance. Stated differently, denial protects us from additional discomfort rather than its initial onset.

Another assumption which is obviously untrue in any real-life situation, and which therefore is maintained for heuristic purposes only, is the yes/no nature of the answers to the meta-questions. It is clearly the case that the answers to all of these meta-questions are ones of degree; a more advanced development of the basic model postulated here must take this into consideration. More and more, the issue of *minimization of stress* stands up as a potent way of reducing psychological impact (see Chapter 1 by Lazarus). Minimization indicates that the threatening properties of the situation are perceived as such, but in a milder form. Any dichotomy allowing only a yes/no analysis of the situation will do injustice to these important continuous phenomena. For analytic purposes, however, and specifically for taxonomic purposes, the simple dichotomies used here may be more appropriate at this stage of our sophistication. At the same time, the progressive nature of these variables has actually been taken into account in the analysis of transition from one stage to another. It was argued that if, at any point, due to additional information coming in, a particular answer, a particular construct cannot be maintained, there comes a point in time when the system has to switch to the next stage of denial. But this by its very nature is an *additive, continuous process*, namely, that the inadequacy of the previous construct has to pass a certain *threshold* before a new stage is initiated.

To sum up then, seven kinds of denial of stress are proposed: denial of personal relevance, denial of urgency, denial of vulnerability or responsibility, denial of affect, denial of affect relevance, denial of threatening information, and finally, denial of information. Moreover, their ordering from A through G reflects the amount of reality distortion involved. (Any kind of denial, even the most minimal one, must of course distort certain aspects of objective reality as perceived by the individual.) *The more advanced the denial is in the sequence postulated by the model, the greater the amount of distortion involved.* In the absence of any change in the objective features of the situation, denial can move only in one way, namely, to more advanced stages.

DYNAMICS OF TRANSITION

There are two possible ways in which the present model can view the transition from one kind of denial to the next:

1. The transition is entirely due to *new information* which makes the present answer to the last meta-question inadequate and raises the salience of the next meta-question. Assuming an ongoing tendency to deny, when the next question is raised, the biased answer is provided as an attempt to further postpone the full realization of the threat.

2. Because of new information the system runs again through the entire sequence leading to anxiety, and it is *anxiety* as such that leads to the next attempt to deny on a different, more advanced level of the process.

The difference between the two conceptualizations of dynamics of transition lies in the role of anxiety, and in the issue of an ongoing general tendency for denial. If the first description is the adequate one, there is no need to expect any periods of anxiety intervening between the various transition points from one kind of denial to another. On the other hand, the second description of the process postulates that it is anxiety, and anxiety only, which keeps the denial tendency operative. Thus one would expect that between any two different kinds of denial, i.e., at any transition point, there will be an experience of anxiety, however brief.

Furthermore, it will be consistent with the underlying assumption of the model to postulate that following a serious experience of anxiety there will be upgrading of the stage of denial used. This is based on the notion of effective learning from experience, namely, that failure of protection against anxiety will lead to a change in the defensive strategy employed. Of course this need not be a single trial learning; a few episodes of anxiety may be necessary.

MEANS AND CONSEQUENCES

Our taxonomy of the seven kinds of denial of stress now makes it possible to analyze the various psychological devices that have to be employed in order to achieve a particular kind of denial. A preliminary analysis of the psychological processes that can be conducive to each of the seven types follows:

Denial of personal relevance (A). In order for a person to view a particular threat as unrelated to him personally, he must psychologically maximize the perceived differences between himself and other individuals involved in the situation. Such maximization of personal differences may lead to a variety of consequences, many of them quite negative. Thus, for instance, the maximization of perceived uniqueness of an individual can make it very difficult for him to maintain good social bonds when he may need them most. It may also lead to a situation where he will find himself unable to model the behavior of others when such modeling could provide a good way to reduce his personal anxiety and increase his sense of safety. It ought to be mentioned in this context that Schachter and others have often demonstrated (Schachter, 1959) that during periods of anxiety and stress we need to affiliate most, and particularly with people who are in the same situation. By taking temporary advantage of denying personal relevance of a threat, the individual may sacrifice his ability to interact with his peers, particularly those who are in similar danger.

The same psychological device can also lead to neglect in many areas, including one's health. The story of medicine, and particularly of preventive medicine, illustrates the potency of this kind of denial. While fully aware of the dangers of certain behaviors or inactions, even an intelligent person may often plead the case of uniqueness, and refrain from taking the right course of action. (At the same time, it must be mentioned that this type of denial is sometimes the basis of courageous acts under duress. By feeling unthreatened and naively exceptional, soldiers or civilians will endanger their own life and protect others without concern or anxiety, which might otherwise inhibit their actions.) The psychological advantages, at least the immediate ones, of such denial of personal relevance are quite obvious; unfortunately, so is their long-term cost.

Denial of urgency (B). Here the psychological process must utilize ways to subjectively slow down time. This can be achieved by a variety of means, such as attempts to differentiate the time left into a greater number of smaller units. In this way a person can perceive the situation as less pressing than before.

Denial of vulnerability (C). In this case, what is called for is a certain maximization of perceived personal strengths. By exaggerating one's image of strength, the illusion can be created of greater control over the events. Another way to achieve denial of vulnerability is by stressing the important role of experience. Since it can be taken for granted that major disasters, including terrible suffering, wounds, and death, were either relatively rare in a person's history or never happened before, by stressing the importance of past experience the person reinforces the belief that whatever was true before is the best predictor for the immediate future. This of course augments the sense of control and produces denial of vulnerability.

It should be stressed, however, that such attempts lead automatically to the neglect of some unique, possibly important features of the present threat. It is only if the present situation is seen as similar to other previously experienced situations that experience as such becomes a meaningful guide for the future. Thus there is a psychological need here to neglect the specific unique features of the present threat and to concentrate on its common denominators with other previously experienced situations. The cost of all this is quite obvious: By sensing the unjustified control over the situation, a person may neglect to take necessary protective action while it is still possible; or, if he cannot deal with it alone, he may fail to ask for the much needed help from other people or organizations.

In the case of a threat that does not leave the person objectively helpless, this Type C denial relates to the opposite of vulnerability, namely, responsibility. In such a situation, what has to be done in order to bring such denial about is to minimize the sense of control over the situation. The person must perceive himself as more helpless than he really is. Such an individual prefers to view the situation as one which is totally out of his personal control, and tends to maximize the perceived similarity between this situation and others in the past in which his control was rather limited. It is also necessary for him to concentrate on those features of the information which support the notion of helplessness. Our concern here is with subjective sense of helplessness, not necessarily based on objective facts, but rather on personal needs. Once again, this kind of denial can be quite costly because it precludes action. It disarms the motive for action and leaves the person passively awaiting his fate.

Denial of affect (D). In order for a person to achieve even a limited sense of neutrality in the face of his own emotional arousal, he must invent procedures which will reduce the affective impact of the threatening situation. There are many ways to do this, such as increased automatization of behavior, development of certain routines which are always followed, stereotypic behavior, and engaging in anything that will distract one's mind from what is in store. Such continuous "neurotic preoccupation" may indeed deflate the emotional impact of the impending danger, at least to some extent. Another, altogether different way to deal with the psychophysiological feedback emanating from the emotional reaction is to explain it away by resorting to nonemotional causes. Thus, for instance, a person may perceive himself as being very tired, attributing the symptoms he senses to fatigue, illness and other similar causes. He or she may even attempt to intellectualize the situation and account for the arousal by a sense of great curiosity, excitement, and interest, instead of threat.

Once more, however, the cost can be quite great. After all, emotions are one of the most reliable triggers of escape and avoidance, and if blunted or reduced or accounted for by irrelevancies, there is always a danger that they will fail to fulfill this very basic function.

Denial of affect relevance (E). Once the emotion itself cannot be explained away by other means, or denied its status, it is still possible to explain it in terms of other causes—anxiety, yes, but not from the threat; fear, yes, but not related to the impending danger. People may engage in diverting their attention to secondary issues and thus try to deemphasize the anxiety-provoking nature of the stressor. For instance, they may use projection, such as claiming that they are terribly worried about somebody else; or, alternatively, about something else; or about another person unduly influenced by their anxiety (therefore *they* are anxious not to show their emotions). People have an incredible capacity to concentrate on secondary issues and focus all their attention and emotion on them in order to deflect their apprehension and anxiety.

Denial of threatening information (F). Psychological theory and experimentation have spent a great deal of effort trying to understand the mechanisms which underlie selective inattention and perception, subception, perceptual defense, and other related phenomena. It is not within the scope of this chapter to analyze the complex issues involved; suffice it to mention that information-processing is conceived as constituting various levels of perceptual analysis and control. One level can influence the subsequent one, and thus progressively reduce the awareness of certain significant stimuli. At the same time, however, in order to eliminate dangerous information which is threatening to the ego, the person must on some level be aware of all information available, including the data to be rejected. It is this partial processing and partial awareness that makes Type F denial possible.

Denial of information (G). Otherwise there would be a transition to Type G denial, which has no problem with selection, since it consists of denial of all information. Type G thus solved the problem of information-filtering by overgeneralization. It is the least sophisticated form of denial, probably very much akin to what Freud called the "primitive stimulus barrier" put between the external environment and the person's psyche.

Whereas denial of threatening information implies the need for continuous on-line monitoring of all information, with very sensitive probes testing at all times whether a particular item of information is neutral, partially threatening, or very threatening, denial of all information is totally indiscriminate. However, the cost of such denial is tremendous. One becomes entirely at the mercy of the internal world, without the much needed corrective features coming from the outside. The psychotic person is a most dramatic illustration of this final stage of denial.

One of the most important criteria for assessing any psychological mechanism is its sensitivity to changes in the situation. Thus, any device, whatever its psychological benefits, which does not allow for its own correction, is bound to be disastrous in the long run. Looking at the various stages of denial, one finds that if there are changes for the better in one's situation (i.e., threat is reduced), the need for denial is likewise reduced, and eventually the person is able to adjust his protection and revert back to a normal appraisal of information coming from external sources. Once having resorted to Type G, however, there is very little room for self-correction. If information from the external world is rejected indiscriminately, there is no way for the person to discover that much of the information is now benign and unthreatening. He may continue to protect himself even when the objective need for it no longer exists. Thus, one of the tragic aspects of psychotic defense is its lack of responsiveness to real changes in one's life; such denial is, in fact, too protective, shielding the person from any reality testing whatsoever.

REFUTABILITY OF THE MODEL

One of the strengths of the proposed model is that it is relatively easy to refute. In order to enhance this property, the model deliberately attempts to state very strong propositions whose truth value can quite easily be ascertained. Instead of just enumerating the seven kinds of denial, there are direct claims concerning their differential intensity and sequence, and the processes underlying their respective formation.

The following illustrates some points for refutation: On the basis of the analysis proposed here, two kinds of denial cannot happen at the same time, at least not concerning the same aspects of the information. After all, according to our reasoning, the person who is using denial must be at a certain stage of the process, and cannot be at the same time in more than one point in the entire sequence described in Figure 1. The only exception to this general rule concerns differentiation of the threatening information. Although within a particular segment of information the process must operate on one specifiable level, and one level only, it is possible to differentiate the information into more specific categories, not all of which have to be treated in exactly the same way. Thus, for instance, a person may relate to one particular feature of the information by denying its threatening implications, and at the same time defend against vulnerability from another cue or another item related to the same threat, but belonging to another aspect of the informational input.

It ought to be relatively easy to study whether a person's behavior is in this sense monomorphic, i.e., exhibits features of defense belonging only to a single level of processing, or whether he indeed shows denials of different kinds at the same time. If such is the case, it will clearly refute one of the underlying principles proposed here.

A closer look at the model indicates that each kind of denial in a sense acts as a short-circuit and keeps the process from advancing to more advanced stages. At each point, by denying the implications of the meta-questions involved, the denial process exits into a circuit which starts from the very beginning. Figure 1 illustrates this very clearly. In this way the person saves himself from the need to face the next meta-question and the ones following it. Thus it is not clear whether the only way to describe denial behaviors within the context of our model is to view them as attempts to avoid rise of immediate anxiety, or whether they fulfill another function, namely, that of protecting the individual from confrontation with subsequent meta-questions.

What is the status of these meta-questions? On the one hand, they can be viewed as analytic tools attempting to explicate the kinds of information-processing that takes place in the various stages of the sequence; at the same time, they can be seen as explicating what is sometimes called "the process of appraisal." Here I ought to mention the important contribution by Lazarus (1966), who views primary appraisal and secondary appraisal as the basic features of psychological stress. While primary appraisal denotes the way a person interprets a particular information as threatening to himself, secondary appraisal constitutes of the cognitive processes which underlie the choice of a particular coping strategy. The meta-questions proposed here deal with these aspects of the situation, but particularly with the question of coping. The threatening aspect of the situation is taken for granted by postulating that the information is, a priori, threatening. By utilizing a stimulus definition of stress, whatever processing occurs from that point on relates to the implications of that information and to possible actions that one may take as a consequence.

Another way to view the meta-questions is to consider the possibility that they indeed depict some of the features of what is essentially sequential information-processing. At any given time, at any given point in the sequence, another aspect of the information becomes the focus of the analysis. The meta-questions describe the content areas of this sequential focusing.

Once again the model is deliberately very explicit about the content areas involved as well as their finite number. Any study that will refute the sequence proposed here, or illustrate the existence of different kinds of denial, ones which do not appear among the seven listed here, will clearly refute the model in its strictest sense. It will also illustrate the need to pose new meta-questions and perhaps add new transition points of sequential focus.

Although the model per se is easily refutable, it may very well survive experimentation by accommodating new information and weakening some of the propositions and assumptions developed here. It is my contention that by starting with a very decisive model, the research in this complicated and rather neglected area of study can profit even if this particular proposal must ultimately be changed beyond recognition.

INDIVIDUAL DIFFERENCES

One shortcoming of the proposed model lies in its total neglect of individual differences. It is concerned only with the central tendency, which may be attributable to all individuals facing threatening information. However, experience teaches that sooner or later a more sophisticated and differentiated approach will be needed.

Thus, for instance, there are personality characteristics which are highly relevant to the process proposed here. Among the most obvious ones are ego strength and vulnerability to anxiety. Individual differences in these characteristics and in a person's ability to manage his own anxiety will clearly monitor the intensity and frequency with which the process of denial is activated.

Another applicable personality variable relates to the distinction between sensitizers and repressors. It is a basic tendency of individuals to confront threatening situations by either trying to learn as much as possible about them, being at all times cued to new information and receptive to it, or on the contrary, by putting barriers between themselves and the information, and protecting themselves from some of its implications. The seven kinds of denial described here all illustrate the operation of the tendency to repress and to protect against external threats. A major advance in this area will obviously necessitate study of individual differences along some of these dimensions.

Yet another individual characteristic relates to the issue of ambiguity and its tolerance. The present model suggests that when a person cannot maintain a particular construct concerning a specific meta-question which is in the focus of the information-processing sequence, he has to change his answer and move to the next meta-question. This is clearly a statement about thresholds. It indicates that only when there is inconsistency beyond a tolerable level between a person's answer to a meta-question and information coming from external sources is there a need to change the present situation. Individual differences in tolerance of ambiguity will therefore influence the likelihood of transition from one state to another. Persons high on intolerance of ambiguity will need to abandon the present level of coping sooner than those who can manage an ambiguous situation with greater ease. Thus, an interesting prediction would be that in the long run intolerance of ambiguity is associated with more advanced stages of denial.

There is one overriding difference between individuals which should be noted—their tendency to engage in denial-like coping in the first place. Already briefly mentioned in conjunction with the repression-sensitization dimension, there might be other components to the same process. Not everyone always copes with threatening information by resorting to denial. There are many other kinds of adaptation and they may all be preferred to denial in various stages of the anticipation situation. It is an open question whether a person who is engaged in Type B denial (denial of urgency), for example, moves to a different, more advanced stage if the need to abandon it becomes obvious, or exits into entirely different modes of coping. The present model indicates that if there is a tendency to *deny*, then the next stage would be denial of vulnerability (or responsibility). In the absence of such an ongoing tendency to engage in denial as a coping mechanism, the individual may indeed exit this system and move to other modes of coping. However, if at any time he returns to the denial tendency, he will once again have to follow the sequential process as indicated here.

It is difficult to predict what the situational determinants that lead to denial or other kinds of coping strategies are. One parameter of the threatening situation, however, already suggests itself at this point of our knowledge. It appears to be a safe assumption that when the *intensity* of the threat is very high, the tendency toward denial may be intensified as well. Threats which clearly indicate a very potent danger usually tend to evoke particularly strong denial-like tendencies. It has also been suggested that the higher the intensity of the threat, the more advanced the stage of denial that will be reached either during an ongoing process, or already in its initial stage. This is tantamount to claiming that if the initial impact of the threatening information is very potent, the denial process described here moves very rapidly into that particular stage where it produces certain positive hedonistic results. The greater the initial threat, the more advanced the first satisfying stage of denial would be.

It is also suggested that when the threatening information is *ambiguous* in its own right, it allows for a greater amount of disconfirmation at any stage of the information-processing. Thus a person may take advantage of inherent ambiguity and use it to maintain a given construct before having to move to a new one. As already stated by Lazarus (see Chapter 1), ambiguity can be an important asset in any stressful situation because it allows a greater amount of cognitive manipulation of the information. I would therefore predict that ambiguous situations will keep the denial process at a lower stage of development than less ambiguous ones.

DENIAL IN PATIENTS WITH A HEART ATTACK: AN ILLUSTRATION

In order to bring the discussion (which until now was abstract) closer to real-life situations, the following illustration will concentrate on patients who experienced a heart attack. The experience of a heart attack is a very dramatic psychological stress which poses a grave danger to the person involved. The chances of using denial-like tendencies in coping with this situation are therefore quite high, and this might allow us to look for the variety of denials as postulated in the present model.

Type A: In their study of a coronary-care unit, Hackett, Cassem, and Wishnie (1968) found that while 11 out of their 50 subjects witnessed a fatal cardiac arrest during their stay in the unit, none identified with the victim. This clearly demonstrates the operation of denial of personal relevance. It is particularly dramatic to witness when the objective personal relevance is quite obvious. It might very well be that there is a need on the part of these patients to maximize the perceived difference between themselves and other patients in similar circumstances in order to ensure themselves that theirs is not a grave condition.

Type B: There is a vast literature on the tendency of many individuals, including those who have experienced a personal emergency — either a heart attack itself or similar symptoms — to delay in calling for help (Hackett and Cassem, 1975; Von Kugelgen, 1975). It seems that many patients could have profited from help much sooner than they actually did, and could have actually saved their lives, if they had consulted a physician or a hospital earlier. This is a classical situation of denial of urgency, in which the person says, "Yes, I sense certain pains in the chest; yes, they may be dangerous or serious, but there is plenty of time. Let me wait for a while and see what happens. Let me see how it develops; there is no need to act immediately."

This denial of urgency can also be seen in the prevalent postponement of change in behavior. Thus, for instance, although many people are sophisticated enough to understand the importance of smoking, overweight, high blood pressure, and lack of exercise or proper diet as major coronary risk factors, there is a clear tendency to refrain from taking immediate action in relation to them. It is not a rare exception to see a person who intellectually understands the threatening aspects of neglect of his personal health, and yet does not act upon it. This denial of urgency takes advantage of the fact that none of the risk factors produce clear indications of growing imminent threat. (In fact, one of the greatest problems of preventive medicine is that the danger from risk factors such as those mentioned in this context lies in their long-term cumulative impact, rather than in any immediate, clearly visible consequence.) It is therefore relatively easy for the individual to utilize denial of urgency in order to reduce the anxiety that might be related to potentially threatening outcomes.

Type C: As is always the case in this kind of denial, we ought to distinguish between two distinct situations. In the instance of objective helplessness, Type C denial relates to denial of vulnerability. In case of objective control over the situation, however, we will deal with denial of responsibility. Let us illustrate them one by one.

Denial of vulnerability. It is often the case that patients who experienced one heart attack and survived tend to exaggerate belief in their control over the situation, beyond that justified by objective data. Thus, they tend to think that by following the physician's prescriptions they not only protect themselves from future similar experiences, but that their physical condition actually becomes better than that of other people who never experienced a heart attack. The motivational advantage of denial of vulnerability in this situation is apparent, and one should be hesitant to tamper with it. A patient who trusts that by engaging in exercise, watching his weight, being very careful in his diet, and giving up smoking he gains total control over his personal destiny, will gladly follow the often difficult regimen prescribed by medicine. And yet, denial it is, and as such can pose a very dangerous trap. The truth of the matter is that those risk factors which are under the control of the individual patient do not account for all of the variance in heart attacks; thus, situations arise in which even those who followed all the prescriptions to the letter may experience another heart attack for reasons unrelated to those risk factors. If such an episode is witnessed in someone else, and even more so, if it happens to the person himself, it may cause a grave psychological breakdown and depression. After all, if it could have happened after all these precautions and difficult changes in one's life, then anything can happen and there is not much use in following the physician's prescriptions.

Denial of responsibility. This, the other side of the same coin, follows almost naturally from what was said above. By abdicating his responsibility over his fate, even though this may indicate a sense of fatalistic passivity, the patient releases himself from the burden of his cardiac condition. Furthermore, in our studies at the University of Haifa (Nitzan, 1977), we have found, contrary to expectation, that many patients view the advent of a heart attack as being totally outside their sphere of control. More frequently than control subjects who did not experience a heart attack, patients claim that what happens to them has nothing to do with their way of conducting their lives. On the contrary, they frequently state that heart attacks are due to luck, fate, and other such uncontrolled factors. While such a belief clearly undermines the ability of the patient to comfort himself concerning his prospects for the future, it at the same time reduces any feeling of guilt.

Type D: In a study of patients who had just experienced a heart attack, it was found that while most of them admitted thoughts of death, only a few admitted experiencing fear during that time (Hackett, Cassem, and Wishnie, 1968). This indicates that these patients must have used the denial of anxiety as a coping device.

Type E: One of the main reasons for dangerous delay in asking for medical help is often the ability of the patient to explain away his own symptoms. Although the signs of illness may be quite evident, and the person is closely familiar with them, he or she may attribute them to other causes, and thus reduce his anxiety over experiencing cardiac problems. Often a patient will attribute his symptoms to such causes as fatigue or some sort of indisposition; he might even engage in vigorous exercise to make his symptoms credible, or alternatively, to convince himself that if he could do so, then it cannot be a heart attack but something much less threatening.

Type F: Out of the variety of different possible ways in which a patient who has experienced a heart attack will resort to biased filtering of relevant information, I wish to concentrate on a single example which is of particular interest. It reflects a situation in which there is a paradoxical influence of protective behavior on the Type F defense mechanism, denial of threatening information.

Consider the case of an individual who engages in a variety of new activities, or refrains from a variety of activities in which he was involved before his heart attack, all with the intention of reducing the danger of another similar experience. *These protective measures, however, have the important property of serving as constant reminders of what happened and what can in principle happen again.* Thus, for instance, a person who starts his early morning activities by engaging in exercise, something which he did not do before his heart attack, is constantly reminded of his problem by the very behavior which serves to protect him. If the individual wants to deny the fact that something very important has changed his normal way of life, and that he has been, so to speak, marked by an important reminder of his vulnerability, he might very well try to refrain from confrontation with other reminders. One of the paradoxical consequences of defending against cues implying his vulnerable condition will be that protective behavior will be reduced. The above may very well be one of the reasons why people often backslide even if they are well aware of the benefits of a particular change in their behavior (see Chapter 2 by Janis).

Protective behavior will be safer in preventing such potential backsliding if it does not dominate one's attention. In other words, only if it does not serve as a reminder can it be maintained safely. The reminding property of a particular behavior depends primarily on whether it is part of a routine or is a specific change due to the heart attack. If it is the former, then the patient may not be reminded by it of his precarious condition, and may profit from it without at the same time having to defend against its implications. There are obviously quite significant practical conclusions to be drawn from the above analysis, but this is out of the scope of the present chapter.

Type G: Denial of all information is such a drastic way of coping, that it is fortunately quite rare. There is, however, one clinical syndrome following a heart attack which might be perhaps related to this sort of denial. It is quite often mentioned in the medical literature that after the initial recovery from the heart attack, deep depression sets in. Such depression during convalescence might indeed indicate the operation of denial in this extreme form. During the depression phase itself, patients often minimize their interaction with their environment and attend mostly to their internal states rather than to external stimulation. In this sense, one may claim that depression always implies a certain amount of Type G denial, namely, denial of positive as well as threatening information coming from one's immediate environment.

In conclusion, it may be stated that a serious threat such as the one posed by a heart condition often leads to denial-like behaviors of a great variety. The model presented here argues that there are essentially seven kinds of denial, all of which find expression in this particular condition. Needless to say, this much neglected area of study requires a great deal of additional research. It is hoped that the model proposed here may serve an important catalytic function in that direction.

REFERENCES

Allport, F. (1955), *Theories of Perception and the Concept of Structure.* New York: Wiley.

Bevan, W. (1964), Subliminal stimulation: A pervasive problem for psychology. *Psychol. Bull.*, 61:81–99.

Goldiamond, I. (1958), Indicators of perception: I. Subliminal perception, subception, unconscious perception: An analysis in terms of psychophysical indicator methodology. *Psychol. Bull.*, 55:373–411.

Hackett, T. P. & Cassem, N. (1975), Psychological management of the myocardial infarction patient. *J. Human Stress*, 1:25–38.

————— ————— & Wishnie, H. A. (1968), The coronary-care unit. *New England J. Med.*, 279:1365–1370.

Lazarus, R. S. (1966), *Psychological Stress and the Coping Process.* New York: McGraw-Hill.

————— & McCleary, R. A. (1951), Autonomic discrimination without awareness: A study of subception. *Psychol. Rev.*, 58:113–122.

Nitzan, N. (1977), Anger, calming down, and personality characteristics of heart disease patients. Unpublished Master's thesis, University of Haifa.

Postman, L. (1953), On the problem of perceptual defense. *Psychol. Rev.*, 60:298–306.

Schachter, S. (1959), *The Psychology of Affiliation.* Stanford: Stanford University Press.

Von Kugelgen, E. (1975), Psychological determinants of the delay in decision to seek aid in cases of myocardial infarction. Unpublished doctoral dissertation, University of California.

DISCUSSION

THE DENIAL MODEL AS A
FRAMEWORK FOR DEBATE

Since the material appearing in Chapters 9 and 10 was presented together, the discussion relates to both of them. In order to facilitate discussion of the model concerning the kinds of denial, Dr. Breznitz started by explicating four propositions. The main goal of these propositions was to present a framework for debate and possible refutation of the model. Consequently, they were phrased in very explicit terms conducive to this purpose.

PROPOSITIONS CONCERNING THE MODEL

Dr. Breznitz: (1) There are only seven kinds of denial. The seven kinds are the ones presented in the model. This is a proposition about the *exhaustiveness* of the model.

Since all of these kinds of denial are perceived as different stages in the sequential processing of threatening information, the following two propositions are based on this notion of *sequentiality*.

(2) The seven kinds of denial are ordered on the dimension of reality distortion. Denial of personal relevance (A) assumes least

reality distortion, whereas denial of information (G) assumes the greatest amount of reality distortion.

(3) Within the context of an individual faced with a particular threat, the order of appearance of the various denial behaviors follows from A to G. Thus, this is a proposition concerning empirical sequentiality.

(4) Some kinds of denial are more stable than others, and a logical and psychological analysis from the point of view of the model presented here makes it possible to predict the stability of any particular kind of denial.

At this point Dr. Koriat suggested another, fifth proposition, based on some of the notions discussed earlier in this volume. The proposition states: The more intense the threat which a particular individual faces, the more advanced the type of denial that he will use. While this fifth proposition can in principle be deduced from the argument of sequentiality, particularly if the threat is becoming gradually more and more imminent, it adds the idea that intensity of the threat may determine the actual stage at which the denial process will begin. Thus, a person facing a very intense threat would enter the sequence directly at a more advanced level.

The discussion that developed focused primarily on these propositions, and the first topic concerned the argument of exhaustiveness of the model. Stated differently, attempts were made to suggest other kinds of denial which do not appear in the list.

Dr. Lazarus: I am concerned with the black/white definitions of denial here, the yes/no dichotomies. It seems to me that many things are a question of degree, for example, I think that there is a specific kind of denial which is missing, one which might be called "minimization." Minimization, while leaving the threat partly there, mitigates it to reduce some of its desperate elements.

Another is the kind of denial which might be called "partial denial," for example, the kind that is a function of social pressure, in which one plays the game with other people; but, it is really a limited kind of denial which operates only when the pressure is there, and once it is off, there is a realization of the threat. This of course relates to the term "middle knowledge" used by Weisman (1972) and illustrates some of the difficulties of a black-and-white definition of the concept.

Dr. Breznitz: The criticism of the dichotomous nature of the answers to the meta-questions is of course well taken, and the need to relax some of the stringent requirements of the simple model has been already mentioned in the chapter itself.

Dr. Horowitz thought that another kind of denial should be included in the list, namely, denial of denial. This implies a situation where a person tries to deny the fact that he is indeed engaged in the process of denial. Other discussants thought, however, that denial of denial is already implied in the concept of denial itself. Since denial is always without awareness, just as repression is a necessary facet of any defense mechanism whatever its nature, so denial of denial is inherent in the concept itself. Nonetheless, this important issue remains open to debate.

Dr. Koriat: If you look at the seven kinds of denial presented here, they all deal with a particular aspect of classification, namely, according to the *object* of the denial. All the kinds of denial described by the model are denials of something, of personal relevance, of urgency, of affect, etc. Therefore, the proposition of exhaustiveness actually amounts to asking to what extent there are possible objects of denial. It may, however, be possible to classify denial according to other principles altogether.

The Argument of Sequentiality

Dr. Janis: I am skeptical whether we can talk fruitfully about these matters in stage terms, a problem which I find with primary appraisal and secondary appraisal as well. It would seem that they are sequential, but I think it's more advantageous to recognize the possibility of many things happening simultaneously.

Dr. Breznitz: It might very well be the case that there is a great deal of overlap in time between some of these kinds of denial. Still, the general sequencing and directionality might hold, particularly if we consider the fact that some of the kinds of denial are so extreme, almost pathological, that they probably do not appear simultaneously with the very sophisticated ones.

Dr. Goldberger: It seems to me that denial of information (G) is a very likely possibility to be the first response, particularly when one thinks of cases of restriction of the ego. Thus, taking, for instance, Witkin's notion of differentiation in a person, there might be certain levels of defense that go on with the undifferentiated person. Babies, for instance, might prefer Type G kind of denial because of their limited stage of development. In addition to developmental constraints, this might also be an individual difference variable.

Dr. Breznitz: The point is, of course, well taken, but one might still claim that the child who goes directly to the last stage, G, cannot use any of the lesser ones. The model does not claim that in order to get to G one first has to be in A, then B, and so on and so forth. It says that *one cannot go back.* One can jump, and maybe when the situation is very threatening, one indeed quickly jumps to a very advanced stage; or if the person is undifferentiated and cannot resort to very sophisticated defenses, he will also start with a very advanced one; but once a particular denial is chosen, there is no way according to this model to later resort to less advanced kinds of denial.

OTHER ISSUES CONCERNING THE PROCESS

Dr. Janis pointed out the similarities between the suggested model and the one proposed in 1977 by Janis and Mann on decision-making. The questions proposed in the Janis and Mann model are somewhat different; thus, the first one is not whether information is threatening, or whether the threat is urgent, or whether a person can cope with it, but rather, to what extent does the person perceive a need to change his ongoing behavior? Instead of being concerned with issues like what is going to happen, which is a typical problem in situations where a person is helplessly anticipating an impending danger, the decision-making model is obviously interested in questions such as: What should I do? What happens if I do it and what happens if I don't? etc. Dr. Janis suggested that the meta-questions proposed by the Breznitz model deal with the micro-processes which underlie the more general questions with which the Janis and Mann model is concerned.

Dr. Lazarus: The one thing left out of both Dr. Breznitz' and Janis and Mann's analysis is person variables. It is very difficult to see how it would be possible to make any predictions without these additional antecedent conditions relating to the person.

Dr. Breznitz: The present model of course cannot be used as a predictor of what a person would answer at any of the choice points. That would depend almost entirely upon what he brings into the situation. However, for the purposes of distinguishing among the kinds of denial and pinpointing some of the underlying information-processing that might be responsible for the various kinds of denial, it might suffice. In terms of a more pragmatic contribution, it can be seen on two levels; on the one hand, it can serve the diagnostic process. Taken in its most stringent sense, the model would predict that if a person responds with one of the more advanced kinds of denial, he is indeed confronted with a major stressor. In addition, there is also a prognostic potential. Unless refuted, the model predicts that if a person exhibits a particular kind of denial, some other specific kinds are expected to follow in the future.

Dr. Janis: We are all familiar with the clinical phenomenon whereby a patient or a client will intellectually deny a threat, and yet, at the same time is showing affective arousal. Often if one is engaged in some kind of therapeutic task, one tries to call attention to that disparity, "Look, you say that you are not the least bit worried about this, and yet you are experiencing anxiety," and the patient responds to that by acknowledging the fact. Thus, it would seem to me that the meta-questions "Am I anxious?" or "Is my anxiety relevant to the threat?" can appear at any stage.

Dr. Breznitz: A partial answer to this obviously central question lies in the distinction between escape versus avoidance. As one's experience with one's own coping devices develop, one might anticipate the fact that following a particular sequence of appraisal will eventually lead to anxiety. Once this learning takes place, a person may try to short-circuit the rise of anxiety by exiting the particular sequence at an earlier point. Thus, both Types F and G attempt to achieve just that. Another possibility worth mentioning is that some kinds of denial are less successful than others. When denial is partial and ineffective, there might be anxiety even if the cognitive understanding is not there. We would then predict that such denial should be relatively short-lived.

EXTERNAL VERSUS INTERNAL SOURCES OF INFORMATION

Dr. Breznitz: The distinction ought to be made between external and internal sources of information. The consequences of these two are obviously quite different. In one case it is as if saying to oneself, "Don't look, don't listen," whereas in the other instance, "Don't think" or "Don't imagine it." These are obviously entirely different processes. In the case of Type G denial, namely, denial of information, we have a situation in which, by putting a barrier between himself and the stimuli around him, the person actually becomes at the mercy of his own images to a greater extent than before. Withdrawing from external reality puts one at the mercy of thoughts, ideas and images coming from within, very often concerning exactly the same threat. It is like running from the Scylla of the external world to the Charybdis of the internal one.

In principle it might be possible to differentially diagnose whether a person is denying information that comes from the outside or inside by certain aspects of his overt behavior. For instance, hectic attempts by the person to distract his mind or be involved continually with external realities so that he has no time to think, so to speak, might indicate that a person tries to deny certain aspects of information coming from within. Hyperactivity, drugs, or anything that makes it more difficult for the person to concentrate might indicate a similar process.

REFERENCES

Janis, I. L. & Mann, L. (1977), *Decision-making: A Psychological Analysis of Conflict, Choice, and Commitment.* New York: Free Press.
Weisman, A. D. (1972), *On Dying and Denying.* New York: Behavioral Publications.

11

METHODOLOGICAL CONSIDERATIONS
IN RESEARCH ON DENIAL

SHLOMO BREZNITZ

Psychological defenses are recognized to be a major source of difficulty in the study of personality functions, particularly within the
context of anxiety-provoking situations. Any item attempting to
measure whether a person is frightened, worried, anxious, or angry
in reponse to a threatening stimulus may yield a negative response
for two diametrically opposed reasons: (1) Either the particular individual does not in fact experience any of these affects; or (2) the
person is so stressed that he or she resorts to powerful psychological defenses leading to active negation of the threat. No such potentially misleading ambiguity exists given a positive response,
which does not lend itself so obviously to alternative interpretations.
The problem in a nutshell is due to the fact that a single response
cannot provide unambiguous answers to two separate questions,
namely: (1) Is the person anxious? and (2) Is he utilizing psychological defenses against anxiety? The issue is not unlike *attempting
to solve one equation with two unknowns* (Rapaport, Gill, and
Schafer, 1968).

Research on denial touches the kernel of this problem; unless satisfactorily solved, it poses the major obstacle to any systematic investigation of the processes and mechanisms involved. Consequently, to empirically establish the case that denial-like behaviors occur, certain methodological considerations must be specified. This chapter provides a preliminary analysis of such considerations. They are deliberately presented as features of an ideal research situation. Needless to say, real-life situations seldom exhibit all the properties of the ideal case. The analytic advantages, however, of presenting the rare but conceptually clear-cut "ideal type," justify this approach.

An Obviously Intense Stressor

In order to be able to investigate whether a particular person employs denial-like defenses against the stressful impact of a given event, there must be no uncertainty as to whether that event is indeed stressful. Some events are more stressful than others, and some people are more stressed by a given stressor than others. In order to qualify as a stressor for everyone, the event in question must be well above a certain threshold in terms of its psychological impact.

Thus, a response definition of stress will not do, in spite of the fact that many scholars in this area favor such an approach (Cannon, 1935; Wolff, Wolf, and Hare, 1950; Withey, 1962; Hinkle, 1974). The main weakness of a response definition of stress in the context of the present argument is that it makes it impossible to distinguish between denial and lack of stress, since in both instances the responses may be identical. *It is only by virtue of having an independent definition of stress that defense becomes a distinctive response category.* A stimulus-based definition of stress is, therefore, vital.

The higher the intensity of the stressor, the better. Powerful stressors ensure that they are above the threshold for everyone. In addition, there seems to be a wealth of evidence indicating that high intensity stressors reduce the contribution of individual differences to the total variance in the reactions studied. Lazarus (1966) claims that "The more severe and basic the harm conveyed by the stimulus, the more universal the stress reaction is likely to be" (p.

57). This makes it more difficult for specific individual reactions to manifest themselves, but such a situational pressure against individual differences increases the importance of those which overcome the barrier. Furthermore, the very notion of defense, and particularly such a serious distortion of reality as implied by *denial, may well be activated only if the psychological stress is sufficiently intense.* A lesser stressor, while still allowing the possibility of response analysis, may well produce only a very limited amount of defensive activity, with the category of denial perhaps entirely absent.

As an obvious corollary to the methodological consideration being discussed, it should be emphasized that due caution needs to be taken to *ensure the perceptual registration of the stressor.* In other words, the stressor must clearly be brought to focal attention of the person under study. What the individual does with it from that point on is his business and indeed the major concern of our entire exercise, but the relevance of denial presumes the initial instigation by the stressor. This last argument leads directly to the second methodological consideration.

DURATION OF THE STRESS

The experience of stress caused by the obviously intense stressor must be of sufficiently long duration for a variety of reasons. One of them follows the previous argument concerning the perceptual registration of the stressor, namely, the logical structure of the denial process itself. To avoid the homunculus position which leads to infinite regress in terms of the controlling agent instigating the defense, the assumption must be made that some anxiety-inducing information is allowed entrance, and that at some stage of the processing sequence, the normal orientation routine is disconnected in favor of a defensive routine on the basis of that information. As in the context of traditional perceptual-defense research (Postman, 1953; Allport, 1955; Goldiamond, 1958; Bevan, 1964; Spence, 1967), the negative aspect of the threatening information must be initially registered before any subsequent blocking, selection, or inhibition can take place. Denial, as well as other defenses acting against external threats, protects a person from *additional* threatening information rather than from its onset. In other words, it is essentially an escape-learning, rather than avoidance-learning, paradigm (even though in some rare instances this may change, leading to dire consequences due to fixation and inability for reality testing).

The two-phasic structure of denial makes it now obvious why the duration of the stress must be sufficiently long. *A brief experience of stress may not provide the opportunity for the defensive mode of reaction to occur or to fully develop.*

Another limiting factor in terms of duration relates to the typical indices that are being investigated. While some denial-like behaviors may take place relatively quickly (e.g., covering the eyes so as not to see, covering the ears so as not to hear, shouting "Oh, no!" in an attempt to negate stressful information, or even fainting, which leads to a temporary complete denial of reality), psychological research of stress often utilizes complex verbal behaviors, sustained emotional patterns, or time-consuming protective behaviors as the main sources of data. All of these require an episode much longer than a brief startle response.

Last but not least, the study of denial-like behaviors needs more than a single time measurement, and the same individual ought to be tested at least twice on different occasions during the basically same stressful experience. The logic of this requirement will be further elaborated in a later section of this chapter, and if justified, *the implications of such repeated measures methodology to the duration issue will be self-evident.*

TEMPORAL CHARACTERISTICS OF THE STRESS

In researching denial it is not sufficient to use intense stresses which have relatively long psychological effects. The advantage of being able to probe the reactions more than once cannot be fully realized without at the same time knowing something about the level of experienced stress over time. Stated differently, *only by knowing the temporal function of a particular stress, can the researcher make the most of a repeated measurement design.* Not having direct access to this information interferes with one's ability to interpret the results. Thus, for instance, is a decrease in overt anxiety indicative of coping, defense, or perhaps habituation? Independent evidence is needed to posit a specific temporal function, which may then serve as a basis for interpreting the findings. A few illustrations may be of some help at this point.

Laboratory experiments on helpless anticipation of danger employing the temporal certainty paradigm all show a typical U-curve function as a result of the threat (Breznitz, 1967; Nomikos, Opton, Averill, and Lazarus, 1968; Epstein and Roupenian, 1970; Elliot, Bankart, and Light, 1970; Folkins, 1970; Mansueto and Desiderato, 1971; Hess and Breznitz, 1971; Averill and Rosenn, 1972; Monat, Averill, and Lazarus, 1972; Petry and Desiderato, 1978). Following the initial reaction to threatening information, which leads to a drastic increase in arousal, there is a relatively rapid recovery, followed by a second gradual increase as the anticipated danger comes closer, with the peak exactly at the moment the danger is assumed to materialize. In longer durations of anticipation, most of the time is spent in the second phase of the increase, depending on the imminence of the threatened danger. Thus, for example, in the field experiment on anticipation of surgery cited in Chapter 9, patients were tested twice: one day before the operation, and on the day of the operation just prior to being given the premedication. The assumption can safely be made that since the patients knew when the surgery was going to take place, they were more stressed when it was imminent than on the preceding day. Likewise in the field experiment on anticipation of oral exams, it follows that the fear reaction during the second test, just minutes before being examined, was higher than during the first test, when the examination was still a few days off. In both of these instances, the assumption is justified by all available research evidence. Studies employing the temporal uncertainty paradigm typically report a gradual recovery function even though the threat may materialize at any moment (Breznitz, 1972; Monat, Averill, and Lazarus, 1972). Studying such situations, whether taken from real-life or the laboratory, one would have to assume that the stress experienced on the first test is lower than on the second, with all that implies for the interpretation of results.

On the other hand, experiments using the discrete warnings paradigm, which is highly relevant to a variety of real-life threats, such as natural disasters, certain medical dangers, war stress, etc., yield different, more complex but reliable temporal functions, which ought to be employed as a basis for interpreting the results on defensive behavior.

When dealing with post-traumatic stress response syndromes

(Horowitz, 1976), the temporal properties of the stress reaction ought also to be studied. Thus, for instance, while we may safely assume that certain features of the stress will be highest during the impact phase and immediately following the impact, certain implications of the trauma may be realized only at some later point in time, leading to a renewed increase in stress. This analysis argues that in the absence of independent evidence concerning the recovery function from a traumatic stressful event, the study of defensive behavior patterns becomes particularly difficult.

Studying the recall of certain factual information may provide an important clue to denial-like processes following a traumatic event. Thus, certain critical items of information can be a priori assumed to be recalled, and inability to do so will indicate a defensive process.

PROCESS METHODOLOGY

From the moment that stress and coping are conceptualized as a continuous transaction between the person and the environment, the need for an idiographic approach to research becomes self-evident (Lazarus and Launier, 1978). Only by the repeated study of individuals over time can the process-oriented researcher observe the evolution of certain typical coping patterns, or the transitions from one state of mind to another (Horowitz, 1976). A within-subject design is therefore the preferred methodology of many students of stress for conceptual as well as substantive reasons.

Interest in denial-like behaviors prescribes a repeated measures approach for yet another important reason, namely, the logical necessity for an independent measure of stress intensity. Continuing our description of the "ideal type" of research on denial, the following illustrates the advantages of having at least two consecutive tests utilizing essentially the same stimulus items.

Let us assume that a person helplessly anticipates a dangerous experience that will take place at some known time (T) in the future. Furthermore, let us assume that the danger is obviously threatening and will remain so until the danger is over. The second test (t_2) is administered when closer to (T) than the first test (t_1). On the basis of all the relevant information, we can assume that the level of stress on t_2 is higher than on t_1. This assumption is made independently of the actual responses (R). Furthermore, *what-*

ever these responses, the ones (R₂) given on t₂ are by definition indicative of greater stress than those (R₁) given on t₁.

Any instance in which there is some dimension of stress intensity whereby $R_2 < R_1$ is thus clearly a case of denial-like behavior. Stated differently, if a person responds as if he were less stressed on the second test than on the first one, even though the danger is more imminent, this indicates the active operation of a psychological defense.

We are now in the position to appreciate the contribution of the various methodological requirements so far. Only by taking them for granted are we able to define denial-like behavior on a purely logical basis.

Needless to say, having access to responses from more than two tests further increases the interpretative power of the design. This is particularly useful considering the fact that in the process of anticipatory stress, anxiety and denial often oscillate quite rapidly, which further complicates the picture. Phasic changes may mistakenly be interpreted as tonic ones, if there are no temporal probes which can measure them separately.

Three tests can in principle provide information about the breakdown of defense. Thus, if there is a third test (t_3) even closer to T than t_2, a response pattern such as $R_1 > R_2 < R_3$ on any stress intensity dimension reflects the instigation of defense on t_2, which the person could not maintain in face of the imminent danger and thus gave up on t_3. While phenotypically R_1 and R_3 may be the same, they indicate entirely different psychological situations. In the first instance, a person may have indicated his anxiety because he or she *did not yet* take recourse to defense. In the second case, during t_3 the anxiety may be due to the fact that *the defense was not successful* in protecting the person. It is, however, only the availability of information from R_2 that allows for such an interpretation. Without it, the responses could have been judged only as psychologically equivalent.

Multilevel Probes

Ideally, the methodology of research on denial can be improved by still another element, that of studying responses on different levels of subjective control. Since denial is never complete because that will remove the motive for its continuation, it may be operating on some levels and not on others. By looking at several levels at once, certain discrepancies may be discovered, and these may then serve as the basis for the definition of denial.

Responses to stress often exhibit interesting and complex desynchrony between the cognitive, affective and behavioral levels. Thus, for instance, in danger situations, there is frequent desynchrony between measures of avoidance behavior and measures of fear reaction (Breznitz, in preparation). Some people engage in protective behavior more than expected on the basis of their fear, whether reported or measured on-line by traditional psychophysiological indices. Is this indicative of denial? In what way?

The multilevel approach can best be utilized if there is an independent criterion for evaluating the degree of conscious control over the responses of the various levels studied. Thus, verbal behavior is often regarded as under greater control than emotional reactions. It has been precisely the discrepancy between these two response channels that served as the basis for the notion of subception (Lazarus and McCleary, 1951). The verbal channel itself is, however, too crude a category, and the distinction between probes consisting of direct questions and those calling for more projective responses has been often found useful in this context. Typically, psychologists will "trust" projective responses more than responses to direct questions that are more under the subjects' personal control. One indication of this differential level of conscious control is the extent to which factors such as social desirability (Crowne and Marlowe, 1960) play an important role in determining the response patterns. The greater the contribution of social desirability, the higher the level of conscious awareness.

The fascinating findings by Spence (see Chapter 4) indicate that verbal probes can be sensitive to denial-like processes in a variety of different ways. His analysis of "leakage" in "defended" versus "non-defended" subjects is of particular interest. It appears that context-free word counts and their particular distributions may be indicative of denial.

If a person is using denial without being aware of the fact — and this is the way the term "denial" is used in this volume — the above approach does not solve our methodological problems. There is no theoretical justification in assuming that high conscious control response levels will be more affected by denial-like processes than low conscious control response levels. If the function of denial is first and foremost to protect a person from anxiety, the emotional channel should not be a priori amenable to the operation of such a defense than the cognitive verbal channel. Thus, the study of *multilevel probes, while providing an important addition to the preceding methodological considerations, cannot replace them.* Standing separately it is at best a very poor alternative; in conjunction with the remaining considerations it yields a wealth of new analytical possibilities.

Many of these issues are solved in the context of intensive clinical investigations. The therapist has access to many repeated probes relating to the same basic stresses, and the clinical method is a within-subject design par excellence. Traditional empirical research must thus attempt to extract from the clinical method its advantages, and at the same time avoid some of its obvious weaknesses. It is argued that the present analysis provides the framework for such a synthesis.

REFERENCES

Allport, F. (1955), *Theories of Perception and the Concept of Structure.* New York: Wiley.

Averill, J. R. & Rosenn, M. (1972), Vigilant and nonvigilant coping strategies and psychophysiological stress reactions during the anticipation of electric shock. *J. Pers. Soc. Psychol.*, 23:128–141.

Bevan, W. (1964), Subliminal stimulation: A pervasive problem for psychology. *Psychol. Bull.*, 61:81–99.

Breznitz, S. (1967), Incubation of threat: Duration of anticipation and false alarm as determinants of fear reaction to an unavoidable frightening event. *J. Exp. Res. Pers.*, 2:173–180.

———— (1972), *The Effect of Frequency and Pacing of Warnings upon the Fear Reaction to a Threatening Event.* Jerusalem: Ford Foundation.

———— (in prep.), *"Cry Wolf": The Psychology of False Alarms.* Hillsdale, N.J.: Erlbaum.

Cannon, W. B. (1935), Stresses and strains of homeostasis. *Amer. J. Med. Sci.*, 189.

Crowne, D. P. & Marlowe, D. A. (1960), A new scale of social desirability independent of psychopathology. *J. Consult. Psychol.*, 24: 349–354.

Elliot, R., Bankart, B. & Light, T. (1970), Differences in the motivational significance of heart rate and palmar conductance. *J. Pers. Soc. Psychol.*, 14:166–172.

Epstein, S. & Roupenian, A. (1970), Heart rate and skin conductance during experimentally induced anxiety: The effects of uncertainty about receiving a noxious stimulus. *J. Pers. Soc. Psychol.*, 16:20-28.

Folkins, C. H. (1970), Temporal factors and the cognitive mediators of stress reaction. *J. Pers. Soc. Psychol.*, 14:173-184.

Goldiamond, I. (1958), Indicators of perception: I. Subliminal perception, subception, unconscious perception: An analysis in terms of psychophysical indicator methodology. *Psychol. Bull.*, 55:373-411.

Hess, A. & Breznitz, S. (1971), Termination of a stressful task reduces fear of an approaching shock. *Psychonomic Sci.*, 23:311-312.

Hinkle, L. E. (1974), The concept of "stress" in the biological and social sciences. *Internat. J. Psychiat. Med.*, 5:355-357.

Horowitz, M. J. (1976), *Stress Response Syndromes.* New York: Aronson.

Lazarus, R. S. (1966), *Psychological Stress and the Coping Process.* New York: McGraw-Hill.

_____ & Launier, R. (1978), Stress-related transactions between person and environment. In: *Perspectives in Interactional Psychology*, ed. L. A. Pervin & M. Lewis. New York: Plenum.

_____ & McCleary, R. A. (1951), Autonomic discrimination without awareness: A study of subception. *Psychol. Rev.*, 58:113-122.

Mansueto, C. S. & Desiderato, O. (1971), External vs. self-produced determinants of fear reaction after shock threat. *J. Exp. Res. Pers.*, 5: 30-36.

Monat, A., Averill, J. R. & Lazarus, R. S. (1972), Anticipatory stress and coping reactions under various conditions of uncertainty. *J. Pers. Soc. Psychol.*, 24:237-253.

Nomikos, M. S., Opton, E. M., Averill, J. R. & Lazarus, R. S. (1968), Surprise versus suspense in the production of stress reaction. *J. Pers. Soc. Psychol.*, 2:204-208.

Petry, H. M. & Desiderato, O. (1978), Changes in heart rate, muscle activity, and anxiety level following shock threat. *Psychophysiol.*, 15: 398-402.

Postman, L. (1953), On the problem of perceptual defense. *Psychol. Rev.*, 60:298-306.

Rapaport, D., Gill, M. M. & Schafer, R. (1968), *Diagnostic Psychological Testing*, ed. R. R. Holt. New York: International Universities Press.

Spence, D. P. (1967), Subliminal perception and perceptual defense: Two sides of a single problem. *Behav. Sci.*, 12:183-193.

Withey, S. B. (1962), Reaction to uncertain threat. In: *Man and Society in Disaster*, ed. G. W. Baker & D. W. Chapman. New York: Basic Books.

Wolff, H. G., Wolf, S. G. & Hare, C. C., Eds. (1950), *Life Stress and Bodily Disease.* Baltimore: Williams & Wilkins.

12

DENIAL VERSUS HOPE:
CONCLUDING REMARKS

SHLOMO BREZNITZ

The denial of stress is such a rich and varied phenomenon that no single volume can hope to do it even partial justice. The many facets of this complex phenomenon, the many aspects of this intriguing process, all await further systematic investigation. The forthcoming research must attack the problem on both empirical and theoretical levels at the same time. The evidence must be based on a longitudinal approach. If there is anything at all in the preceding chapters with which everyone seems to agree, it is the clear understanding that denial is a dynamic phenomenon, ever changing, always elusive to the simple tools of the researcher.

Much has been said about the costs and effectiveness of denial. No longer seen as the "black sheep," as always negative because it implies distortion of reality, this pervasive and important mechanism of coping is rehabilitated in the present volume. The costs are manifold and sometimes prohibitive, but one must not lose sight of the possible advantages to the individual who is overwhelmed by what is often a situation of total helplessness. The more sophisticated our analysis, the more difficult it becomes to answer what appeared to be a simple question: When is denial worthwhile and what are some of its more important benefits? Starting from the very first chapter, this volume tries to explicate some of the problems that any such complicated quest indeed must deal with. Needless to say, ours is not an exhaustive list of the problems to be encountered; nor is it necessarily the most important one. Given the background of almost total neglect of this important form of coping, however, the contribution might yet turn out to be worthwhile.

Even this preliminary account of cost-effectiveness of denial would not be adequate without considering the problem of *behavioral alternatives*. More specifically, instead of asking the question: What are the positive and negative effects of a particular kind of denial of stress, we should pose another question, namely, if not denial, then what? What would the individual do instead of denying? It is only by putting denial into the perspective of its most probable alternatives that its status and adaptive value can be ascertained. The evaluation of denial will surely pose no problem at all if its main probable alternative was effective active coping with an impending stressor. Under such circumstances, there would be very little doubt that denial is ineffective and prevents behavior that is much more conducive to higher levels of adaptation. But how can we know whether the most probable alternative to denial is effective instrumental coping? In fact, many situations which promote denial tendencies are ones in which the individual is objectively helpless and consequently cannot engage in effective active coping. What, then, are the alternatives in such a case? If there are no alternatives, then again there is very little to discuss regarding the advantages or disadvantages of behavior that is entirely predetermined and cannot be changed into anything else. Thus, the analysis of the alternatives is the crux of the matter; there is little meaning in discussing cost-effectiveness without a more explicit knowledge about these alternatives.

The present state of our knowledge does not, of course, allow any specific comparisons. We simply do not know enough about these things, and they must await further investigation. We believe that analysis of the behavioral alternatives to denial may well turn out to be the best research investment in this complex area. During the conference on which this volume is based, the participants on many occasions called for such an investigation as a prerequisite for a more sophisticated analysis of denial. On the level of speculation, some ideas were proposed which clearly deserve to be taken seriously in future investigations. It is one such idea that I wish to develop to some extent in my closing comments.

DENIAL VERSUS HOPE

A threatening situation is never totally negative. Even in the darkest hour there might be found a ray of light, a ray of hope. Sometimes more clearly visible, but often covered by the darker side of the situation, the positive side can be found only by actively looking for it. The hedonistic principle can therefore be served in two distinctly different ways: On the one hand, a person may try to deny the negative aspects of a particular piece of threatening information, and on the other hand, he may try to extract the positive aspects of the information and concentrate on them. In the present context, this is seen as an act of hoping. The two distinct ways of coping with what is essentially a threatening situation are schematically presented in Table 1.

The two modes of coping as presented in Table 1 are conceived as independent, thus, yielding four distinct behavior patterns. This schematic dichotomization is only a rough preliminary sketch of what clearly must be continuous dimensions. A few remarks about each of the four types might be appropriate. At first, however, some of the features in which we conceive of hope ought to be made more explicit.

Firstly, the distinction ought to be clarified between hopelessness and hopefulness on the one hand, and helplessness and control on the other hand. Although recently there has been a growing interest in the notion of learned helplessness (Seligman, 1975), hopelessness is an entirely different phenomenon. A person may be in a situation in which he is entirely helpless, and yet be quite hopeful about the eventual outcome. In such an instance, it will not be due to his efforts or his direct intervention that the threatening situation will change for the better, but somehow, from somewhere, help will arrive. Thus, we *view hope as a more pervasive and basic phenomenon than the more specific question of control.*

Hope is a very active state. By concentrating on certain posi-

TABLE 1
DENIAL VERSUS HOPE

Denial	Hope	
	Yes	No
Yes	1	2
No	3	4

tive features of a situation, the person tries actively to dwell upon it, to preoccupy his mind with it, to imagine it, to provide lucky scenarios for the eventual outcome, etc. *Hope, therefore, implies awareness.* Unlike denial, a person cannot hope for something without knowing what is it that he is hoping for.

One of the main problems with denying facets of objective reality is that the reality will not go away simply because it is unwanted. Therefore, there is always the danger that sooner or later the objective facts will be able to pierce through the protective veil of illusion, and the person will be found totally unprepared.

However, that is not the situation in case of hope, particularly if the hope is not based on false illusion. Looking at Table 1, a distinction is made between Types 1 and 3. In both instances there is hope, but in Type 1 the hope is based to a great extent on denying certain negative aspects of objective reality, which is not so in Type 3. The question can be raised: How can one hope without denying; how is it possible to concentrate on something positive when there is so little of it? In other words, is Type 3 behavior at all realistic, or can hope exist only in conjunction with a certain amount of denial? We posit that hope is always possible, even without denial. Naturally, when a person is well aware of what is in store for him, the hope will turn out to be of a more minimal nature. Instead of hoping that everything will turn out for the best, the person may hope that something positive will happen before the final breakdown, or simply that he will live for one or two years, or months, or weeks, or days. Hope can shrink, but it need not disappear altogether. What is important, however, is the cognitive preoccupation with the positive rather than with the negative. As an initial working hypothesis we would submit that Type 3 is a better way of coping than Type 1 because one does not need to continually invest in bolstering one's hopes in the face of objective reality. Type 1 behavior, on the other hand, can be actually labeled as *false hope* because it is not based upon true facts, but rather on distorted ones. Such false hope, albeit very pleasing while it lasts, forces the individual to continuously defend against information to the contrary.

Type 2 behavior illustrates one of the major disadvantages of denial. *By denying a threat, the person is also often denied the chances to consider some of its positive aspects.* Extreme forms of denial thus make it very difficult for a person to actively engage in bolstering his hopes.

In terms of adjustment, Type 4 is probably the worst of all possibilities. This is particularly so if the situation is one of objective helplessness. In the absence of any active coping, a person who does not even put up a psychological fight against the disastrous implications of particular information may very well be psychologically lost. Looking more closely at some of the fascinating reports which claim that denial-like tendencies can play an important role in saving one's life in highly critical situations (Hackett, Cassem, and Wishnie, 1968; Schmale and Iker, 1971; Gentry, Foster, and Haney, 1972; Cousins, 1976), the possibility should be raised that it was not the absence of denial which caused major problems, but rather the absence of denial and hope in conjunction. Type 4 behavior indicates that a person has given up all fight, and that he or she is indeed psychologically defenseless. Even inadequate defense, even unwarranted denial, indicate that there are some "psychological vital signs," the absence of which indicate depression, and possibly, death.

Thus, one important behavioral alternative to denying, is hoping. While practitioners in all the helping professions take it as virtually self-evident that hope plays a major role in recovery, there is practically no systematic research on this phenomenon. Therefore the conclusion of our exposition is the beginning of a new one. This is, of course, as it should be.

REFERENCES

Cousins, N. (1976), Anatomy of an illness (as perceived by the patient). *New England J. Med.*, 295:1458–1463.
Gentry, W. D., Foster, S. & Haney, T. (1972), Denial as a determinant of anxiety and perceived health status in the coronary care unit. *Psychosom. Med.*, 34:39–44.

Hackett, T. P., Cassem, N. H. & Wishnie, H. A. (1968), The coronary-care unit. *New England J. Med.*, 279:1365–1570.

Schmale, A. H. & Iker, H. (1971), Hopelessness as a predictor of cervical cancer. *Soc. Sci. Med.*, 5:95–100.

Seligman, M. E. P. (1975), *Helplessness: On Depression, Development and Death.* San Francisco: Freeman.

Subject Index

Accurate reality testing, 1, 7, 100
Active memory storage, 144–145, 146
Adaptive denial, 35–37, 89–91
Affect, denial of, 262, 265–266, 269, 277–278
Affective-impulse regulations, 149–150. *See also* Controls
Affect relevance, denial of, 262, 265–266, 269, 278
Aggression, denial and, 234
Anticipatory stress, denial and, 225–226
  experiment design, 228–232
    dependent variables, 229–230
    subjects and controls, 230–232
  experiment results, 233–253
    categorization of WAT results, 232–233
    changes in modes of reacting to anticipatory stress, 238–241
    facets of denial, 251–253
    operational definitions of denial, 233–236
    prevalence of denial, 236–237
    response reproduction, 237–238
    stages in coping with anticipatory stress, 243–251
    taxonomic value of categories, 241–243
  presurgery, 227–228
  stress and coping under "temporal certainty," 226–227
Anxiety, 239, 246
Apprehension, denial and, 234, 239
Asthma, vigilance and avoidance and, 18
Atlanta methanol poisoning (1951), 63–64
Attentional processes in denial, 172–179

Attention-focusing functions, 149–150. *See also* Controls
Avoidance, 10, 235, 244–246
  of associational connections, defined, 134
  defensive, 37–39
  measurement of, 17–18
Avoiders, 105–107
Awareness, denial and, 99–100

Backsliding
  as denial, 81
  stress inoculation and, 42–43, 46–51, 56–58
Bad dreams, defined, 136
Beliefs, systems of, 2
Bereavement, denial and, 32, 139–144
Blocking, denial and, 234, 245
Breast lumps, 18
The Brothers Karamazov (Dostoevski), 6
Buddhism, 215–216, 220, 224
Burn victims, 19
Byrne Repression-Sensitization Scale, 20, 58, 105–107

Cancer, denial in, 12, 20, 89–90, 108–122, 125–127
Catastrophe theory, 192
Childbirth, stress inoculation for, 40, 60
Children, stress inoculation for, 81–82
Christianity, 217–221
Cognitive approach to defense (discussion), 197–198
Cognitive-behavior modification, stress inoculation and, 49–50
Cognitive controls, *see* Controls
Cognitive coping devices, stress inoculation and, 47

Cognitive functions, 144, 149

Cognitive schemata, effects of serious life events on, 138–141

Cognitive/semantic model of personality and motivation, 179–189

Commitment, stress inoculation and, 47, 79–80

Compartmentalization, denial and, 234, 244–245

Completion tendency, 144–145

Compulsive repetition, 143, 147

Concentration camps, denial in, 7, 199–211

Concerned patients, see Language, choice of

Conflict model of coping, 52–54
    hypotheses, 68–69
    personality predisposition and, 61–62

Conscious detachment, 170

Controls, 145–148, 168
    character variation, 157
    vs. defense mechanism, 148
    defined, 147–148
    of format, 154–157
    of information flow, 151
    of schemata, 153
    that select information, 150–152
    that select self-images and role relationship models, 152–154
    serious life events and, 144
    varieties of, 148–150
    see also Information-processing aspects of denial

Coper-versus-Avoider Test, 58–59

Coping, problem-focused and emotion-focused, 24. See also Denial-like processes; Stress inoculation

Coping patterns, 52–53
    selection of, 53
    theoretical model of, 51–56

Coping suggestion, see Stress inoculation

Coronary disease, denial and, 20, 89–90, 275–279
    denial rating scale for, 15–16
    stress inoculation, 62–63

Crown-Marlow Social Desirability Scale, 105–107

Cynicism, 171

Decision-making, denial and, 17

stress inoculation, 43

Defended patients, see Language, choice of

Defense, cognitive vs. psychodynamic approaches to (discussion), 197–198

Defense mechanism
    defined, 148
    denial as, 85
    see also Controls

Defensive avoidance
    as coping pattern, 52–53, 55
    predisposition, 59, 61, 63–64
    subpatterns, 38–39

Delayed response, 149

Denial
    as an active process, 100–101
    adaptive, 35–37, 89–91
    of affect, 262, 265–266, 269, 277–278
    of affect relevance, 262, 265–266, 269, 278
    anticipatory stress and, 225–253
    attentional and memory processes in, 172–179
    avoidance and, 10, 235, 244–246
    awareness in, role of, 99–100
    backsliding as, 81
    beneficial, 19–23, 25–26, 35–37
    bereavement and, 32
    cognitive/semantic model of personality and motivation applied to analysis of, 180–189
    in concentration camps, 199–211
    concept of, history of, 14–15
    defined, 10, 35–36, 84–87, 98–99, 168, 213–214
    definitional problems (discussion), 97–101
    of denial, 283
    as a diverse set of processes, 13–14
    of facts, 12
    first-order, 12
    fragmentary registration and, 106
    vs. hope, 297–301
    of implications, 12
    of information, 263, 265–266, 270–271, 279, 283–284, 285
    information-processing aspects of, 167–193
    language, choice of, and disease process (experiment), 108–122

leakage and, 103–110, 213
levels of, 169–172
major, 90–91
mediation of, 106–107
methodological considerations in research, 287–295
minimal, 90
minimization, 25, 35–37, 265, 282
negative connotations of, 97–98
neurosis and, 86–87
nonpathological, 36
paradox of, 103–122
partial, 90, 282
pathogenic, 37–38, 43–44
pathological, 16–19, 25–26, 35–36
personality differences and, 91–92, 273–275
of personal relevance, 261, 265–266, 267, 275–276
preoccupation with trivial detail, 106
psychosis and, 86–87
psychosomatic disorders and, 88
rationalization and, 106–107, 235
reality and, 223–224
vs. reality testing, 1, 7, 100
religion and, 213–221
repression and, 10, 85
of responsibility, 261–262, 265–266, 268–269, 276–277
second-order, 12
seven kinds of, 257–279
    assumptions and constraints, 263–266
    dynamics of transition, 266
    exhaustiveness of, 281–283
    heart attack patients, 275–279
    individual differences, 273–275
    Janis and Mason decision-making model and, 284–285
    means and consequences, 267–271
    model, 258–260
    model as framework for debate (discussion), 281–286
    refutability of model, 271–273
    sequentiality, 281, 283–284
signs and symptoms, 131, 133, 134, 135
stress inoculation and, see Stress inoculation
third-order, 12
of threatening information, 262–263,

265–266, 270, 278–279, 285
time-related implications, 24–25
types of, 169–172
as unconscious defense mechanism, 85
unwitting incorporation of the target stimulus, 107
or urgency, 261, 265–266, 267–268, 276
varieties of, 35–39
in various facets of health (discussion), 31–33
of vulnerability, 261–262, 265–266, 268–269, 276–277
well-consolidated, 11
wishful thinking and, 235, 239, 241, 248, 253
Denial-like processes
with constructive outcomes, studies of, 19–23
with damaging outcomes, studies of, 16–19
as a form of self-deception, 10–15
principles concerning costs and benefits of, 23–26
research on, 15–16
Denial state
controls and, 145–157
explanation of, 138–141
explanation of state changes, 141–147
frequency and means of signs and symptoms of, 135
operational definitions of signs and symptoms of, 134
phases, 130–131, 132
signs and symptoms during, 131, 133
transition process (discussion), 161–165
Dieting, stress inoculation and, 51, 55–56
Difficulty in dispelling ideas, defined, 136
Discrete warnings paradigm, 291
Dissociation, denial and, 234
Doctors in concentration camps, 206–208
Dosing, 178

Echo, denial and, 235
Emotion-focused coping, 24, 78–79
Endorphin-B, secretion, 22–23, 32–33

Examination, oral, anticipatory stress and (experiment), 227–253
Explanation, denial and, 235
Extreme life situations, positive and negative functions of denial in, 199–211

False hope, 301
Fear-arousing information, see Stress inoculation
Fear of flying, 49–50
Fear of losing bodily control or hyperactivity in any bodily system, defined, 136
Fiction, illusion and reality in, 2–7
Fictional finalism, 8
First-order denial, 12
Format, control of, 154–157
Fragmentary registration, 106

Grieving, denial and, 16–17

Hallucinations and pseudohallucinations, defined, 137
Heart attacks, see Coronary disease
Henry IV (Pirandello), 4–5
Hinduism, 215, 217, 220, 221
Hiroshima victims, 19–20
Holocaust survivors, 7, 171, 199–211
Hope vs. denial, 297–301
Hypervigilance, 43
    as a coping pattern, 52–53, 55
    defined, 136
    predisposition, 60, 61, 64

The Iceman Cometh (O'Neill), 2–3
The Idiot (Dostoevski), 6
Illusion
    defined, 136
    reality and, in fiction, 2–7
    reality and, in psychological thought, 7–10
    self-deception and, 1–2
The Illusionless Man (Wheelis), 3–4
Inattention, daze, defined, 134
Individual differences, see Personality differences
    Inflexibility or constriction of thought, defined, 134
Information
    denial of, 263, 265–266, 270–271, 279,

283–284, 285
    external and internal sources of, 285–286
Information flow, control of, 151
Information-processing, model of, 174
Information-processing aspects of denial, 167–168
    application of the cognitive/semantic model of personality and motivation to the analysis of denial, 180–189
    attentional and memory processes in denial, 172–179
    cognitive/semantic model of personality and motivation, 179–180
    toward a mathematical description of the information-processing approach to denial, 189–193
    types of levels of denial, 169–172
Intellectualization, denial and, 234, 244
Intentional stereotypy, 249
Intrusion state
    contents, 133, 138
    controls and, 145–157
    explanation of, 138–141
    explanation of state changes, 141–147
    frequency and means of signs and symptoms, 137
    operational definitions of signs and symptoms, 136–137
    phases, 130–131, 132
    signs and symptoms during, 131–133, 135
    transition process (discussion), 161–165
Intrusive ideas in word form, defined, 136
Intrusive images, defined, 136
It Is So! (If You Think So) (Pirandello), 5

Language, choice of, disease process and (experiment), 108–110
    discussion of, 119–122, 125–127
    methodology, 110–112
    results, 112–118
Leakage, denial and, 103–110, 213
Leukemia patients, 21–22
Lexical leakage, 109
Liolà (Pirandello), 5
Literature, reality and illusion in, 2–7

Long-term memory (LTM), 178–190.
      See also Information-processing
      aspects of denial
Lookers, 105–107
Loss of reality appropriateness of
      thought
   by sliding means, defined, 134
   by switching attitudes, defined, 134
   by use of disavowal, defined, 134
Loss of train of thought, defined, 134

Major denial, 90–91
Man of La Mancha (Wasserman), 3
Marker words, *see* Language, choice of
Meaning in life, need for, 7
Memory failure, defined, 134
Memory processes in denial, 172–179
Minimal denial, 90
Minimization, 25, 35–37, 265, 282
Morale vs. social functioning and so-
      matic well-being, 31
Motivated perception, 169
Motivation, cognitive/semantic model
      of, 179–189
Myocardial infarction, 20, 89–90

Nazis, *see* Concentration camps
Neurosis, denial and, 86–87
New Look movement, 7, 223–224
Nonpathological denial, 36. *See also*
      Adaptive denial; Pathogenic denial
Numbness, defined, 134

Oral examination, anticipatory stress
      and (experiment), 227–253, 291

Pain, stress inoculation for, 41
Pangs of emotion, defined, 136
Partial denial, 90, 282
Pathogenic denial, 37–38
   stress inoculation and, 43–44
Pathological denial, 16–19, 25–26, 35–
      36
Peekers, 105–107
Perceived control, stress inoculation
      and, 48–49
Personality, cognitive/semantic model
      of, 179–189
Personality differences
   denial and, 91–92, 273–275
   stress inoculation and, 58–65

Personal relevance, denial of, 261, 265–
      266, 267, 275–276
Phobic situations, stress inoculation for,
      41
Polio patients, 19
The Power of Positive Thinking (Peale),
      26
Predicting adverse events in advance,
      positive effects of, 47–48
Predisposition
   denial and, 91–92
   stress inoculation and, 58–65
Preoccupation with trivial detail, 106
Presurgery patients
   anticipatory stress and, 227–253, 291
   stress inoculation for, 39–40, 41–42,
      58–60
   vigilance and avoidance, 21
Prisoners, *see* Concentration camps
Problem-solving coping, 24, 78–79
Procrastination, 38
Projection, denial and, 234, 244
Psychodynamic approach to defense
      (discussion), 197–198
Psychological thought, illusion and
      reality in, 7–10
Psychosis, denial and, 86–87

Rationalization, denial and, 106–107,
      235
Reality
   ambiguity in meaning and content of,
      8
   denial and, 223–224
   illusion and, in fiction, 2–7
   illusion and, in psychological thought,
      7–10
   ongoing process of construing, 12–13
Reality testing, 1, 7, 100
Reduced level of feeling responses to
      outer stimuli, defined, 134
Reenactments, defined, 136
Religion, denial and, 213–221
Repression, denial and, 10, 85
Research, "ideal type," 287–295
Responsibility, denial of, 261–262, 265–
      266, 268–269, 276–277
Reversal, denial and, 235, 239, 241
Rigidly role-adherent or stereotyped,
      defined, 134
Role relationships, controls that select,

152–154
Rumination or preoccupation, defined,
136

Second-order denial, 12
Selective exposure, 39
Self-deception
  denial process as a form of, 10–15
  illusion and, 1–2
  need for, 9–10
Self-esteem, stress inoculation and, 64–
  65
Self-images
  controls that select, 152–154
  intrusion and denial states, 139–141
Self-imposed stress inoculation, 80
Semantic memory, hierarchical structure of portion of, 176
Serious life events, psychological response to, 129–157
  cognitive processes, 144
  completion tendency and active me-
    mory storage, 144–145, 146
  compulsive repetition, 143
  controls, 144, 145–157
  controls of information-processing,
    147–157
  effects on cognitive schemata, 138–
    141
  ego and id functions, 143–144
  explanation of states, 138–141
  processing the meanings of, 141–147
  states that follow, 130–138
  see also Extreme life situations
Shifting of reponsibility, 38
Short-term memory (STM), 179
Skepticism, 171
Skin conductance, denial and, 170–171
Smoking, stress inoculation to stop, 55–
  56
Social functioning vs. morale and somatic well-being, 31
Startle reaction, defined, 136
Stereotypy, 235, 239, 248–249, 253
Stress
  anticipatory, see Anticipatory stress
  controls, see Controls
  defined, 89
  duration of, 289–290
  stimulus-based definition of, 288–289

temporal characteristics of, 290–292
Stress inoculation
  backsliding and, 42–43
  with children, 81–82
  cognitive reappraisal and, 49–50
  denial, varieties of, 35–39
  discussion of, 77–82
  dosage of fear-arousing information,
    44–46
  future of research, 65–68
  hypotheses, 68–69
  inappropriate, 41
  individual differences and predisposi-
    tional factors, 58–65
  information, role of, 80–81
  preventing maladaptive reactions to
    subsequent setbacks and crises,
    46–51
  research on, 39–41
  selective denial and, 126–127
  self-imposed, 80
  theoretical model of coping patterns,
    51–56
  three essential steps, 56–58
Stress response syndrome, signs and
  symptoms of, 135
Stroke victims, 22
Suicide, 220
Synonym, denial and, 235

Target stimulus, unwitting incorpora-
  tion of, 107
Temporal certainty paradigm, 290–292
  stress and coping under, 226–227
Third-order denial, 12
Threat, trauma and, 225. See also Stress
  inoculation
Threatening information, denial of,
  262–263, 265–266, 270, 278–279,
  285
Transition process, denial and intrusion
  states (discussion), 161–165
Trauma, threat and, 225
Trivial detail, preoccupation with, 106
Type-A behavior, 31

Unconflicted adherence, 52, 61
Unconflicted change, 52, 61
Unrealistic narrowing of attention,
  vagueness, or disavowal of stimuli,
  defined, 134

Urgency, denial of, 261, 265–266, 267–268, 276

Value-expectancy models of decision-making, 53
Verleugnung, 85, 213, 216, 219
Verneinung, 213, 216, 219
Vigilance
    as coping pattern, 52–53
    essential conditions for, 54
    measurement of, 17–18
    predisposition, 59–60, 61
    stress inoculation and, 43
The Visit (Dürrenmatt), 4
Vulnerability, denial of, 261–262, 265–266, 268–269, 276–277
Warding off trains of reality-oriented

thought by use of fantasy, defined, 134
Warnings, *see* Stress inoculation
WAT, *see* Anticipatory stress
The Wild Duck (Ibsen), 3
Wishful thinking, 235, 239, 241, 248, 253
Word association test (WAT), *see* Anticipatory stress
Work decision, stress inoculation for, 40–41
"Working through," as a process (discussion), 161–166
"Work of worrying," 17, 42

Zen Buddhism, 224

Author Index

Note: Numerals in *italics* indicate complete citation in References;
numerals in **boldface** indicate participation in Discussions.

Adams, J. E., 19, *28,* 130, *158*
Adelsberger, L., 200, *211*
Adler, A., 8–9
Adler, H. G., 201, *211*
Adler, N. E., 35, *70*
Aitken-Swan, J., 89, *93*
Alfert, E., 25, *28,* 48, *73*
Allport, F., 263, *279,* 289, *295*
Allport, G. W., 169, *193*
Alvarez, W., 131, *158*
Andrew, J. M., 17, *26,* 58, 59, *70,* 228, *253*
Ansbacher, H. L., 8, *26*
Ansbacher, R. R., 8, *26*
Arieti, S., 177, *193*
Arkoff, A., 45, *72*
Atthowe, J., 43, *70*
Auerbach, S. M., 228, *253, 255*
Averrill, J. R., 20, *28,* 48, *70,* 84, *94,* 169, *194,* 226, 250, *253, 255,* 291, *295, 296*

Baade, E., 170, *195*
Baker, G. W., 226, *253*
Ball, K., 43, 48, *70*
Ball, T. S., *70*
Bandura, A., 65, *70*
Bankart, B., 225, *254,* 291, *295*
Bartlett, F. C., 172, *193*
Bateson, G., 171, *193*
Battit, G., 40, *71*
Becker, E., 2, 10, *26,* 84, *93*
Becker, M. H., 45, *70*
Becker, S., 144, *158*
Beecher, H. K., 22, *26*
Bem, D. I., 2, *26*
Benner, P., 7, *26*
Bentley, E., 5–6, 7, *26*
Bergmann, T., 14, *27*

Bernstein, D. A., 43, *70*
Bettelheim, B., 200, *211*
Bevan, W., 263, *279,* 289, *295*
Bibring, E., 143, *157*
Bigelow, D. A., 40, *76*
Binstock, W. A., 91, *94*
Blanck, G., 149, *157*
Blanck, R., 149, *157*
Blinder, B., 104, *123*
Bloom, F., 22, *27*
Bobey, M. J., 59, *71*
Bokert, E. G., 108, *123*
Borus, J. F., 153, *158*
Bowers, K. G., 48, *70*
Bowlby, J., 16, *27*
Boydstun, J. A., 211, *212*
Breen, D., 40, *70*
Breger, L., 17, *27*
Brehm, S., 47, *70*
Breuer, J., 130, 142, *158*
Breznitz, S., **32,** 51, 57, *70,* **79–80, 99–100, 101, 125, 126–127, 163–164,** 225, 226, 237, 250, *253–254,* **281–286,** 291, 294, *295, 296*
Broen, W. E., Jr., 237, *254*
Buchsbaum, M., 178, *193*
Byrne, D., 58, *70*

Cameron, R., 49, *74*
Cannon, W. B., 288, *295*
Caplan, G., 46, *70*
Cassem, N. H., 15–16, 19, 20, *28,* 63, *72,* 90, *93,* 204, *212,* 275, 276, 278, *280,* 301, *302*
Chamberlain, K., 204, *212*
Chapman, D. W., 226, *253*
Chapman, R. C., 228, *254*
Charcot, J. M., 142, *158*
Chu, C. C., 46, *70*

311

Clark, R. L., 20, *27*
Clarke, S., 48, *71,* 225, *254*
Cobb, B., 20, *27*
Coelho, G. V., 130, *158*
Cohen, E. A., 200, *212,* 233, *254*
Cohen, F., 17, 21, *27,* 35, 36, 59–60, *70,* 228, *254*
Cohen, J. B., 26, *29*
Collins, A. M., 176, *193*
Cousins, N., 301, *301*
Cox, G. B., 228, *254*
Cramer, P., 232, *254*
Croog, S. H., 90, *93*
Crowne, D. P., 294, *295*

Dabbs, J., 48, *75,* 228, *255*
Davidson, P. O., 59, *71*
Davidson, R. J., 92, *94*
Davis, F., 19, *27*
Deckner, W. C., 46, *75*
DeGroza, S., 19, *28,* 41, *72*
DeLong, R. D., 17, *27,* 40, 58, 59, *71*
Dembo, T., 16, *27*
Desiderato, O., 250, *255,* 291, *296*
DeWitt G., 226, *253*
Dinardo, Q. E., 20, *27*
Dirks, J. F., 18, *30*
Dostoevski, F., 6
Dubitzky, M., 43, *75*
Dunkel-Schetter, C., 16, *30*
Dunn, T. M., 228, *255*
Dürrenmatt, F., 4

Easson, E. C., 89, *93*
Egbert, L., 40, *71*
Eitinger, L., 208, *212*
Elkes, J., **31, 33, 166, 198**
Elliot, R., 225, *254,* 291, *295*
Enelow, A. J., 66, *71*
Epstein, S., 48, *71,* 225, 230, *254,* 291, *295*
Erdelyi, M. H., 168, *193*
Erikson, E. H., 1, *27,* 138, *158*

Federu, P., 35, *71*
Feinberg, C., 104, *123*
Fenichel, O., 14, *27*
Fenz, W. D., 170, *193,* 226, 230, *254*
Feshbach, S., 44, *72*
Festinger, L., 9, *27*

Field, P., 40, *71*
Fine, B. D., 15, *27*
Fiore, N., 121, *123*
Fischer, R., 157, *158*
Fish, R., 87, *95*
Fishbein, M., 45, *71*
Fisher, C., 88, *93*
Flaxman, J., 43, *71*
Folkins, C. H., 225, *254,* 291, *296*
Folkman, S. K., 7, 24, 26, *27, 29*
Foster, S., 63, *71,* 301, *301*
Frankl, V. E., 7, *27,* 200, 212
Freedman, D. X., 19, *29*
Freud, A., 10, 14, 15, *27,* 35, *71,* 84, 85, *93,* 149, *158,* 177, *193,* 199, *212*
Freud, S., 10, 14, 84, 86–87, *93,* 104, *123,* 130, 142, *158*
Friedman, S., *71*
Freidman, S. B., 21, *28, 30,* 91, *95*
Froese, A., 204, *212*

Gal, R., **101**
Galin, D., 89, *93*
Gallagher, T. G., 18, *28*
Genest, M., 49, *76*
Gentry, W. D., 63, *71,* 301, *301*
Gilbertson, V. A., 89–90, *93*
Gill, M., 237, 250, *255,* 287, *296*
Ging, R., 204, *212*
Ginsberg, E., 109, *123*
Giora, Z., **126**
Girodo, M., 39, 48, 49, 69, *71*
Glad, D. D., 92, *93*
Gladstone, A. I., 47, *72*
Goldberger, L., **78, 164, 224, 283–284**
Goldiamond, I., 263, *279,* 289, *296*
Goldstein, M. J., 17, 20, *27,* 58, *71*
Gomersall, E. R., 40, *71*
Goss, M. E., 19, *30*
Grinker, R. R., 233, *254*
Gruneberg, M. M., 172, *193*
Guillemin, R., 22, *27*
Gur, R. C., 88, 92, *93, 94*
Gur, R. E., 92, *93*

Haan, N., 1, *28, 148*–149, 150, *158*
Hackett, T. P., 11, 15–16, 19, 20, *28,* 63, *72,* 90, *93, 204, 212,* 275, 276, 278, *280,* 301, *302*
Haley, J., 171, *193*
Hall, C. S., 9, *28*

Hamburg, B., 19, *28,* 36, 41, *72*
Hamburg, D. A., 19, *28, 30,* 41, *72,* 130, *158*
Hamilton, V., 168, 178, 179, 190, *193,* **198**
Hammen, L., 43, 47, 67, *74*
Haney, T., 63, *71,* 301, *301*
Hare, C. C., 288, *296*
Hartmann, H., 143, *158*
Haynes, R. B., 43, *75*
Hebb, D. O., 180, 182, *194*
Hellman, L., 18, *28*
Henderson, J. B., 66, *71*
Hess, A., 291, *296*
Hesse, H., 6
Hinkle, L. E., 288, *296*
Hochbaum, G., 45, *72*
Hofer, M. A., 21, *28, 30,* 91, *95*
Holmes, T. H., 21, *30*
Horowitz, L. M., 13, *28*
Horowitz, M. J., 17, *28,* **32,** 88, *94,* **99, 127,** 130, 131, 133, 139, 141, 144, 150, 156, 157, *158,* **161–165,** 177, *194,* 226, *254,* 292, *296*
Houston, B. K., 48, *72*
Hovland, C. I., 45, *72*
Howard, J., 46, *72*
Howe, C. D., 20, *27*
Hunt, W. A., 43, *72*

Ibsen, H., 3
Iker, H., 108–109, *123,* 301, *302*
Insko, C. A., 45, *72*
Insko, V. M., 45, *72*
Isbell, G. M., 226, *255*
Israel, N. R., 92, *94*

Jackson, D., 171, *193*
Jacobson, E., 14, *28,* 84, *94*
Jahoda, M., 1, *28*
Janis, I. L., 17, *28,* **32–33,** 35–45 *passim,* 47–58 *passim,* 60, 62, 68, 69, *72, 73, 75,* **77–82,** 84, 91, *94,* 120–121, *123,* 126, 130, *158,* **163,** 226, 228, 233, 252, *254,* **283–285**
Johnson, J. E., 40, 48, 49, *73, 75,* 228, *255*
Jones, S., 45, 46, *73*
Joseph, E. D., 15, *27*

Kafka, F., 6

Kahn, R. I., 36, *76,* 84, *95,* 199, *212*
Kahnman, D., 170, *194*
Kaltreider, N., 131, *158*
Kanfer, F., 48, *73*
Kanner, A., 26, *29*
Kanungo, R. N., 7, *28*
Kasl, S. V., 66, *73*
Katz, J. L., 18, *28*
Kautsky, K., 201, *212*
Kellett, D., 48, *76*
Kelley, H. H., 45, *72*
Kernberg, O., 149, *159*
Keutzer, C. S., 43, *73*
Kiesler, C. A., 47, *73*
Killilea, M., 46, *70*
Kinsman, R. A., 18, *30*
Kogon, E., 201, *212*
Kohut, H., 149, *159*
Koriat, A., 169, *194,* **197–198, 282, 283**
Kral, V. A., 208, *212*
Kroll, P., 204, *212*
Kübler-Ross, E., 20, *28,* 84, *94,* 110–119, *123*

Lacey, J. I., 92, *94*
Langbein, H., 201, *211, 212*
Langer, E., 40, 44, 49, 50, 51, 64, *73*
Lapidus, L. B., 60, *73*
Launier, R., 24, 26, *29,* 292, *296*
Lazarus, R. S., 7, 12, 17, 20, 21, 24, 25, *26, 27, 28,* **31–32,** 35, 36, 48, 59–60, *70, 73,* **77, 78–79,** 84, 89, *94,* **98–99,** 100, 101, 130, *159,* **161–162,** 169–170, 171, *194,* 204, *212,* **223–224,** 225, 226, 228, 250, *254, 255,* 258, 263, 272, *280,* **282,** 288, 291, 292, 294, *296*
Lebovitz, B. Z., 19, *30*
Lefcourt, H. M., 20, *29*
Leventhal, H., 40, 44, 45, 46, 48, 60, *73,* 228, *255*
Levine, J., 22, *29*
Levine, S., 90, *93,* 170, *195*
Leviton, G. L., 16, *27*
Levy, J. M., 40, *73*
Lewin, B. D., 84, *94*
Lewin, K., 53, *73*
Lichtenstein, E., 43, *73*
Liebert, R., 228, *255*
Lifton, R. J., 19–20, *29,* 84, *94*
Light, T., 225, *254,* 291, *295*

Lindemann, E., 16, *29,* 35, *73*
Lindsey, G., 9, *28*
Ling, N., 22, *27*
Lingens, E., 201, *211*
Lipowski, Z. J., 15, 19, 25, *29*
Luborsky, L., 104, 105, *123*
Luchterhand, E., 208, *212*
Lumsdaine, A. H., 47, *72*

Mack, J. E., 91, *94*
Mackenzie, J. M., 91, *94*
Maddocks, M., 83, *94*
Maer, F., 92, *94*
Mages, N. L., 35, *73*
Mahoney, M. J., 67, *74*
Maiman, L. A., 45, *70*
Mann, L., 17, *28,* 38, 39, 42, 43, 47, 52, 53, 54, 58, 60, 62, 68, *72,* 284, *286*
Mansueto, C. S., 250, *255,* 291, *296*
Marlowe, D. A., 294, *295*
Martindale, C., 180, *194*
Martinez-Urrutia, A., 228, *255*
Maslow, A. H., 1, *29*
Mason, J. W. A., 21, *28, 30,* 91, *95*
Matarazzo, A., 43, *72*
Mausner, B., 43, *74*
McCleary, R. A., 263, *280,* 294, *296*
McDaniel, J. W., 16, *29*
McFall, R. M., 43, 47, 67, *74*
McGee, R. K., 40, *73*
McGill, 63, *74*
McGuire, C., 20, *27*
McGuire, W. J., 44, 45, 47, *74*
McLoone, J. B., 20, *30*
Mechanic, D., 23, *29,* 226, 228, 233, 250, 251, *255*
Mees, H. L., 43, *73*
Meichenbaum, D., 39, 41, 44, 48, 49, 69, *74*
Melamed, B. G., 40, *74*
Melkman, R., 169, *194*
Mendelsohn, G., 35, *73*
Menninger, K., 1, *29*
Mewborn, C. R., 44, 45, 46, *75*
Meyers, M. S., 40, *71*
Milgram, N., **81, 97-98**
Minick, S., 22, *27*
Mischel, W., 62, *74,* 180, *194*
Monat, A., 225-226, *255,* 291, *296*
Moore, B. E., 84, *94*

Moran, P. A., 40, *74*
Morris, L., 228, *255*
Morris, P. E., 172, *193*

Nagler, S., **81, 161**
Neisser, U., 168, *194*
Niemela, P., 225, *255*
Nitzan, N., 277, *280*
Nomikos, M. S., 25, *29,* 250, *255,* 291, *296*
Norman, D. A., 183, *194*

O'Brien, L., 226, *253*
Offer, D., 19, *29*
Oken, D., 11, *29*
Olson, J. M., 59, *74*
O'Neill, E., 2-3
Opton, E. M., Jr., 20, 25, *28, 29,* 84, *94,* 250, *255,* 291, *296*
Orne, M. T., 91, *95*

Parad, H., 130, *159*
Parad, L., 130, *159*
Parkes, C. M., 36, *74,* 130, 139, *159*
Pasale, L., 20, *30*
Peale, N. V., 26
Pervin, L. A., 48, *75*
Peterfreund, E., 177, *195*
Petry, H. M., 291, *296*
Piaget, J., 138, *159*
Pirandello, L., 4-6, *29*
Postman, L., 169, *193,* 263, *280,* 289, *296*
Powell, J. W., 64, *75*
Pranulis, M., 48, 49, *75*
Pylyshyn, Z. W., 180, *195*

Quillian, M. R., 176, *193*
Quinlan, D. M., 65, *72, 75*

Rabe, A. J., 211, *212*
Rangell, L., 143, *159*
Rank, O., 9, *29*
Rankin, N. O., 25, *29*
Rapaport, D., 237, 250, *255,* 287, *296*
Resnick, H., 130, *159*
Riskind, J., 51, *75*
Rivier, C., 22, *27*
Rodin, J., 42, 47, 48, *72*
Roehl, J., 49, *71*
Roessler, R., 91, *94*

Rogers, R. W., 44, 45, 46, 75
Rokeach, M., 1, 29
Rosenbaum, M., **80**
Rosenberg, M., 45, 75
Rosenn, M., 291, 295
Rosenstock, I. M., 45, 53, 75
Roskies, E., 7, 26
Rossier, J., 22, 27
Roupenian, A., 225, 254, 291, 295
Rubinfine, D. L., 84, 94

Sachar, E. J., 91, 94
Sachnowitz, H., 201, 212
Sackeim, H. A., 88, 92, 94
Sackett, D. L., 43, 75
Safer, M., **79, 125–126**
Sampson, H., 13, 28
Sandman, C. C., 92, 94
Sarason, I., 228, 255
Sarnoff, I., 171, 195
Scarborough, H., 109, 123
Schachter, S., 267, 280
Schaefer, C., 7, 26, 29
Schafer, R., 237, 250, 255, 287, 296
Schäfer, W., 201, 212
Schimek, J., 104, 123
Schmale, A. H., 108–109, 123, 301, 302
Schmidt, R. L., 40, 75
Schmitt, F. E., 40, 75
Schulz, R., 40, 75
Schur, M., 143, 159
Schwartz, G. E., 48, 76, 89, 92, 94
Schwartz, J. L., 43, 75
Sechrest, L., 62, 75
Seider, M. L., 48, 73
Seligman, M. E. P., 48, 75, 299, 302
Selye, H., 250–251, 255
Sexton, A. W., 16, 29
Seymour, P. H. K., 183, 195
Shannon, I. L., 226, 255
Shapiro, D. C., 90, 93
Shewchuk, L. A., 43, 75
Siegel, L. J., 40, 74
Siegelman, E. Y., 13, 28
Silk, K., 204, 212
Silverman, L. H., 190, 195
Sime, A. M., 60, 76
Singer, R. E., 45, 46, 73
Sjöbäck, H., 14, 29, 84, 94
Sledge, H., 211, 212
Sobel, R., 37, 76

Spector, S. L., 18, 30
Spence, D. P., 32, 104, 109, 123, 126, 223, 289, 296
Spiegel, J. P., 233, 254
Spielberger, C. D., 228, 255
Spinoza, B., 200
Staub, E., 48, 76
Staudenmayer, H., 18, 30
Stern, M. J., 20, 30
Stone, G. C., 35, 70
Storms, L. H., 237, 254
Strauss, A., 46, 72
Sykes, R. N., 172, 193

Taulbee, E. S., 228, 255
Terwilliger, R., 45, 73
Thistlethwaite, D. L., 45, 46, 75
Thom, R., 192, 195
Townes, B. D., 21, 30
Turk, D. C., 48, 49, 74, 76
Tursky, B., 48, 76

Ursin, H., 170, 195

Vaihinger, H., 8–9, 30
Vaillant, G., 1, 30
Vale, W., 22, 27
Vargo, T., 22, 27
Vernon, D. T. A., 40, 76
Visintainer, M. A., 40, 76
Visotsky, H. M., 19, 30
Vogler, R. E., 48, 70
Von Kugelgen, E., 19, 30, 276, 280

Wadsworth, A. P., 228, 255
Waelder, L., 143, 159
Waelder, R., 84, 94
Waid, W. M., 91, 95
Waldhorn, H. F., 15, 27
Wallerstein, R. S., 147–148, 159
Wangaard, C., 18, 30
Wangensteen, O. H., 90, 93
Wanous, J. P., 40, 76
Warburton, D. M., 171, 195
Wasserman, D., 3
Watslawick, P., 6, 7–8, 12, 30, 87, 95
Weakland, J., 87, 95, 171, 193
Weimer, H., 18, 28
Weinstein, E. A., 36, 76, 84, 95, 199, 212
Weisman, A. D., 11, 12, 28, 30, 84, 95,

282, *286*
Weiss, J., 13, *28*
Weiss, J. M., 48, *76*
Weiss, S. M., 66, *76*
Welch, C., 40, *71*
Werblowsky, R. S. Z., **126, 198, 224**
Wheelis, A., 3–4, *30*
Wilner, N., 131, *158*
Wilson, S. K., 91, *95*
Wishnie, H. A., 20, *28,* 63, *72,* 90, *93,*
    275, 278, *280,* 301, *302*
Withey, S. B., 288, *296*
Wittkower, E., 36, *76*
Wold, D. A., 21, *30*

Wolfer, J., 40, 44, 49, 50, 51, 69, *73, 76*
Wolff, C. T., 21, *30,* 91, *95*
Wolff, E. T., 21, *28*
Wolff, H. G., 288, *296*
Wolff, S. G., 288, *296*
Wolfson, A., 13, *28*
Wooldridge, P. J., 40, *75*
Wortman, C. B., 16, *30*
Wright, B. A., 16, *27, 30*
Wyller, T., 201, *212*

Zanna, M. P., 59, *74*
Zeeman, E. L., 190–192, *195*
Zigler, E., 22, *29*